Mancunians

Manchester University Press

Mancunians

Where do we start, where do I begin?

David Scott

Manchester University Press

Published by Manchester University Press
Oxford Road, Manchester M13 9PL
www.manchesteruniversitypress.co.uk

British Library Cataloguing-in-Publication Data
A catalogue record for this book is available from the British Library

ISBN 978 1 5261 6150 5 hardback

First published 2023

Typeset by Newgen Publishing UK
Printed in Great Britain by Bell & Bain Ltd, Glasgow

For My Family, those near and far,
present and departed, you are forever cherished.
Although we may be separated by distance,
time, or circumstance, it is your love, guidance,
and memories which continue to shape
who I am and all I do.

‘Things are never how oft perceived,
Allowed others to shape what you believe
Beautiful, *you* should know me better than that.

’Twas only when it became home no more
should I ever *meander* from your shore...’

from ‘Tassle Alley’ by Keelan Reilly, in
Lost Letters from Lentsholme

Contents

Contributors

Steve Armstrong is a former business executive, now known for, amongst other things, selling the *United We Stand* fanzine and rescuing dogs.

Tunde Babalola is a musician and part of the Grammy Award-nominated production duo Future Cut. He has gone from the underground Drum and Bass scene to curating some of pop's biggest hits, to writing a new Broadway musical titled *The Ten*, which will be directed by Tony Award winner Ruben Santiago-Hudson.

Badly Drawn Boy is an English indie singer-songwriter and multi-instrumentalist, whose first album won the 2000 Mercury Music Prize.

Marsha Bell works within the local authority as well as being a community volunteer, but most importantly is a mum to a son.

Tom Bloxham MBE is chair and founder of the award-winning regeneration company Urban Splash, and founding chair of Manchester International Festival.

Emily Brobyn is a journalist, sports presenter, and broadcaster.

Contributors

Nooruddean Choudry is an author and writer for the Republic of Mancunia blog and the *Guardian*.

Stan Chow is an artist and illustrator, known for his distinctive portraits of musicians, film and sports personalities, including many beloved Mancunians.

JP Dolan is the son of Bob Dolan (of Bob's Gym, Levenshulme), and a Man City fan.

Rob Drummond is a Reader in Sociolinguistics at Manchester Metropolitan University.

Elliot Eastwick is a former Haçienda DJ, now running a rapidly blossoming hot sauce business.

Karen Gabay is a broadcaster, TV producer, podcast host and producer, award-winning filmmaker, exhibition curator, and radio presenter of one of the BBC's longest-running shows, *The People*.

Guy Garvey is the lead singer and lyricist with Elbow, winners of the Mercury Prize, a BRIT Award, and three Ivor Novello Awards. He is also a broadcaster with his own show on BBC Radio 6 Music and a music TV show on Sky Arts.

Emma Goswell is a radio producer and hosts *The Weekend Outing* on Virgin Radio Pride, as well as presenting cover shows for BBC Radio Manchester.

Len Grant is a freelance photographer.

Contributors

Andy Hargreaves is the drummer from I Am Kloot. He is currently teaching drums and recording and playing live with various artists.

Dave Haslam is a writer, broadcaster, and DJ. He DJed over 450 times at the Haçienda nightclub in Manchester.

Dan Hett is a digital artist, writer, and games designer.

Ste Howson is a British Army veteran, loyal Stretford Ender, and Droylsden native.

Aziz Ibrahim is best known for his work as guitarist with Simply Red, The Stone Roses, and their former vocalist Ian Brown, in whose band he regularly performs.

Richard Jupp is a lecturer at LIPA in Liverpool and former co-founder, co-songwriter, and drummer with the award-winning band Elbow.

Rachel Kelly is a secondary English teacher in East Cheshire.

Darren Lewis is a musician and part of the Grammy Award-nominated production duo Future Cut.

Steph Lonsdale is a poet, educator, and performer.

Sacha Lord is a co-creator of Parklife festival and The Warehouse Project. He is also the Night Time Economy Adviser for Greater Manchester.

Mary McGuigan works as a freelancer and is the sister of Paul 'Guigsy' McGuigan, former member of Oasis.

Phil Mealey is an actor and writer, known for *The Royle Family*, *Early Doors*, and *Sunshine*.

Leon Mike is an English football manager and former professional player.

Nathan Miles is an experienced commercial lead working in the Civil Service.

Andy Mitten is a journalist and author. He founded the best-selling *United We Stand* fanzine at the age of fifteen. He has interviewed over 500 footballers, past and present, and his work has taken him to over 100 countries. Born and bred in Manchester, he divides his time between his city of birth and Barcelona, Spain.

Justin Moorhouse is a comedian, actor, writer, and radio presenter.

John Moss is a retired firefighter, having served twenty-eight years with Greater Manchester Fire and Rescue Service.

Jay Motty is a journalist and co-owner of Manchester United YouTube channel Stretford Paddock, and spent years as Key 103's Manchester reporter.

Kurtis-Lee Spittle is a forty-year-old mixed-race diva from Gorton, as well as being a dancer, a singer, and a worker in Manchester's hospitality sector running nightclubs and restaurants.

Ged Tarpey played professional football for Manchester City in the 1990s, and is now the managing director of global media and entertainment at Twitter.

Jay Taylor is currently the English National Coordinator for the Music Venue Trust and Chair of the Greater Manchester Music Commission. He contributes to the Greater Manchester Night Time Economy Task Force and the Manchester Music City partnership.

Sylvia Tella is a is a British singer, who worked as a backing vocalist for Boney M and then embarked on a successful solo career.

John Thomson is an actor, comedian, and drummer, best known for his work on *Cold Feet*, *The Fast Show*, *Coronation Street*, and *Men Behaving Badly*.

Andy Votel is a musician, DJ, record producer, graphic designer, and co-founder of Twisted Nerve Records and the reissue label Finders Keepers Records.

Jim White is a journalist, who has worked for the *Independent*, the *Guardian*, and the *Telegraph*, writing mainly about sport. As well as extensive broadcasting, he has written twelve books.

Tash Willcocks is a graphic designer. She has designed album covers for Elbow, skateboards with Linder Sterling, and led graphic design courses at Salford University.

Natalie-Eve Williams is a broadcast journalist and Manchester music contributor for various media and publications, including her current role with the BBC.

Anne Worthington is the last Manchester clay tobacco pipe maker and is a retired customer service advisor. She is a volunteer guide at Manchester Cathedral and secretary of St George's Youth and Community Centre.

Preface: A view from the Low

Less than 10 miles east of Manchester city centre lies Werneth Low, a 915 foot hill that borders Stockport and Tameside. At its highest points, you can see Derbyshire, the Cheshire Plains, the South Pennines, and the Welsh Mountains (so I'm told), and stealing centre stage is Manchester. At its peak, there is a stone compass to direct walkers to landmarks they can spot in the landscape, a welcome aid to the weather that often tries its best to ruin the view. Yet even at its bleakest, the sky provides a grey contrast to allow nature's greens, browns, oranges, purples to pop out. The landmark on the Low is the Cenotaph commemorating the lives lost in the Great War; there are usually battles around the monument as golfers bemoan dogs disturbing their teeing off on the course, which runs parallel.

For the past two decades, I've been dragging my arse up here. It originally began as a challenge to banish a hangover. At the height of my drinking days, I would often make these pacts with myself when faced with the fear which followed a heavy session. Over the years, I'd convinced myself that if I took on an arduous act, at its completion, it would cure my ills. These would range from painting rooms, fixing broken objects or cleaning the house, to hitting the gym and long walks along the canal. They were a penance for pints consumed; if I was going to drink into oblivion, I would have to punish myself the following day. Writing this now, I wonder if this is some deep-seated influence from my heavily Catholic Irish grandmother who dragged me to church as a kid. They were also ways to distract me from the paranoia while my body and time worked their magic to restore the damage done. It would only be years later I would understand the best way to stop a hangover was not to drink; a book in itself, yet within these pages lie some clues to why alcohol became such a crutch for my peers and me.

One particularly woeful Sunday morning when there wasn't a wall in need of a lick of paint or a device that needed repairing, I took on Werneth Low for the first time. No matter which way you go up the Low, it is a bastard of an incline. Throw into the mix that I was unfit, had had two hours' sleep, and carried the contents of a booze cabinet in my gut, 915 feet may as well have been Everest. If anyone had offered me oxygen as I ascended that morning, I'd have been on it, sweating, coughing, aching, yet persevering through the demons in my head and the pains in my body to the top. A path leads you from the entrance to the peak, and halfway between them is a bench (a lifeline that particular morning). As I sat catching a breath, swearing at myself, trying my best not to look like a corpse to the jovial walkers in bright coloured coats saying hello as they passed, I noticed her for the first time, in total panorama: Mamucium. Manchester. Home. The place I'd lived in for decades yet only ever seen from within it. The hangover was ruinous, the weather conforming to type, so it wasn't an enlightening moment, but it did make me think of how things look differently the further we are away from them.

While my drinking has subsided to special occasions, this walk has become a therapeutic ritual. From here, I can see how both I and Manchester have changed over the years. The bench that first gave me salvation has also been the best seat to watch the slowest game of monopoly unfold. In the years I've come up here, I've watched a skyline that once only boasted the Arndale Tower become a playground for cranes. The Beetham Tower then became the most prominent building, followed by Deansgate South, and by the time this book is published, another skyscraper will take dominance. A cynical friend once quipped to me 'Big Property, Small Pecker', but it's not just the size of the buildings but the sheer number of them that now dominate: new apartment blocks, student accommodations, business buildings. In the town centre, they are noticeable by their inconvenience; you walk in their shadows, your pathway diverted to take other routes as they are assembled, but you cannot take in their collective magnitude when you're stood underneath them.

During the height of the COVID-19 pandemic, Werneth Low, more than ever, was an escape for my family and me. Every single day we were up on the Low. We never saw another person. It felt like we were suspended in a void, dependent on nothing external but each other, detached from everything and everyone else. Stripped of real life's complexities and the influences an outside world brings, unplugged from the news channels, it was one of the most blissful periods of my life. Mother Nature showed her devious side and offered up a blistering summer when we were supposed to be inside for twenty-three hours a day. Every evening we would go back to the Low to watch the most glorious sunsets; within an hour, the sky became a Monet over Manchester; it bled from blue to orange, deep red before fading to the night. One evening I took a photograph of my eldest daughter running wild with the sun setting behind her. When we returned home, I opened my photos to look at the image I'd caught of her innocent and free when I noticed I'd also captured a silhouette of Manchester in the same shot. Reality kicked in. The reminder that none of this was real – it's just a pause button.

At some point, life would have to resume. But how would that future look? I stared at the image and said to myself, 'That place will never be the same after all this.'

The following day I was interviewed by the Inspiral Carpets' Clint Boon for his *Humans of XS Manchester* podcast. The premise is for recognised Mancunians to describe their experiences of growing up in the city; what they thought of it then and now. I have known Clint a while; I was franker than usual, more chatting to a mate than being under interrogation. I've always forced myself not to be nostalgic as a mechanism to push me forward in my career and life, to concentrate on what is coming ahead rather than staring in the rearview. Looking backward always felt like a waste of time. I reeled off anecdotes of my loves and loathes, and it dawned on me how little I'd taken account of my past. Outside of the name and body, the person I talked about no longer existed; he was somebody I used to be.

Similarly, the Manchester these stories took place in, outside of name and geography, didn't exist. It was somewhere I used to know; this eased the fear from the previous night that Manchester wouldn't be the same following the pandemic. It has never been stationary. Places and people are constantly in flux, yet our memories are crystallised. 'It's not how it used to be' is something I often hear from long-lived Mancunians. The past romanticised as idyllic. Manchester is not the same as it was, but neither is Liverpool, Sheffield, or Newcastle. It's just that those cities don't have such flagpoles of concrete to mark their change. But how much of Manchester's past do we remember? Do we remember things for how they once were? Are we not all guilty of dressing the past like my daughters do their dolls? There is a touch of colour here to make it stand out; a bit of make-up to cover the blemishes; add a few accessories to embellish the ensemble. We're happy to promote our successes, but how often do we bare our scars?

Preface

Like many of the inmates' coronavirus made of us, I took in a lot of podcasts, books, radio, and TV shows about Manchester to pass what felt like limitless time. I found no new stories. Oasis, Haçienda, Factory Records, Madchester, Man United Treble Winning Season. The same talking heads, telling the same stories, about the same period. All significant cultural events and people, all things that I revel in and celebrate as a Mancunian, yet they didn't fully represent the city. It wasn't where I grew up. The Manchester portrayed by those musicians, footballers, and actors wasn't my home. There needs to be a skewed narrative to suit a documentary's purpose. But to look at my city through this lens distorts how it is received to those that lived outside of the city. I asked a few friends and put a call out on Twitter for reflections on what Manchester meant for people who didn't grow up here.

> As a kid growing up in the Midlands, Manchester was this mythical distant land – and everything we knew about it came from Oasis and the Gallagher brothers. We assumed everyone strutted about in parkas and City shirts, telling everyone how 'mad fer it' they were. It felt like a city where real people could become superstars, and the party went on until morning. When I finally visited the city in the late nineties, I wasn't ready and found it too big – unlike Nottingham where I was living at the time which I knew like the back of my hand. Even walking from Piccadilly to Whitworth Street seemed to take an age, never mind trying to get my head round the different quarters and the surrounding boroughs, never mind working out how to get a tram or a night bus. I just assumed Manchester was like what I saw on TV – namely Oasis and *Shameless* – until I moved here.
>
> – Bill Rice, sports editor, BBC Radio Manchester[1]

> I was in Year 8/9 at school in very boring and quiet Oxfordshire … I remember going to London for the day and seeing the video for 'Live Forever' on a big screen and I was totally spellbound with them

[Oasis] and then Manchester. The idea of this big, exciting, but totally unapologetic place.

– Linda Walker, journalist, BBC Radio 4[2]

The Oasis thing felt like a weird boorish boozy cult, football culture crashing head first into music culture and inevitably presenting as less than both. Luckily Manchester is diverse and so there has always been a strong counter-culture.

– @thefibreman, Twitter response[3]

Manchester always felt dangerous, seedy and yet cool as fook. I got mugged in Manchester and took down an alleyway, the police asked me if I wanted to do a line up, I wouldn't have recognised them anyway as I was too drunk. I was still back in Manchester the next weekend. Because that was the pull of the place, the shopping centres, the mysterious labyrinth of Affleck's Palace with a million pin badges to wade through, back alley pubs that were once toilets and others that were still toilets, jukeboxes, pool tables and a collective spirit of the people, whether you were indie, emo, goth, towny. It didn't matter, everyone was equally accepted as they were ridiculed in that fair city.

– @mrseed2022, Twitter response[4]

It felt prior to Oasis, that nothing happened up here – and by 'up here' I meant the North – and although Newcastle is a few hours' drive from Manchester, it felt that things were pulled closer for the very first time. It was the first time you could hear songs and things that you could relate to. I'm not going to over-egg it and say that me and my friends were walking around pretending that we were Mancs – it wasn't like that – but it showed us that there was a possibility there. That everything didn't have to come out of London.

– Andy Bell, journalist[5]

At that formative age – sixteen, seventeen, eighteen – in your life, you just don't think about other cities. I don't think that I'd ever thought about Manchester until Oasis came on the scene, because I had a really strong relationship with Oasis in terms of their music, and I remember listening to *Definitely Maybe* for the first time and it wasn't about Manchester, that album, it was about growing up and wanting to be something you're not, and I think that was the first album that spoke to me as a person, and I sat up and went 'someone has written music for me here'. Culturally, I saw no real difference between what was happening in Manchester to what was happening in Camberley, Surrey at the time, which couldn't have been two more different places in the nineties. Camberley was all commuter belt, bankers and it was a relatively wealthy area and I've seen images of Manchester looking back around the time of the IRA bomb; it wasn't the shiniest, brightest of places. I wasn't drawn to Oasis because they were from Manchester, or even because of who they were as individuals, because that very much came later. The music came first for me, but the more I became aware of them as individuals – and they were these big personalities, and they had the Manchester thing, that was kind of what they shouted about. That then did become Manchester. So it was the swagger, it was the attitude, it was the bucket hat, it was the little round glasses, it was the parka jackets. That became, for me, exactly what Manchester was at the time. Before I moved here in 2000, it felt like a city with a buzz, a city that was developing and growing. It had this sort of creative exciting culture around it, and it had a bit of edge as well. And I think that's important when you're looking at creativity as a drawing point. Because if you're safe, and you're happy, and you're in a bubble without anything challenging you then you're not going to push against that. And that's where good creativity comes from, it comes from when you've got to overcome an obstacle, battle something or manoeuvre around something. That's where it comes from. So for a city to have that sort of spark, it needs that sort of edge, it needs that sort of spikiness to it, and Manchester definitely had that. And I don't mean creativity in terms of just the art, music or culture. Something that flows through the city is the creativity from the grafters who are looking at entrepreneurial ways to make business or opportunities, and I think that's really cool.

– Jim Salveson, XS Manchester[6]

> In the mid- to late nineties I hadn't travelled far outside my hometown of Southampton. We had no cool bands and no culture to speak of. Thanks to bands like Oasis, the Smiths, the Charlatans and the Stone Roses, and TV programmes like *The Word* with Terry Christian and *TFI Friday* with Chris Evans, we southerners put Manchester on a bit of a pedestal. We liked the humour and the swagger. This resulted in a focus on, and a veneration of, Manc culture and Manc celebrities to the detriment of others. I tended to group bands and celebrities into two categories: 'From Manchester' or 'From somewhere-other-than-Manchester'. Even massive bands like Blur – I vaguely knew they were from London but it wasn't a point of interest. In fact, I couldn't tell you where any of my other favourite nineties' bands were from if it wasn't Manchester.
>
> – Claire Moruzzi, content editor[7]

Oasis clouds all. These aren't wrong or right views; they are interpretations made from media representations, celebrity triumphs, or brief city visits. They don't paint the whole picture. An omnipresent perspective is impossible, but that doesn't mean we shouldn't add more dimensions to the narrative. The past, like landscapes, is also best viewed from a distance. Only when we travel in years between events do we begin to look at things differently. It is never within the moment that we know what it means, but only after it has occurred. It is only then stories stand out against the transparency of time. But who chooses which stories are important, which moments, and how we remember them? Oasis had left Manchester by 1996, yet where are the stories of Mancunians that stood in their shadow? What stories did they have to tell? What tales haven't we told? I looked back once more at my own life and asked myself how had the city shaped me? How had Manchester formed my identity? The more I looked at life events through the lens of the city, the more it became apparent how intrinsic Manchester had been to my growing up. The drink, the drugs, the songs, the sport, the crime, and the culture had moulded me more than I'd imagined. I began picking at the threads of these themes and realised so much of this period remains undocumented, overlooked, dismissed. I wondered if I told parts of my life through these themes, could it tell an alternative story of Manchester? But my story alone wouldn't be enough. It would be one more person telling a single account. It would be a bold task, but could I possibly collect different impressions simultaneously? Would that give a better portrayal, if not a full one? Would it even be possible? I wanted to find out.

There are countless great books on Manchester, but few first-hand accounts of what it was like living here at the turn of the millennium, and none that did what I wanted to attempt: take a story told in broad strokes and rewrite it with a fine paintbrush, held by multiple people. What was it like to be a musician trying to do something different to the mainstream? Did the IRA bomb kickstart the regeneration? How was Manchester's nightlife after the Haçienda? Why did Manchester seem to be the home of the binge drinkers of the country? What was it like to be involved in gang wars? How did the city's school system fail its youth? What is a Mancunian, if not the stereotype? These were questions that I wanted to find answers to. In total I interviewed 106 people for this book, a mixture of names you will know and some that you won't; people that didn't want their names printing and names that have been changed for legal purposes. There are names that didn't make the final cut, a decision based on editorial reasoning, but their input still had an influence, their voices just as authentic, and many opened new lines of questioning as the contributors grew. Collating the stories of other Mancunians has opened my eyes beyond what I knew of my city. We shared the city simultaneously; we may have shared similar experiences, but how we receive them is always in isolation.

The vignettes of my life that run throughout are of My Manchester. The kind people that contributed parts of their story show us their Manchester. Some views may contrast, some may concur, but they are all the points of view of people with a real lived experience of the city at the time. Bound together, I hope these collected impressions of Manchester at the turn of the century give you a portrait of what it was like to be there, then.

Thank you for taking the time to read it.

David Scott

1

'Manchester was miserable'

15 JUNE 1996

> Manchester was miserable before the bomb. There wasn't a lot going on. When people used to leave work in the evening – I don't know if you're old enough to remember – but the entire city centre was just mobbed by starlings. Horrible big clouds of starlings. I mean filthy, horrible, dirty, street urchin birds that spend all day on canals, and then at night they would swoop in. It would go dark with these clouds of birds, genuinely. It was awful, horrible. They would all congregate around Piccadilly Plaza hotel ... It was fucking miserable.
>
> –Justin Moorhouse, comedian[1]

Jackson Pollocked in bird shit, Queen Victoria was the first face to welcome me off the 192 bus into town. Almost black in the sun, the statue's sombre face cut a contrast to the cast of Mancunians hurrying about the city centre in the early morning. Double-decker buses would arrive from the suburbs to drop shoppers outside of Piccadilly Gardens; unlike the unwelcoming monstrosity it would become, it was once a garden in the truest sense. Trees would outline the top level, and within a few steps down, you could enjoy the flowers in bloom. The continuous square bench around the perimeter of the lower level was where all walks of life sat next to each other: gossiping women with trolleys, men marking horses in their papers, drunks passed out, punks looking pissed off, and youths pounding tunes from a ghettoblaster in a corner. Little kids would splash and toss coins into the fountain as mothers took the weight off their feet. Manchester city centre was busy every weekend, but 15 June 1996 was the Saturday before Father's Day, and town was heaving with shoppers.

The beacon that beckons them is the Arndale. Paris has the Eiffel Tower, New York has the Empire State Building, and Manchester had Arndale House. A 295-foot skyscraper covered in bile-coloured tiles. It was billed as the flagpole of the future when it opened in 1975, but by 1996 it looked like God's own toilet. Each side is reminiscent of a pub's urinals. However, don't judge a building by its piss-stained teeth; it is the mall underneath which holds shoppers' attention. Each weekend thousands filled up its aisles; several national chains make up the stores here, and there was a busy indoor market, but the majority was made up by an assortment of regional and local shops. There were shops such as Chelsea Girl and Dolcis, whose names suggested the clothes were en vogue, but the closest they came to a catwalk was at Pet Paradise around the corner. Anyone wanting to get close to the new look from Milan would have to hit House of Fraser, an expensive department store on Deansgate where the staff were always snotty if you didn't fit in with the Didsbury set which was their demographic. Security guards would often kick my friends and I out because we were presumed shoplifters when we were there to check out the latest Tommy Hilfiger and Helly Hansen coats we'd seen in rap videos on MTV. These designer labels were not available anywhere else.

One of the biggest shops inside the Arndale was the Warner Bros. store; outside, it had a fountain adorned with Bugs Bunny, Daffy Duck, and other cartoon figures to entice young kids and their parents inside. The Warner Bros. store was expensive but often used as a bribing technique by mothers trying to keep their kids quiet as they shopped. 'If you're well behaved, I'll take you to the Warner Bros. shop before we go home' could often be heard. For the teens less impressed with cartoons, there was The Gadget Store, a shop that housed the most impressively useless technology that you dared not touch due to its fragility but would watch in awe during the demonstrations as a toy helicopter would take off without remote control but soon crash to the floor and smash to pieces. There was WHSmith and Clinton Cards for gifts and cards for occasions. These had recently found a competitor with Birthdays founded by a local businessman; Manchester United captain Bryan Robson had recently become a significant shareholder, which hugely raised its profile. There didn't seem to be the same competition between the local businesses as there is today; I don't recall shopping around when I would go to town with my Mum. She knew where she was going for each item. Trainers, JD Sports; jewellery, The Gold Centre; butterfly clips and school uniforms, C&A – if there wasn't a store for what you were after, then there was Argos. Some stores didn't bother using fancy names to attract shoppers and went the Ronseal route: The Perfume Shop, The Sweater Shop, The Sock Shop, Tie Rack, all sold what they said on the door. Urban urchins like myself often hit Stolen from Ivor. A shop as famed for its yellow and black plastic bags as it was for the clothes. You could find Stolen from Ivor in the Arndale by following your ears. It was constantly blasting out big, heavy bass lines. Young teens with wet gel curtain haircuts would loiter outside, chatting up the girls with biker shorts and short skirts. Stolen from Ivor was the shop for clubbers' clothes, cheap garments with logos based on drug symbolism, available in one size: baggy.

When you were looking for something to eat, most people headed to Voyagers, an 800-seater food court. Voyagers opened in 1993 to much fanfare; costing £9 million to build, it promised exotic plates from far-flung places – the experience was to replicate a voyage around the world. There was a Spud-u-Like, a McDonalds, and Chinese and Indian eateries which may say something about an ambition to expand flavours in town. However, the food served up was more school canteen than Cantonese; authentic Eastern dishes they were not.

Market Street, as it is today, is the main retail strip that runs through the city centre; the biggest store here was the three-floor HMV Megastore, opened in 1993 by Simply Red's Mick Hucknall. HMV was always busy. The ground floor was where all the popular music was; the second floor was for computer games – afternoons could be spent up here queuing for a turn to play Tekken 2 on the new Playstation. The basement was for world music, obviously not the taste for most Mancunians as it was always quiet, which made it a good place for shoplifters. Joanne, a girl from around the way, used to steal from HMV to order – any CD for a fiver. She'd pick it up, remove the alarm tag while perusing Miles Davis, put it down her pants on the escalator back up, and be out the door. I got banned from HMV on a few occasions, but not for shoplifting. I loved US Hip Hop, but most of it only came in as American imports which were expensive; you could pay up to £20 for a five-track EP. I'd buy the CD, record them at home on tape, and then return them and get my money back; one weekend, I tried to do it twice in a day and got caught. Aside from cottoning on to my little scheme, the staff were useless, part-timers turning up for a pay-packet, and many did not have a clue about music other than it was a product they sold. The places to go with a serious music interest would be the independent record shops such as Piccadilly Records, Vinyl Exchange, or Eastern Bloc. The people here were cool: they gave a toss about their jobs, the music they were selling, would advise on what was worth checking out, and weren't afraid to take the piss out of you if you picked up anything they deemed awful.

John Lewis and Debenhams were the two largest department stores in town, and faced each other at the top of Market Street. Different in name but not so much in nature. They both sold the same stuff; as much as I could tell from being dragged around them by my Mum, one offered watch repairs, whereas the other provided piercings. They both were a walkthrough on the way home where we'd douse ourselves in aftershave testers (despite not yet shaving). A year earlier, I'd joined my sister as she got her ears pierced at Debenhams, and the women doing it threatened to 'do my nose', to which I told her to 'Do one!' and legged it out of the store, once more being chased by a security guard presuming I was on the rob. It was no easy task to explain I'd done nothing wrong but try to prevent a hole in my nostril.

Smokers would cough and queue outside the Index Catalogue Shop to exchange part of their lung capacity for household appliances. Benson & Hedges ran a promotion that gave away gratis points with every box of cigarettes smoked. These points could be saved and cashed in against household products. For example, if you were to tan 800 cigs, you could get money off a brand new toaster. It doesn't seem like much of a payoff, but times were hard; a lot of my friends' parents would have to furnish their house on credit from sofas to ovens, so anything that seemed like it was saving money was attractive (I mean they could've just stopped smoking, but who am I to judge?). Home media systems were also an expensive commodity, so those out of pocket who wanted a telly would head to Radio Rentals to hire a TV and VHS player. Manchester United winger Ryan Giggs was the poster boy for the store and could be seen in the adverts promoting the latest Sony widescreen, yours for just £4 a week (with four weeks' deposit upfront). It felt like Ryan Giggs was the face of everything at that time, from Radio Rentals to Reebok, the

Arndale to Quorn Burgers, where he featured in an advert as bland as the burger. His influence was such that your author had the same long curled haircut as his childhood idol (albeit not the same ability on the ball).

The Corn Exchange at the back of the Arndale was an old bazaar of mystery. Locals would have many left-field stalls selling the weird and wonderful. I would spend hours walking through the poorly lit aisles, looking through dusty windows and meeting eccentric shop owners. Here you could peruse old comic books, trinkets from lost time, exotic posters with scantily clad women, and the draw for teenage boys, dangerous objects. We would often be here to buy pellet guns and sling-shots with promises that 'we wouldn't get up to no good' with them.

The Millennium Quarter (the Northern Quarter, as it's now known) was the moody part of town. It was full of prostitutes, pimps, pushers, pet and porn shops. Tib Street became that ingrained in our young minds as the red light district that no playground insult was complete without claiming to have seen someone's mum working there. It's always the mums that get the brunt of it. There were only two reasons I would visit that part of town during my high school years: Dr Hermans, where you could buy magic mushrooms legally if you were eighteen-plus (if you were underage, a plea in the doorway to someone going in always resulted in getting Shrooms), and more often than not I'd be here for Affleck's Palace, arguably the only building that has remained the same in Manchester. It was a world unto itself then, and now it feels like the world outside is assimilating to Affleck's. A maze of independent market stalls for the alternative, a sanctum for your author when he used to skip school. I was fascinated by the staff and shoppers at Affleck's Palace. I was always trying so many different masks on to fit in with groups when I was younger that to see these lot dressed like they were out of a sci-fi movie blew my young mind; white people with dreads, body piercings, tattoos, the smell of Nag Champa in the air to disguise the aroma of weed. It was like you were walking the set of *Blade Runner*. How these people dressed would just not slide in my part of town, but within the confines of Affleck's Palace, if you were wearing brands or trying too hard to look cool, you were very much the odd one out. Being different was normal. The people who ran the shops didn't seem much older than us and didn't care we were wagging school, as long as we weren't causing trouble to them.

The population of Manchester city centre was by and large white. The only indication that you were in a multi-cultural city at the centre was Chinatown. The first Chinese restaurants had opened not long after the Second World War, but it wasn't until the eighties that this small rectangular area became immersed in the city. In 1987, a year after Manchester twinned with Wuhan, the *paifang* on Faulkner Street was built. This 'Arch of Chinatown' adorned with dragons and painted in red and gold soon became a landmark and a tourist attraction. We would always come to town to celebrate Chinese New Year, but that was as diverse as the town centre got, despite our migrant population.

The Industrial Revolution kick-started large-scale immigration, beginning with Irish migrants taking up work in the mills and followed by Jewish migrants fleeing persecution in Eastern Europe. Moving ahead to the middle of the twentieth century, migrants generally arrived in this country because of problems in their countries of birth, such as war, civil unrest, discrimination, and, like the Irish migrants a century before, poverty. The main immigrants between 1951 and 1971 were Irish, Caribbean (particularly Jamaicans), South Africans, East African Asians from Kenya, and people from India and Pakistan.[2]

For evidence of this migrant history of Manchester and to see its multitude proper, you would have to venture outside the centre. The inner-city areas across Manchester became recognisable by the ethnic enclaves they had evolved into through periods of migration. People with similar cultures settled together to build lives that reflected their heritage: Rusholme's Asian community, Prestwich's Jewish neighbourhoods, the Irish of Levenshulme, the Caribbean culture in Moss Side. Cheetham Hill was so eclectic that you could hear Salaam, Shalom, or See You Later just by walking ten minutes down the main road. There were many different cultures, cuisines, and colours across Manchester, yet their representation within the town centre didn't exist.

On 15 June 1996, however, people celebrated their heritage in town but weren't part of the local population. A massive influx of football fans had travelled in from the Continent for the European Championships that started this weekend. Manchester was a host city with the games taking place at Manchester United's Old Trafford Stadium. Scores of Germans, Czechs, Italians, and Russians were in town with banners, face paint, and joie de vivre. Due to previous tensions stemming from England's rivalry with Germany, there was an increase in police presence on patrol should trouble arise. This conflict has always seemed one-sided to me and driven by English media; the only beef the Germans were worried about came on a plate. At the time, the UK was at odds with the rest of Europe on whether eating British meat could lead to people contracting the human version of Mad Cow disease. The German national team were taking no risks and brought their own chef, with their German produce, to prepare the squad's meals. In a bid to convince German fans his meat was safe, a food seller outside Old Trafford put up a sign offering a guarantee that he was selling 'kein englisches Rindfleisch' (No English Beef).

I was also in town that morning for football reasons. The upcoming summer I was having trials at Bolton Wanderers and needed some new boots. I had got in early, went to JD Sports to drool over the Adidas Predators (£120 RRP) and left with a pair of Puma Kings (£30 RRP).

- *It's the foot inside the boot that matters, David.*

By 10am, I was back in Longsight playing football in Crowcroft Park. During the last international tournament (USA World Cup '94), we'd come up with the idea of pairing off into doubles, with two players going up against each other as a game to play. Each duo would represent a nation in the competition; your team was given to you by which country you looked like you might originate from. As someone with olive skin and jet-black hair, the list was endless, but it never included England; for Euro '96 I was Romania, Portugal, Spain, and Italy.

After an hour of playing, we'd decided to head home to get ready for the England and Scotland game that was on later that day. One of the lads, Wes, had a free house so we'd be able to get pissed and watch in there. We walked up Stovell Avenue from Longsight to Levenshulme from the park, discussing the Euros. As we turned up Matthews Lane, which splits the two areas, we felt a huge rumble. We presumed it was roadworks close by, thought nothing more of it, said our goodbyes, and I crossed into Levenshulme, down our street and home. I opened the front door to see my Mum in the hallway holding one of those old cordless handsets with an antenna so large you had to duck when the person holding it turned around. My Mum was in bits.

- *What's happened, Mum?*
- *There's been a bomb in town! Kelly's gone in to get your Dad a present …*

There had been bomb scares in the past, but it never crossed my mind that we might have felt the effects of one only moments earlier. The alarms for IRA bombs had become so common that kids at my school used to phone in with mock-Irish accents, threatening there was a device on the grounds so they would have to evacuate the pupils and we'd get a day off. I thought this would be a similar prank; never did anyone imagine there would be an actual bomb attack in Manchester.

> We were on the day shift, I would say around about 9.30, and we got a first call to a suspected bomb. So we all piled down to near the Arndale Centre, just a way off Cross Street and then we hung around there for a little while. Over that period of time we got a lot of calls for the Arndale Centre with like incendiary devices – they told you like a holding point for a while, and then they release certain pumps. So they just kept one pump parked on Cateaton Street. We left the site, got released, and then we turned out to a place on Deansgate. About five or ten minutes later there's a little bit more action and you start seeing helicopters and we thought all that strange. They usually just check it out and say everything's OK and you're back to normal. But the helicopter was coming over, and you could hear like a loudspeaker and then there was more and more appliances coming into town from Salford, Broughton, and Moss Side.
>
> –John Moss, firefighter (retired)[3]

Due to the number of false alarms for attacks in the past, many shoppers dismissed the requests to evacuate. It was difficult for shop owners to clear their premises and get them to safety, so managers began setting off fire alarms to hurry them out. The staff that remained were on the look out for anything that seemed out of the ordinary on their premises.

> We'd been evacuated before, it'd happened so many times and we used to get bomb warnings quite regularly and we would get a 111 code and would have to all go round looking for a 'suspicious package'. We were all like, 'What are we actually looking for?' To me a bomb

was a black round ball with a wick hanging out at the end of it. I don't know what I was looking for, but we all just evacuated as we have done before. Not really thinking much about it.

– Rachel Kelly, teacher (then WHSmith employee and student)[4]

We didn't realise at that point that to get rid of the people out of the shops and the offices, they were pressing the fire alarms; rather than say it was a bomb, they wanted to give the impression it was to evacuate for a fire. That was the only way they deemed they could do it. So there's loads and loads of calls going into control with the firefighters heading into town thinking it's a fire alarm going off. We dealt with the Deansgate one, a smoke alarm in the kitchen. We got some call to the Britannia Hotel in Portland Street, another fire alarm. It was not coming over the airwaves that something was happening with a bomb. We then got another call to the Ramada Hotel, which meant we had to go down Corporation Street where the lorry holding the bomb was. We go past and onto Deansgate and into the underground carpark of the Ramada. Then over the radio we get news that there's gonna be a controlled explosion. So I thought, oh right, okay, you know, usually they just do the detonator, whatever. We're just about to step off the appliance … and then boom!

– John Moss[5]

At 11.16am, bomb disposal officers with a remote-controlled robot tried to defuse an explosive inside a truck parked on Corporation Street. Their attempt failed. A 3,300lb bomb exploded in Manchester city centre, the biggest detonation in the UK since the Second World War. The impact was felt in the surrounding suburbs; people heard the explosion 15 miles away, the mushroom cloud it created was 1,000 feet high and visible across Greater Manchester.

So we went on the floor because the shockwave has just come straight down on us, we look at each other – you can imagine what we said to each other as we looked up at the concrete, expecting that it's going to come down on us! It took a couple of seconds to get our bearings. A security woman shouted, 'My partner is in Longridge House!' We

> come out from underneath the loading bay and it's just a big cloud of dust and you can't … you can't see your hand in front of your face for all the dust …
>
> – John Moss[6]

Many office workers ignored the advice to leave their buildings and remained on-site and in office blocks when the bomb exploded; thankfully for them, due to the heightened police presence in town and the extra number of fire engines in town attending false fire alarms, the emergency services were equipped with numbers to help with their injuries.

> Someone said there's something going on in Manchester, his dad's phoned in and the police are ordering you to keep away from the windows. They think it's a car bomb. From what we heard, we thought it was near Lewis's, so we're working away. We was in the centre of one of the floors, nowhere near the windows, and then all of a sudden, this, well, I still can't describe it, because it was like a silence … then this suction, if you know what I mean. And then the debris falling from the false ceilings. I just hid under my desk. I think if they realised how big it was, they'd have got us all down in the basement. Apparently someone was looking out of the window and they got hit by the suction of the windows going in. There was a couple of windows come out on the side that was facing the bomb. It was just mayhem and then we was sent down into the basement. It was just a crazy day.
>
> – Anne Worthington, customer service adviser (retired)[7]

> We exit up to Longridge House with the first aid kit. The first pump crew had already gone into that building 'cause they could hear people screaming and the majority were told to wait on the second floor where they'd gone to the windows to look out at what was happening. So they copped the force of the blast. About 20 people were all told to stay in there – with hindsight, if they'd gone underneath the tables they would probably have been safe. I mean it was carnage from the blast. The lifts were all twisted, the doors and everything

were mangled. We find this security guard, his head is sort of sliced, it's just skin flapping off where the glass has gone and cut his forehead. We bandaged him up. Then there was quite a lot of girls under their desks that won't get out through fear. So we're dragging them out, saying, 'Look, we need to get you out, everything's OK. Let's just get you out of here!' The one thing that struck us – 'cause you don't see that kind of devastation – was when we go inside the Arndale Centre and it's like the blow-torch effect. You could see where the blast's petered out as it's gone down the malls. So nearest to the blast it's obviously gone and pushed everything out, and then going up towards Piccadilly Gardens, that end of the Arndale, it just like tapered out. The top end at the back was fine but anything near the bomb, it just tore through it.

–John Moss[8]

The blast destroyed parts of the Arndale and Marks and Spencer's. Manchester Cathedral had part of its roof torn off, the bus station was gone, and the historic buildings in Shambles Square were damaged. In a preservation task The Old Wellington and Sinclair's Oyster Bar (built in the 1700s), were painstakingly dismantled, relocated 100 metres away, and meticulously reassembled to their original form. The Royal Exchange was devastated. The glass roof of Victoria Station shattered with shards raining on those who had taken refuge inside. The structural damage to the Corn Exchange required two years of redevelopment and many of the independent businesses that operated inside would never return. There were over 650 buildings damaged to the tune of an estimated £700 million (£1.7 billion today).

A few weeks later I got a phone call from Bootle Street Police Station saying that they had recovered loads of items from different shops that obviously had been left in there. My purse had been in there, they'd been able to identify it and did I want to come down and collect my stuff. I always remember when it was because it had been my birthday that week and it was coming up to Father's Day. So I had my birthday money in my purse and I was like, brilliant, I thought I'd lost my birthday money, and WHSmith were claiming for that on their insurance anyway. But then I went down to the Police Station and got my bag back but they're not allowed to take anything out – they can only look in your bag to identify whose it is. So everything was in there, including my sandwiches from that day! So literally everything had to go in the bin – I was like, oh for God's sake, this was a really nice bag, and a really nice purse and it all went in the bin – but I did get me money back, and then I got the money back on the insurance as well. So I did pretty well! I never got the Adidas top back which I left, which I was gutted about. It was probably ripped to pieces. It was gorgeous. It was a cornflower blue with orange stripes down the sleeves and it was gone. Gone! I don't remember what was in the sandwich – when I got the bag back it was just a bag of black mould! It was quite emotional going and getting my stuff. I'm thinking that I've lost stuff, but you know, it's only a bag. It could have been a lot worse, couldn't it?

– Rachel Kelly[9]

We were absolutely sweltering, you've got your full fire gear on with big rubber boots. It was a boiling hot day. You're running up and down buildings and I remember there was a fountain, like a circular fountain – where the new one is built. At the end of the day for a breather, we all sat tunics off with our feet in this fountain, still in a little bit of disbelief, and shocked that despite all the devastation surrounding us there was still no confirmed reports of any deaths, or life-threatening injuries.

– John Moss[10]

The increased number of emergency services in the city centre at the time of the bomb was the reason for the low number of casualties. Had there not been the extra police presence in town for the Euros, had business owners not set off false alarms calling in fire engines, then it may not have been the case. In total, 216 people were injured in the blast.

Many of those injured were outside the police cordon. Seventy bystanders were ferried to three hospitals in ambulances. Others

> walked or were taken by friends. A consultant at Hope Hospital said most of the seriously injured – including a pregnant woman thrown 15 ft (4.6 m) into the air – had suffered deep glass wounds which would require surgery.
>
> – BBC report[11]

The police stopped all transport in and out of town; there was no way to leave other than by foot; with only landline phones available as a way to communicate their safety, many families sat in fear of what might have happened. The people at home only had the news to follow for what was going on. My Mum and I were included in the audience. It was around 3pm when we heard the front door go when our fears alleviated. My fourteen-year-old sister walked into the living room, oblivious to events.

- *Are you OK?*
- *Yeah. What's happened?*
- *What do you mean, 'What's happened?' The bomb in town?!*
- *What bomb? We went to Stockport instead, better shops …*

Miraculously, there were no fatalities on the day, but the aftermath of the disaster did take a life. In 2015, father-of-two Stuart Packard died from cancer caused by the asbestos in the air following the clean-up. Stuart worked as part of the security team during the clean-up, where he was working as a security guard. Unequipped with the correct clothing to wear, almost two decades after the event, his life was tragically cut short at the age of forty.[12] Addressing the attack, Prime Minister John Major condemned the act, closing his statement with 'We shall spare no effort to bring those responsible to justice'.[13] To this day there have been no arrests in connection to the attack. Greater Manchester Police are now resigned that there may never be.

While the buildings surrounding the bomb felt the full force, as the debris fell from the sky, a postbox next to where the truck was parked remained intact. It has since become a symbol of Mancunians, resolute to not waiver in tragic circumstances. It wasn't just the postbox that held strong:

> What did make us laugh, the police had been in and filmed the aftermath and sent it to all the different shops, and one of our bosses let us watch it. You know when you go into a bookshop and they have cardboard stands to promote the new titles? They would never stay up. They were always falling over, and we had to constantly rebuild them to keep these books in place. In the police video, much to our disbelief, was one of them still standing. They fell down on us every single week, but managed to stay up after the impact of a bomb! So it wasn't just the postbox that was left undisturbed, there was also a cardboard book stand at WHSmith that never fell.
>
> – Rachel Kelly[14]

Mancunians didn't allow the explosion to deter them from venturing into town. On the very same night, people were back in Manchester city centre to watch the football and go out; they refused to let a terrorist attack put their life on hold.

> 'I'm not gonna be stopped what I'm doing by the IRA' was my attitude, and my son was in a marching band and was playing in the Marple Carnival that afternoon. England was playing Scotland. We was gonna do that, and then find a pub to watch the football match. I said, 'I'm not spoiling my plans for the bloody IRA' – so I went to get out. The security said, 'We're not supposed to let you out – but if you go out you go out it's on your own accord and risk.' 'Sure, whatever,' I said, 'you want me to sign something, I will, but I am going out, I'm not staying in this building!' And then they directed me to walk away from the building. And then I saw the girls from Littlewoods – I could recognise the uniforms – and the state that they was in … And it's only after you saw the plume of smoke that was still going when we got home that I realised how big it was. It was weird. But we carried on our day. We went up to the Marple Carnival, and then had our Saturday night out in town to watch the football. We knew town was closed up to a certain area, but we said, 'We'll go and find out, there'll

> be somewhere open', and we had to walk through on the perimeter. I remember going past the Arndale. The alarms was still going off. It was weird because it was silent except for all the car alarms ... I find it very hard to say that it was a good thing, because it was shocking. It was shocking what happened ... But Manchester proved that it could come back from anything, and we proved that and we came back better. But I'll never say that the bomb was a good thing for Manchester.
>
> – Anne Worthington[15]

> The bombing happened at a time when funding from the Millennium Commission was available for regeneration projects. In addition, much of the work on public spaces such as Cathedral Gardens, Exchange Square and Piccadilly Gardens would have happened regardless of the bomb, as Manchester was due to host the Commonwealth Games in 2002.
>
> – Dr Joanne Massey, senior lecturer[16]

The popular notion that surrounds the IRA bomb is that it was the catalyst for Manchester's change. That's a creation myth. That Manchester had its version of the Big Bang and what followed was a new beginning. It's the sort of tragedy over triumph you would expect from a Hollywood blockbuster. A plucky Northern town hit by disaster to rise from the ashes. It's a good story; it's a romantic story; it's a fictional story.

> It isn't at all true. Manchester regeneration had already started with Manchester Arena, with the Bridgewater Hall, with Hulme redevelopment, and other things would have been in the pipeline. When the bomb went off, the partnerships were already in place, which meant the intervention was that much quicker.
>
> – Len Grant, photographer[17]

> A lot of people put the regeneration down to the IRA bomb. I think that's wrong. Some people put it down to the Commonwealth Games, and that's wrong. I put it down to the Olympic Games bid much earlier on. The Olympic Games bid – although we lost both

> bids – it was the first time Graham Stringer bought a suit, went down to London, and started being confident. Even when we lost the Olympic bid, people were celebrating in Castlefield by tens of thousands. For the first time, Manchester realised we weren't trying to compete with Bradford or Birmingham or Burnley, but we were competing with the great second cities like Barcelona, Los Angeles, and Sydney. And there was a sense of civic pride that came up.
>
> – Tom Bloxham MBE, chair of Urban Splash and founding chair of Manchester International Festival[18]

The idea that Manchester was bidding for the Olympics was met with mixed emotions; some felt that it was ambitious of the city and possible, others felt it was a waste of time and money that would be better spent elsewhere. The National Archives have recently released documents containing a post-mortem on the failed bid where Tory MP Damian Green claims, 'The reason for Manchester's failure is the obvious one: that no one in their right mind would spend three weeks in Manchester.'[19] But unknown to Damian Green, a failed bid could also be a success.

> I always thought it was a bit bizarre that Manchester should be bidding for the Olympics. I thought we haven't got a chance – I think there was a lot of scepticism at that time – we haven't got a cat in hell's chance, why are we doing this? I don't think many realised that it was just putting Manchester on the international stage, 'cause that's what the Council leaders, the city fathers if you like – and they were fathers rather than mothers – were trying to do. It wasn't really a case of 'oh, we think we'll win this'. It was raising the profile. Wherever it is announced alongside all these other cities, Sydney, San Francisco, and whoever else, and then they have Manchester, you've obviously got people around the world saying where the hell is Manchester? And I suspect it was probably [Chief Executive of Manchester City Council, Howard] Bernstein that could see the bigger picture.
>
> – Len Grant[20]

> What the bomb did was accelerate a change that was already in place. It was a huge opportunity that, to Manchester's credit, it grabbed with both hands and actually used it to accelerate the change. So all those little ideas went a lot, lot quicker. Every city is different, other cities would maybe have been standing around a year later arguing who was supposed to lead, who was going to be on the board of the task force, worrying where they would get the money. Manchester didn't do that. It said, 'Let's come up with a plan, let's worry about the money later.' What was important at that time was the relationships between the City Council and national government. It was a Tory Government at that stage, and the public and private sector were all well embedded, so everybody was working together with a common purpose.
>
> – Tom Bloxham[21]

Given the facts, the truth is far more impressive and telling of Manchester and its people. This was a place that only a decade previous had been hit with recession. This was a city that had almost been crippled by de-industrialisation, 'leaving worklessness, poverty and low ambition entrenched in many communities'.[22] Under Margaret Thatcher, economic decline accelerated alarmingly.

> Like lumbering dinosaurs who suddenly met their meteorite, the big heavy industries of east Manchester toppled into extinction. Wire works, engineering firms, factories of all kinds went out of business, throwing hundreds of men at a time – and they were mainly men – onto the dole. In east Manchester, a district full of people in skilled and semi-skilled employment became a place where there were hardly any jobs at all.[23]

Michael Gove, who in 2022 would be appointed Secretary of State for Levelling Up, Housing and Communities, celebrated Thatcher's impact at the time: 'We are at last experiencing a new empire, an empire where the happy south stamps over the cruel, dirty toothless face of the northerner.'[24] Even Tony Wilson said his home town 'felt like a piece of history that had been spat out. It was really grimy and dirty. Dirty old town'.[25]

Manchester's response to the economic decline that pre-dates the IRA bomb is the true beginning of our regeneration. The IRA does not deserve a single bit of credit for what we were to become; it was the city's leaders and key decision-makers that sought not only to get Manchester out of austerity but to push us beyond what many thought possible. This is the rags-to-riches story we should celebrate. In response to the political adversity, the city not only got back on its feet but swung for the fences and came out on top, against the odds. The explosion on 15 June 1996 was a hurdle in an ambitious race that Manchester had already long started. The terrorist attack may have accelerated the process, but the bomb on Corporation Street was not the catalyst for change that many perceive it to be.

> In other cities like Liverpool, they were militantly controlled by Labour but there was still a lot of political infighting, and they hated the Thatcher government, quite rightly, but what was happening in Manchester, local politicians were being more pragmatic about what was going on in the central government. In the early nineties it was Graham Stringer before Richard Leese, he was the leader of the council … rather than saying, 'We're not going to play ball with central government', they would say, 'Right, OK, we will work with you. We'll take your money, thank you very much.' One example of that was an organisation called the Central Manchester Development Corporation which was set up by the government. Stringer sat on the board of that, and it brought in investment, which kickstarted Castlefield, which started Piccadilly Village. Central Manchester Development Corporation put in their money and they were also behind the investment into Central Manchester, which developed the Bridgewater Hall and so on. Manchester's local politicians said, 'OK, for the benefit of our city, we'll work with you.' That's what was happening in Manchester politically at that time, and that's why they were keen to do the Olympic bids. Manchester was ambitious. Manchester wanted to see itself as a European city.
>
> – Len Grant[26]

The rebuilding seemed to begin as quickly as the dust settled. Grey exteriors became glass fronts; more tramlines snaked across the city, international stores opened, new buildings were built. The Printworks, a multipurpose venue with restaurants, clubs, and a cinema, was opened by the odd pairing of Sir Alex Ferguson and Lionel Richie. Quickly, there were more and more reasons to come into town.

> I realised that I was documenting something significant. I had access to some of the viewpoints where you could see this city that was devastated, every building being wrapped up in plastic, and I realised I was documenting something unique. I was doing it for about two years, and it did feel like every scaffolding pole and every piece of plastic that was available in the northwest was being used in Manchester centre, the place was void of shoppers. It was still accessible for people to walk around, but it was full of workmen. The best fun I had on a shoot was on the demolition of Maxwell House, which became the Printworks, and the only thing that was left of Maxwell House was the wall, the façade, and everything else behind it was being demolished. The façade was pinned up with scaffolding but the whole interior was being demolished. I loved going and photographing the gangs of demolition guys who were working on that. The demolition workers are a breed apart from construction workers. The Printworks was very incongruous with the rest of town, but it was terribly false. We had New Cathedral Street, we had Harvey Nics, a shop I think I've probably only been in once in twenty-odd years. I think the only other one outside of London was in Leeds so we got Harvey Nics, we got a Selfridges, again it was the first time Selfridges had moved out of London. You felt when you were walking down New Cathedral Street – although these shops weren't necessarily something you'd want to go into – that the city had advanced, had moved up. It did feel as if it was becoming part of a world stage. Much of the city centre was designed by local architects, but we also had certain things where we had international architects coming in, working in the city for the first time, and the remodelling of it.
>
> – Len Grant[27]

The foundations of what Manchester was to become were more and more visible. This newfound affluence, however, wasn't felt in the surrounding districts. Change outside of the city centre was conspicuous by its absence. If this new vision of Manchester was to bring more opportunities for future generations, then it wasn't evident for the young people growing up.

2

'The city that lets down its pupils'

YOUTH

After eighteen years in charge, the Conservative Party had lost control of the country. As with many of my peers ready to leave school, my political awareness was minimal. The only MPs I recognised were those satirised in *Spitting Image*; the context of sketches was beyond me, but the puppets' behaviour did pique the interest of someone who had begun heavily smoking weed. It was only when D:Ream's 'Things Can Only Get Better' was rammed down everyone's ears that my attention extended beyond John Major's grey caricature. The song, and Tony Blair, was everywhere. From newspaper front covers I'd deliver on my paper round to appearing on every terrestrial TV station – Labour's campaign was inescapable. The song was horrendous, and Tony's face represented dragging a heavy bag of Sunday papers around Longsight. What things were going to get better? Hindsight affords you a comparison, whereas in your youth, there are no alternatives; things just are. There was never a suggestion that some greater power had created the framework within which I lived. I wasn't aware that political decisions made 200 miles away had any significance. Everything I experienced as a teenager never felt anything other than normal.

Following their 1997 General Election win New Labour implemented a programme of local authority inspections across the UK. The report on Manchester was damning. The city was failing across all areas, and the *Independent* declared it a 'city that lets down its pupils'.[1] Manchester was 127th out of 132 areas for GCSE performance. One Manchester school in the report stood out for how badly it was performing: Spurley Hey High School. My high school.

As Tony Blair moved into Number 10, I was leaving Spurley Hey, just as it made the national news as one of the country's worst schools. The truancy rates, expulsion numbers, and exam grades were in the relegation zone in the school league tables. The national average for GCSEs was 45 per cent of the school year to achieve five or more A–C grades; Spurley Hey High School had just 6 per cent. There was a running joke that more people left pregnant than with GCSEs which I can't substantiate as a fact, but I'm aware of the number of us that left as expectant parents compared to those that went on to further education.

Spurley Hey's minimal academic achievements may suggest that school was difficult; some may think of it as an intimidating place with disinterested teachers; this is partly true. I have regrets about not getting better schooling, but I wonder at what expense it would have been? As a sixteen-year-old lad who spent his schooldays chasing footballs and girls, I was blissfully unaware I was being let down by the state. I've read biographies of people who went to a public school, institutions guaranteed to enlighten and sharpen young minds, but they sounded like such miserable places run by totalitarian regimes; no thanks! But which teenager compares their education? Did I have a single concern? No. Which teenager pulls their parents aside to ask for better schooling?

- *Mum, Dad. I'm not sure my teachers are as good as they can be – can I go somewhere stricter, where I'm forced to listen, study more, and pay attention. I don't like the freedom I'm getting at school.*

That doesn't happen. And besides, I was happy. I may not have had the best education, but the social skills I acquired from my peers remain invaluable to this day. My school, unintentionally, was preparing me to live in Manchester, not to go to Oxford, Cambridge, or any university. How I learned to communicate with fellow pupils and negotiate myself around trouble seemed more vital than learning Pythagoras. Quick wit will get you out of a fight faster than a maths calculation. Besides, it's not like I was privy to how dysfunctional it was; I presumed all schools were the same. My reports never gave my parents cause for concern, and I was doing well across most subjects, despite having some of the most maladjusted teachers Manchester had seen:

Mr D, an ageing RE teacher, would keep cider in his drawer. He looked like Uncle Monty from Withnail and I and would try to tell us about the Bible while being half-cut. He was nice to us most of the time, until the one time a pupil stole his drink and started necking it in class.

> - *Thou Shall Not Covet Another's Possession, Rosie.*
> - *Thou Shouldn't Get Pissed in Class, Sir!*

There were the PE teachers, Messrs C, M, and F. Mr C was a stern bastard who would make you do class in your keks if you forgot your kit – nicknamed Caveman for his great beard and unkempt hair. Mr M would wet his index finger with his mouth and ram it down your ear if you were behind on shuttle runs, something he referred to as 'giving a wet willy', and would start most lessons asking, 'Who wants one?' Then there was Mr F, who seemed like a decent teacher for the majority of school, but by the last year, he was suspended for throwing his keys at a pupil's face and nearly blinding him. On his return he was under investigation for inappropriately touching a female pupil. For Music, there was the creepy Mr W who would use his tongue as a metronome so you would learn how to keep time.

He'd stick out this little moist pink morsel from his mouth and count to four by flicking it left-right-left-right. That was enough for me, regrettably, not to choose Music as a GCSE option.

For Science, Mr H was a tattooed, long-haired, Harley-Davidson rock 'n' roller type. He was always really sound with students, partly because of his chilled demeanour; he always stunk of skunk, which probably helped with the kids he tried to control.

The Headteacher was mousey Miss P, a non-existent entity outside of the school assembly. It was her Deputy, Mr B, that everyone feared. A former prison warden, Mr B patrolled the corridors and dealt with bad behaviour as if he was walking a wing on Strangeways. The naughty pupils – those that got caught – hated Mr B because he was where we were sent for discipline. The truth is he had a fair but firm policy; whilst he may have come across as a daunting figure, he cared about our welfare. One weekend, I'd been hanging around a car park in Levenshulme with some girls that were from out of the area when a local lad with gang affiliations tried to embarrass me by putting a machete to my throat. He threatened that if I didn't get him some money by Friday, then he'd have my head. As you'd expect, that somewhat shook the shit out of me. My parents had two modes to deal with this: 1) tell Mr B and 2) load a van of people outside the school by Friday's deadline. Mr B was unbelievably calm about it and alleviated a lot of my fears. The kid didn't turn up, and unknown to me, Mr B and my family were in cahoots should anything have happened. After school, he walked over to the van my Dad had with his friends in and knocked on the window, saying, 'I think we're alright here, but I'll look after him from now on.'

There were good teachers! Mr M1, who taught IT, was a 6 foot 5 basketball enthusiast who on the face could be presumed intimidating, but he was really a big friendly bear, with the loudest infectious laugh. The surroundings never daunted him. He would never lose his temper, never swear at the kids, nor chuck something at us because we were misbehaving – something that happened in other subjects – he operated the class incredibly well, spoke to us on a level with respect, which students would reciprocate. He was the only teacher I remember talking to about rap music; although he didn't like the gangster stuff we were into, he put me on to The Roots, which remains one of my favourite bands to this day. As the only black teacher at Spurley Hey, it was apparent how the black pupils warmed to him more than other teachers.

> It was a great morale booster as he was the first person of colour in a professional role in my young mind. Information Technology was my favourite subject in school and he was part of the reason. A great teacher with a colourful personality. He passed on a few years back. I remember bumping into him about twelve years ago at his daughter's graduation and he was so proud. We had a really good chat and that memory is cherished forever.
>
> – Nathan Miles, author's friend[2]

My favourite teacher was Miss E who taught English. She was popular amongst boys as she would always wear low-cut tops and often bend over your desk to help. Now, this wasn't why she was my favourite – I won't deny a schoolboy crush – but Miss E was the one teacher that gave a damn about my creative ambition and was so encouraging in my work. It was only her class that I excelled in during my time at school, and part of the reason you're reading this today.

By my final year, many young supply teachers came in on rotation to fill in for the teachers off because of heart attacks, nervous breakdowns, and court cases. If the thick-skinned seasoned teachers struggled to get through to us, then this fresh-faced bunch straight out of Uni stood no chance – we ran wild. It was an unruly school, and it would be quick to point the finger at the teachers; we saw it as a youth club – it cannot have been an easy job.

Spurley Hey wasn't an exception, it was emblematic of the problems Manchester's high schools faced. North Manchester for Boys and Moston Brook joined my high school for the worst three state schools for achievements, but the issues were widespread. Truancy was rife across the city, ten pupils a day were being excluded, with one school temporarily excluding 782 pupils over a three-year period. One hundred and forty kids had been permanently expelled from the school system, with no alternative education provided. The school budget deficits were the highest in the country, the exam results were worryingly low. An Ofsted inspection of Manchester said, 'The LEA is beset with problems. Some are inherent in the nature of the city, others are the political and managerial responsibility of the LEA. Too many decisions have been put off for too long, so that problems have grown to a size that makes them increasingly difficult to tackle.'[3]

Spurley Hey failed us with education, but it did excel when it came to integrating people from different cultural backgrounds; due to its location, it benefited from having diverse students. The school was positioned between Longsight, Levenshulme, and Gorton in South Manchester, and it allowed me to interact and learn about other people's heritages. That was always the noticeable difference between the north and south of Manchester. Outside of Cheetham Hill (a multi-ethnic community since the mid-nineteenth century), areas such as Moston, Clayton, and Miles Platting were densely White British. In South Manchester, the streets I ran through in Levenshulme, much like my school, were a migrants mash-up. I have always been a culture vulture and expanding my horizons into how other people live has always fascinated me. To go through my friends' front doors was to step into different worlds, with new music, customs, and so much fantastic food.

> I always loved Leve [Levenshulme] because it was a picture of immigration in Manchester. There was a lot of Irish at first, then Irish and Caribbean and then Indian and Pakistani. The mix of the people was brilliant. Our school was the best because we would celebrate every single religious holiday. I felt like there was a party every week! Perhaps it is because of where we grew up or because we are all immigrants from somewhere, but we'd all celebrate together. My street had people of all shapes, colours, creeds, religions; people would take food round to each other's house. Our next-door neighbour was Jamaican and when they made a goat curry, they would bring it to our door; there was a Pakistani family, that had knocked three houses through, and at Eid they would bring loads of treats to neighbours. They'd bake all these cakes and distribute them along the street. I've moved to places like Stratford-upon-Avon – you couldn't get more white middle class – and it's not an immigrant city at all, and it just felt really alien to me. I couldn't stand it and had to leave.
>
> – Mary McGuigan, freelancer[4]

> When I was younger I lived in Hulme and that is a big black community. A lot of streets of black families, and going to my Mum's friends I was playing with all black kids, it was a tight-knit community. When I came over to the south of Manchester, it was more mixed. My school was very mixed and diverse, most of my friends then were probably as many white as black. What I did notice is that when I used to go and see my cousins who lived in Hulme they lived a different lifestyle to how we lived in South Manchester. I think that was why we came south because my Grandma wanted us to live in a more mixed area for us to be able to progress, and perhaps not fall into certain trappings. Like it was tight-knit, but perhaps too tight-knit, to the extent that you might not get that open-minded view of how people live in the wider city. There was still all the culture, the music, the rum punches, cut down chickens on a Sunday. We still had that, but also

> being surrounded by more Asian and white people gave us a more holistic view of how the city, and its people, worked.
>
> – Nathan Miles[5]

The schools that did perform well, as they ever did, were Manchester's grammar schools; if you were financially fortunate, or passed your eleven-plus to attend, you were going to get a better education. The flipside being that these institutions didn't offer the same multi-cultured environment as large parts of Manchester; if you attended a school where you were in the overwhelming minority, it left those young people facing a sense of alienation and gravitating towards familiarity wherever they could find it.

> We were from what you would call a 'rough area', a council estate, and I used to get the bus to Urmston Grammar School. It was forty-five minutes away and I passed my eleven-plus and got into grammar school. I was one of basically two black or mixed-race kids, like an Asian girl and a couple of Asian lads. A lot of them did come from middle-class backgrounds, middle-class families, and I got on with some of those people as well but the people I got on with the best were the kids from my similar economic situation. My good mates were all from working-class environments. So you weren't in a position that you were getting grief if you were a bit skint, if you got a meal ticket for dinner, you're not having the piss taken out of you. So you would naturally gravitate toward those people.
>
> – Jay Motty, journalist[6]

> When I left primary school, my Asian mates went to school in Cheetham Hill and Cravenwood, and my parents put me in for grammar schools and to do the eleven-plus. I got into Bury Grammar but the problem was there were hardly any Asian people. In a year that might have been maybe one black and two Asian pupils. All my Asian friends had gone to the feeder school so it was an alienating environment to be in. Obviously, around Bury there's a large Jewish community, to the extent that they had their own assembly at the school. You would have the White assembly, and a Jewish assembly but nothing

accommodating anything else. So if anything, the closest I felt to having an affinity with people was with the Jewish lads, 'cause at least they were a little bit different to the majority, and Islam and Judaism are both Abrahamic faiths and have similar ways. So there was that small similarity I could attach to, but that alienation made me keener to hang around with my proper mates outside of school.

– Nooruddean Choudry, author and writer[7]

I lived in Cheetham Hill until I was nine and that was more Asian back then so I'd been in that diverse area and then I moved to Clayton and that is white, I mean you couldn't get more white. There were like three black families in the area so I'd never really experienced a black community. The only time we had aside from that to be surrounded by predominantly black people was at family functions. I think that's why my sister and I went searching for our culture, like going to watch the Manchester Giants basketball team. We met people there who were ethnic minorities and we were like, 'Ooh, this is different', because all our friends in school were white, so we branched out from there trying to find more. That was why I decided to go to Loreto College because we needed to embrace that culture and it was probably one of the most important decisions we made.

– Marsha Bell, author's friend[8]

Outside of school, there were few organisations to occupy our time. There was only one youth club that was run at the Bethshan Tabernacle by some well-intended religious folk, but the facilities were dire – cheap orange juice, broken pool cues, table tennis with no balls – their evenings always came with some undercurrent of converting us would-be sinners to the Lord's salvation. There were the RAF cadets around the corner from my house run by despot Poundshop army rejects that would bark orders at young kids in grey uniforms. I went once with a keen friend on the promise that we'd get to shoot guns, but inside the only shots fired were in the form of abuse from the elders. It was horrible.

Fortunately (for me) my friend quickly lost control of his bowels when some bully in a beret spit-shouted in his face. Never have I been so pleased to see someone fill their keks; we quickly left and never returned.

In Levenshulme, there was Bob's Gym which was opened by former pro-boxer Bob Dolan in 1980 at the old community centre on Chapel Street. Bob's Gym had countless youngsters through the doors over the years, giving sanctuary and support to many that may not have had it at home. I would go down to Bob's a lot as a teenager but hardly got involved in the sparring; I was too fond of my face and too bad at boxing to put the gloves on too many times. His work with kids in the area over four decades meant he was regarded as a local legend by the people of Levenshulme. Bob passed away at the time of writing this book and the vast number that attended his funeral is testament to his influence in the area. Bob Dolan's story typifies what will be a theme in this book, and one you'll find in most Mancunians of note; a person whose family was from somewhere else (Ireland) that made their mark in Manchester by giving back to the people that live in the city. Nowhere outside Bob's Gym offered anywhere to expand our interests. The last thing a teenager holed up in a school five days a week is going to do is seek more of the same. It felt like everywhere we went tried to discipline us, to add more constraints on how we were to behave; with no entertainment forthcoming, we found our own.

> I grew up on the edge of town, maybe like three miles out and when I was growing up it was a very white area, extremely white and parochial, and people didn't move out of the areas. I mean, it's been massively gentrified now and it was never a terrible area but even so, it was parochial. So everybody knew everybody's family. There was a real community spirit. There was an undercurrent of violence, I would say. It was a bit, I wouldn't say lawless, it's different to how it is now – I

> think in hindsight, especially when I look at my own kids and pupils I teach now, we were given too much freedom.
>
> – Steph Lonsdale, assistant headteacher and poet[9]

If drink is the curse of the working classes, then boredom is the blight of their children. It was the lack of choice that brought alcohol into our hands. Life revolved around solving three problems: where can we play football, where can we meet girls, and where can we get drunk? One place answered all: the local park. A crushed plastic bottle rotates on the asphalt. The smell of weed floats across the grass – motorbikes speed outside, followed by the sound of sirens. The bottle spins. A spliff passed. White Lightning swigged. A football comes over from the five-a-side into the circle of friends and bounces back out. Someone insults a mum. Punches fly. The bottle stops. Her again. I've got to kiss her. Again. This scene would play out weekly.

> Alcohol, our society's most problematic drug, is consumed by the vast majority. Although cider and beer are the most popular drinks rather than alcopops, the industry has increasingly targeted young people in the last decade. The '90s have seen alcohol featuring more and more as a gateway to illicit drugs. He [Dr Chris Luke, Accident and Emergency consultant at the Royal Liverpool University Hospital] emphasised the scale of consumption among young people, stating that:
>
> - 29 per cent of boys and 26 per cent of girls aged 10 to 13 consume alcohol, three quarters of whom reported being drunk
> - 1,000 children under 14 and over are hospitalised every year with alcohol-related presentations
> - 'Virtually all' 15–16 year olds have consumed alcohol.
>
> *Institute of Alcohol Studies*, Issue 3, 1998[10]

> It was just normal. That's what you do. We were just going out in the streets doing mad stuff. Weekends in the parks, drinking White Lightning, getting pissed and just having a laugh, chasing after girls.

We didn't expect it to be any other way because we didn't know it to be any other way.

– Nathan Miles[11]

All my mates were quite similar. We all got into smoking cigs and weed quite early – it was easy to get hold of 'cause where I grew up, that was one of the pathways for me personally. You know, when we were 14, 15, 16 and started drinking on a weekend, the cider and cigs, get £10 of draw between you, all chipping in. That eventually led to the rave scene and everything else. I know it's a horrible term, but I suppose it could be seen like 'laddish culture': the football, drinking, getting into girls, and that sort of stuff. We were very much like just lads, you know. It wasn't very violent. I did have a few fights, especially dealing with racism stuff, but I don't look at that time and think that when I was growing up as a teenager, I was fighting a lot. I wasn't really, it was more a case of I was enjoying myself a bit too much!

– Jay Motty[12]

I was out on the streets every evening, but then so were my friends from school who were more well off. There was much more of a culture that if you were at secondary school then you just went to the park, or wherever, on a Friday, got beer from a shop, and got pissed. We called it jibbing. It was mixed where I grew up, so I went to a proper comp and you had kids coming in off the precinct, and in off Langley Road which was a bit rougher. You had the odd kid that was bussing it in from Ordsall. You'd have the kids off the council estates in Weaste, but then you had the kids from the nicer houses whose dads ran their own business – they were also going out to the park and drinking. It was just the culture where you'd have these massive packs of teenagers outside drinking. And then you'd walk about and discover little spots where you knew you could be left alone. We didn't drink in the park because the police were more likely to move you on so we had these little dead spots where no one could find us. It sounds ridiculous now because it's just wasteland … you know the areas you'd expect the homeless to hang around and we'd sit there and drink; and there'd be twenty or thirty of you, maybe more. People coming and checking out

> what you were up to. It wasn't gangs in the crime sense but just large tribes that would rub up against each other.
>
> – Steph Lonsdale[13]

We were tribes of teens drifting aimlessly through the drizzled streets of Manchester. Gangs as in large numbers, but not gangs that gave their group a name. It wasn't The Warriors. Our postcodes labelled us with reputations perceived by stereotypes. Working-class areas housed scallies; if you were from an affluent area, you were considered a towny. Scallies were trouble-makers from broken homes, susceptible to minor crimes, and all dressed in tracksuits; townies were well educated, well off, and often dressed in expensive clothes with terrible taste in music. The gang I hung around with ran the gamut between the two. Some dressed in Nicholas Deakins boots, Ben Sherman shirts, and North Sails coats; others would wear nothing else but Adidas trackies and Nike Air Max trainers. Some broke the law, but many did not. I also knew lads that lived in the sort of mansions we'd see on *MTV Cribs* from Poynton who dressed and behaved with more scally traits than anyone I knew in South Manchester. The reality is that most teenagers rarely fit the typecast, regardless of where they live, but those that do go on and amplify an area's image for the rest of us and, as we shall discuss later in the book, such is Manchester's greatest curse: parody trumps portrait. Your parents' income did little to influence what you got up to outside the house. If they were rich, you had money to do nothing; if they were poor, you had no money to do nothing. Alcohol was the great equaliser.

> It was so unsupervised. It was quite common for kids to have to get their stomachs pumped – and it was usually the middle-class ones – whereas if that happened now it would be a mega deal with safeguarding and social services being involved. But that used to happen a few times a year, it was almost a given. I remember the

> last day of school we used to have these assemblies in the big school hall and there was a big kerfuffle at the back near the canteen shutters – and some lad had come in absolutely bladdered and collapsed and they had to get an ambulance to take him out and carry on the assembly.
>
> – Steph Lonsdale[14]

I never got my stomach pumped, although I knew plenty that did. Without any funds to buy any alcohol, one weekend my friend Paddy had decided to pilfer his parents' homemade Poitín – a homemade Irish moonshine with ABV varying between forty and ninety per cent – which tasted like the sort of white spirits you clean paint brushes with. The resulting outcome from drinking it wasn't too dissimilar. Not too long after drinking he had to be rushed into Manchester Royal Infirmary to get his stomach pumped.

> You'd always be able to get someone to go in and get you some booze on the regular and by the age of thirteen or fourteen you knew which shops would sell to you. One near us would always if you were a girl, but not a boy. So quite often I was buying because I'd hit puberty dead early and had massive boobs by the time I was in Year 8. And there'd be shopkeepers that would just sell to you so I used to be responsible for buying. We'd get the bus in to Shalimar on Chapel Street, they would literally sell you whatever you wanted, and then we'd get the bus back to where I live and then we'd all drink.
>
> – Steph Lonsdale[15]

> I think the lack of opportunities is part of it. I don't think there was much to do, there was a youth club. It was a bit of a mooch, but we used to go there sometimes. But the majority of the time you'd be hanging around the streets. That's what you did.
>
> – Jay Motty[16]

> My drinking habits stemmed from school. I was, like everyone else, a street drinker. There was nothing to do when we were younger. The

> interesting thing is that now I'm the biggest drinker of my friends and I was brought up in a white area. I don't know whether my drinking culture came from being in a predominantly white area, because I speak to people now who are ethnic minority and they didn't have the same thing. They look at me like 'What!? You used to drink on the streets?' My Dad's not from that culture, so every week I had to stay at my friends' houses where it was facilitated and allowed within her family; they'd let me stay every weekend and we'd get absolutely hammered and off our faces and the next Sunday they'd be making us a full English. It felt like it was normal behaviour.
>
> – Marsha Bell[17]

It seemed the alcohol industry targeted teenagers with the introduction of new brands. We had started on cheap cider such as White Lightning, but pretty soon the local off-licence had an array of drinks that shared the same high sugar content and garish colours that you would find in sweets. Hooch Lemon, Bacardi Breezer, Mad Dog 20/20. It was Willy Wonka's Factory for Winos.

We had places to drink, we had shops that would sell us drink; the only problem was finding the funds to buy it. A bottle of cider only costing £1.60, it was hardly an expense to get pissed but, still, we would find alternative ways to make money. I had a paper round, but as I started drinking and smoking weed more, the less inclined I was to get up at the crack of dawn to carry a load of papers around every morning for £5 a week. My first proper job was working at JD Sports in the stock room upstairs, then folding clothes and giving customer service downstairs. The store was in Stockport and most of my fellow employees lived there, too; these were rich kids (townies) from places like Bramhall, Hazel Grove, and Cheadle; they were also little thieving bastards. Once the shop had closed, they'd all, to a member, take a few items to the changing room, untag the security badge, and put clothes underneath their uniform without the store manager noticing a thing. It got to the point where they were coming into work with knackered old Reebok Classics at the beginning of a shift and walking out with brand new Nike Air Max as they clocked off. I'm a fan of ingenuity and found the brass neck of it all hilarious. Sorry, JD Sports! Another job I had was shifting counterfeit clothes for an older lad called Faisal that I'd met in Crowcroft Park. His old man owned a factory where Faisal had bribed a seamstress to sew fashion labels onto clothes – Emporio Armani, Calvin Klein, Hugo Boss – he would sell these at Dickenson Road Market in Longsight twice a week. With him being Asian, Faisal figured I might be better than him to take these around pubs and flog them to people on the piss. It was a decent earner for a while. I would make £5 on the £25 for the tops, and if I could convince a customer to pay more, that was more money for me, but, given the quality of the tops, this venture didn't last long. I returned to a pub where the previous week I'd sold a Polo top for £30. Instead of it being Lacoste, it read Lactose – I mean you should check before buying anything in a pub! After that, like my peers, I was hired by Greater Manchester Police.

> Your first job was usually a paper round or some shit, but for me, one of my first proper earners, I think it was my friend Daniel that told me about it, was doing these [police] ID parades. He said, 'You should try it out', so I went down there, did a couple and thought yeah, this is alright. You have to give them your details and then they'd call you to be part of a line-up at the station. It became a regular thing, three or four times a week, I was going to do an ID parade and was getting £50 a week, and that went on for ages. It was weird, because to start with, it was a nice little hustle I thought I had on the side, but before I knew it, half of Manchester was turning up, so you'd see all your mates from school or football there doing the line-up alongside the suspect. You had to stand straight-faced and everything. Nine times out of ten the suspect always got chosen, but it was a top little earner. My Mum didn't like me doing it because she was fearful that as a black

> kid, I might get set up, but she wasn't giving me the sort of money I was making, so why wouldn't I?
>
> – Nathan Miles[18]

Greater Manchester Police, the same organisation that used to chase us off the streets for being pissed, were the same people that were lacing our mitts with the money to do it. A few ID parades would see you with enough dough to get your drink, weed, and a new CD every weekend. When word spread around, the job market got saturated, and your calls decreased, but while it lasted, it was surreal to earn that much by standing in a line. It wasn't always as fun with the police. How they dealt with us outside the line-ups was problematic. The stop and searches did target youths of colour. There were countless times I had been with a group, and they would pick on the black or Asian kids amongst us; the friendly local copper that came to school to deter us from anything criminal they were not.

Between 1996/97 and 2002/03 'in terms of differential rates, the Greater Manchester police stopped and searched 19 times more black people'.[19]

> You'd match the description of someone, so it's basically where they pull over and ask, 'Where are you going and what you doing? Where do you live?' and all that shit. It was more prevalent in the nineties, the stop and search, to everyone all over the place, but the police were regularly stopping and searching us a lot, especially the black and Asian kids.
>
> – Nathan Miles[20]

> The only time I remember experiencing racism was at the hands of the police and my younger brother that would get stopped and harassed every day on the way to college because he was black in a predominantly white area. It took my Mum having to go down to the police station to make a complaint to get them to stop it.
>
> – Marsha Bell[21]

We were a source of entertainment for the local police on their shift to pass the time. Two police officers in particular relentlessly tormented my group of friends. We were never doing anything illegal that required them to bother us or send us away from where we were hanging out, yet, nevertheless, that's what these two would do. The frustration in this would usually boil over into one of us calling them a dickhead, and then we would be in for it. Instead of arresting us they would bang you into the back of their van, drive you to the far part of Stockport, give you a going over, which would be pulling your arm as far up your back whilst the other one walked up and down it; this was extremely painful but left no evidence. Finally, they'd confiscate whatever you had on you, and with no mobile and no money, you'd have to either face the eight-mile trek home or try sneaking on the 192 bus back. This cat-and-mouse game got particularly moody when one gang decided to get revenge and set a massive firework off underneath a police van outside the old Levenshulme Police Station.

The only serious problem I ever got into with the law came at the hands of a blind shopkeeper. Despite my looking closer to attending primary school than the local pub I had been getting served at Abbas Off Licence on Hemmons Road, Longsight since I was thirteen. We never needed to go anywhere else. Whether it was his failing eyesight or lack of care for the legal age, everybody got served by Abbas. This was our spot for booze, therefore it was also our spot to hang out; the traffic was that minimal so street football was possible, and we had a massive wall with graffiti goal-posts. The same summer as the IRA bomb, we'd play football all day and get pissed every night as we had no school. A friend of a friend started hanging around with us. He would drive down from Gorton each night on a different stolen motorbike, trying to show off; all this peacock dancing, the gesturing, and posturing to show he was some sort of bad boy. One evening we were all just sat on the wall debating who United was going to sign that summer and drinking. A normal night. Next minute this dickhead comes storming out of Abbas' shop and boots the absolute shit out of his Ford Granada parked outside. Knocking wing mirrors off, dinting the side of the doors, throwing stuff on top of the windscreen, putting in the lights. The next minute old Abbas pokes his head out the door like a mole from its hole and says he's calling the police. I still haven't a clue what happened inside the store, but I sat there thinking, this will be interesting. I hadn't done anything wrong, so I stayed, fully expecting the lad who did it to be on his bike back to wherever he came from. But he didn't move either and sat next to us, literally calling the blind man's bluff!

Before long the boys in blue turn up, go into the store, then the two coppers and the blind shopkeeper walk over to us with Abbas raising his walking stick at three of us, saying it was him. Now the three lads he pointed at were similar in height, hair and age but that was where the similarities ended. One was a black lad with hair braids, one was a fat kid with the sort of fluorescent pink skin an Irish man turns in the sun, and then me, Ryan Giggs barnet with more dark tan than olive skin due to the weather. I'd been going into Abbas' store for three years, always polite, always respectful, and here he is misplacing me for being the dickhead that did his car motor. Next minute we're all in the police car.

Fast forward three hours and I'm sat with my Mum in Longsight Police Station with a free legal counsel aid, who looked four years older than me, wearing an ill-fitting suit with shoulders powdered with dandruff, advising me to admit to it and take the warning. If I went to court I would be looking at charges of Criminal Damage and ABH with a potential stint at a Young Offender Institution.

- *I didn't do it though?*
- *That doesn't matter at this point, David. It would be best for all concerned if you say sorry and we can all walk away.*
- *He said he didn't do it, he is not pleading guilty! He won't be having any record before he finishes school.*

My Mum gave me a bollocking when I got home for being stupid enough to stay at the scene, but within the interview room of the police station, she was not going to let her son take the blame for something he hadn't done. It would be on him to prove it to the court; that he so quickly wavered under her interrogation was not a good sign. I lasted longer under her questioning and I had no legal training.

- *Well, who did the damage then?*
- *It wasn't me!*
- *If you say who it was then …*
- *He is not a grass!*

Thirty minutes later, we were home, with my Mum more frustrated at the incompetent brief than she was at me.

Months passed. I forgot about what had happened to the point that I was back buying booze from Abbas, and I presumed it was all behind me. It was December, and my Mum had taken my sister and brother to Tenerife for a week. I wanted to stay at home, and my Auntie Ann would look after me. One evening I'd left our group to head home from our usual spot but stopped to grab something to eat on the way back from Trawlers Chippy. I'd got my chips and gravy, stepped out the door, and bumped into Anne, a girl I had been flirting with for most of the year. One thing led to another; before I'd had time to tuck into my dinner, I was taken into the alley behind the chippy for a bit of tongue tennis. A few minutes later, the kissing was abruptly brought to a halt by a thick Irish accent shouting at me from the alley entrance.

- *Oi, Dickhead.*

The silhouettes of two opposing figures stood at the top – one small and round, one tall and wiry. It was the fat kid from the summer, who I'd not seen since we both ended up in cuffs.

- *What are you gonna say in court?*
- *What do you mean?*

My mind at this point on two things, my chips going cold and is this going to stop me getting into Anne.

- *Don't you be grassing me up?*
- *What?! I'm pleading Not Guilty. Why would I gra…*

SPARK! The streaky tall bastard decided that despite my having no intention of grassing anyone up, I should get a taste of what would happen if I did. He caught me straight in the jaw; I fell to the ground, instinctively curled up into my knees like a foetus in the womb. A kick to the ribs flipped me on my back; then it was a flurry of legs stabbing into me from every direction. I put my hands up to protect my face, but it was useless. I looked up as the sole of a boot caught me clean in the face as the back of my head rebounded against the frozen concrete. Up and down. Up and down. My head the squash ball to their paddle of a foot. I became numb to the pain. Blood poured from my nose, and I felt the wetness of it coming out of the back of my head. Then Anne let out a scream.

- *That's enough. Leave 'im alone now.*

And the three of them left. I got to my feet, stumbled out into the street, leaving the chips and gravy steaming from the ground behind me as I headed home. I sat in my room, my tears diluting the crusted blood from my face, one of my eyes immediately swollen preventing me from seeing out of it. I played Tupac's 'Hit 'Em Up' continuously that night, fantasising a revenge I knew I would never act out. I felt isolated. Embarrassed someone was able to do this to me. Again. There were incidents before this and I doubted this would be the last; everyone was always kicking off. I was tired of the bullying. The name calling. The snide remarks. I didn't see a rhyme or reason to be here. I wanted to escape. I stayed at home for weeks after the attack. I couldn't deal with whatever was going around the grapevine. Two people beating me up would have brought more ridicule than concern. I told my auntie I'd got into a fight but not what caused it. My face was a mess but would recover by the time my parents got back off holiday. For fear of causing any emotional pain that may match my physical pain, I never told my parents about the incident.

Fast forward half a year later, the same week I finished the final GCSE exam, I was in court. The pressure of both wanting to get into college and not go into YOI had mounted. I had been shitting myself for months about both outcomes and the threat of getting locked up undoubtedly affected my revision for my GCSEs. To add some unintentional comedy to the day of the trial, my Mum had bought me a horrendous outfit to wear. This itchy white wool cable-knitted jumper to go over a red check shirt combination. I looked ridiculous.

- *You're not going in there dressed like a tramp! You need to make an impression.*

My Mum apparently had the belief that looking like a wicket-keeper would go down well with the judge. We went into court and I was so disappointed. After years of seeing crime dramas on TV I was expecting all the black gowns and daft wigs, but it was a judge in a white shirt with thick red vertical stripes; he was just missing the straw boater hat. I sniggered and whispered to my Mum, 'I bet he drinks Pimm's', which cost me an elbow to the arm. We sat there and waited. Nothing happened. The other kid hadn't turned up. I couldn't see Abbas. The solicitors started talking to the judge, then a policeman was summoned in. Abbas hadn't turned up. The police had to phone him and couldn't get through. I sat in court for an hour as they went to the corner shop to ask him why he wasn't there. He said he no longer wanted to press charges, which upset the boatsman up top no end. The judge then apologised to me for having to go through this ordeal. You have no idea, mate, I thought to myself, you have no idea! But it was over. I wasn't going to YOI. I ditched the cricket outfit, kissed my Mum on her forehead, went to Abbas' shop, bought a bottle of cider and drank to every bit of relief flowing through my body.

There is a stigma that the hordes of kids wandering the streets of Manchester were from broken homes, that this behaviour stemmed from absent parents, that our drinking was a reaction to neglect. Nothing could be further from the truth. I have never known either my Mum or Dad not to be working. We weren't rich, but I've never wanted for anything; whether emotional or financial support. They were always there for me in everything that I told them. My Mum is just seventeen years older than me, and since I was born she has always held down a job, and my Dad continues to this day to be one of the hardest working people I know. My parents weren't the exception. Across all the friends I had growing up, there wasn't one that came from a house where their parents weren't working.

> My Dad was strict! He would kick off if he ever caught me drunk – I used to have to stay out because he would hit the roof. I remember the one time I went home and my Dad found out I'd been drinking, all hell broke loose. He was furious, screaming downstairs, 'She's been drinking!' I was so hungover, he grounded me for life.
>
> – Marsha Bell[22]

> For me personally, I used to quite enjoy my life. I'm not gonna sit here and pretend it was grim growing up. I had a good set of mates, I had a good time, and I had a very loving and supportive family that did everything for me. You know, we may not have had a lot of money and

may have had to struggle at times – not the latest fashions, gadgets, or whatever – but who did? And the main thing is, and this sounds schmaltzy, but it's beyond material stuff, you know my family were quite young, my Mum's only sixteen years older than me. So yeah, you might look back and think it was rough – it wasn't. I look at my childhood as a good example of the sort I want to give my kids in terms of the family dynamic. We all got on and I always felt loved. You know what I mean? I always felt that, and that's what I'm trying to carry on with my kids. We might not have all the money, but as long as there was support and love, that carried me through years of trouble.

– Jay Motty[23]

What my Mum did, in terms of raising three lads on her own, holding down a good job, with all the madness that was going on in Longsight at the time is incredible. There's stereotypes about single mothers, and even though I didn't have a dad in my life, I think that my Mum went beyond what anyone could expect of her. She gave us morals and principles and that perhaps goes back to my Grandma as well – she had such core values in terms of how you should behave and foresaw how things may be for black people in Manchester. But my Mum is an incredible woman, she's so strong, so resilient … it's just mad when you look at the cards she was dealt that she managed to keep sane, let alone raise us three! We've all gone on to have respectable jobs and it was all down to my Mum. She stopped us falling into certain traps. You look at some people I knew that didn't have the same support and how it affected their lives …

– Nathan Miles[24] (see Chapter 3 for more)

On the last day of school, a couple of friends and I met my Dad at his local pub, the Farmers Arms, to celebrate where he bought us our first 'legal' pint.

- He's not old enough.

- He is!

- He's got his uniform on, Wayne!

- *It was his last day today, Kim.*
- *That right? Well, he can have this one on me.*

And so went my introduction to pub culture; the three of us sat around a table trying to blend in while wearing shirts that only an hour earlier were tagged in marker pen by our classmates. Up to that point, my experience of drinking didn't venture beyond the stuff we'd swig on the streets. The landlady handing over a pint of Foster's, with a conspiratorial wink, was a welcome to the World of Men. Then I took my first sip of what I can best describe as a pint of gassy cat piss.

- *That's minging! I don't like that!*
- *Don't worry love, you will. You will.*

Few graduated from high school to college; but all of us advanced from getting pissed in the park to down the pub. It was a natural progression from the lifestyle and routine we'd developed. We just moved our playground. We joined the adults, content to push the roundabout of working week and wasted weekends as fast and hard as we could. Some of us would hold on too tight until the drink returned the favour, some of us enjoyed the rotation, and some fell off, unable to keep up with the pace, but very few didn't stay on the ride they first got on in their local park.

In 1998 David Blunkett announced New Labour would provide an additional £19 billion spending on schools and pledged that education would be the new Government's number one priority and 'give everyone in our society the opportunity to realise their full potential'.[25] Maybe things would get better, but it was too late for my generation; we had been neglected by what was on offer within our schools, and outside of it we self-governed in our own Mancunian *Lord of the Flies*. Should it be of any surprise that those who didn't have the support at home would then escalate to the same murderous outcomes as William Golding's novel?

3

'It's the world of the drama series *The Wire*'

CRIME

In 1995, at a birthday party in Bristol, eighteen-year-old Leah Betts took an ecstasy tablet and drank approximately seven litres of water within a ninety-minute period. Shortly afterwards she fell into a coma from which she would not recover. Leah's death sparked a controversial new anti-drugs campaign when the family gave the press a harrowing photo of her.

Ecstasy, a source of hedonism for Manchester's earlier youth culture, was given a very different image for mine. The national press, my teachers, and my parents all towed the same line: ecstasy is dangerous. You will die if you take it. It's difficult to say if the government's shock tactics worked. For the latter part of the nineties I don't recall ever being offered ecstasy or it being mentioned, nor was it taken in places where other drugs were. When it came to narcotic use, the staple for us as teenagers was weed. Whatever money we hadn't spent on drink was divvied up and used to buy 'some solid'. This was usually blocks of Red Leb you would have to burn to break before putting into a joint. The downside of smoking solids wasn't in the effect of the drug but the hot rocks of weed that would fall out and burn little holes in your clothes. The amount of good tops I'd lost to a hot rock. Whizz was also common, cheap to buy, gave you a load of energy for a couple of hours and stomach cramps for days – a pay-off that wasn't worth it, although many of my mates felt otherwise. From time to time there would be a lack of availability of weed; dealers had supply lines cut off. It was often during these 'droughts' that the golden fleece of drugs would find their way into our circle. LSD, better known to us as trips, came in perforated sheets with bright technicolour designs with names such as Strawberry Dips, Smileys, Purple Ohms, Buddhas. We would often trip out during school excursions or at orienteering when a teacher would find us lying in the woods discussing the futility of life and the chameleon skin of Michael Jackson. LSD has provided me with some of the best drug experiences, from throwing a tennis ball around to watch the trails, to out-of-body experiences, to hallucinating that I saw Jackie Chan working behind the bar in a nightclub because he needed to raise money for a new film. It's also given me some of the worst, when one of our party was that freaked by what was going on in his head he set fire to someone else's hair with deodorant and a lighter. It was almost impossible to tell how strong they were other than take your dealer's word, and if they'd misjudged your tolerance it was too late and you'd better hold tight for the next ten to twelve hours.

The first time I took ecstasy was on the closing night of the old Granada Studios in 1999. Two close family friends had hired the venue for their wedding and after the nuptials were signed it was opened into a musical festival on a film set. I was having a pint in the Rovers Return, enjoying the music, when I felt tingles over my body and started to get really hot. Having the experience of coming up on other drugs, I knew from the waves something was afoot, but was unsure what. Pulling at my collar I turned to Paddy, my plus-one for the evening:

- *Proper hot in here, mate. I'm sure someone has put something in my drink.*

His raised eyebrows and grin confirming he was the guilty party.

- *You bastard!*
- *Chill out, you dick. They're sound.*

My first thought was Leah Betts. A deep-seated paranoia instilled many years earlier kicked in. My Mum and Dad were at the same wedding; if the pill didn't kill me then they certainly would. As I was coming up my MO was to try and stay busy and ride it out, keep my mind off the drug, keep moving, keep talking with people, and to keep away from my parents. Then it kicked in and every fear was stripped away like bark from a tree – I loved everything and everyone. I was in a sweet little sweaty state pilling away on the cobbles of Coronation Street. The following week I was offered a pill in 42nd Street, bought it, dropped it, and felt nothing other than a loss of five quid.

When buying drugs, a lot of trust is placed in your supplier. Rare is the dealer that admits they cut their gear with aspirin, bath salts, caffeine, glass, washing powder. And if your man didn't cut it with anything then you can be sure as shit someone did on the way to it reaching your palm – they deal in drugs, and profit margins. It becomes particularly problematic when you're buying stuff from someone you don't know. If you're not familiar with buying drugs, then imagine the anxiety when you go to a new barbers or hairdressers, your fate is in the lap of the gods but there's potentially more damage in store than a dodgy barnet. Every drug dealer says theirs is the best gear, it's the safest, and at the end of the nineties when it came to pills, safe they were not:

> Pills went to shit when we were nineteen or twenty – there was a lot of dodgy ones. We was at Bowlers one night and people were collapsing, and I mean a lot of people. Loads of ambulances were coming, people getting dragged out. And it was down to these Spice Girls pills. Apparently they were a bad batch and people had been dropping from them. I remember being stood there in the chill-out room, chatting to my mate, going under, 'cause I'd had six of 'em! Like waiting for my heart attack or something … Everybody asking: 'What's going on here?' It was them pills. 'Some Spice Girls … The fucking Spice

> Girls have started to make people sick!' I'd just ate two, they'd done fuck all, and gone for another two, nothing's happening, another two … And then everyone's fucking dropping, you know, but the pills were just getting well too dodgy. That for me was when sniff began to take over …
>
> – Jay Motty[1]

A report from the UK Drug Policy Commission in 2007 summarised the shift in recreational drug use as a move from pills to powder cocaine.

> Since the late 1990s [there had been an increase] in the use of powder cocaine among young people. The increase in cocaine use has been attributed partly to the falling price of the drug. According to the Serious Organised Crime Agency's latest assessment, the average street price of a gram of cocaine fell from £69 in 2000 to £49 in December [2006]. Another factor may be changes in the image of the drug and its pattern of diffusion among young people. From being an exclusive drug, used only by the wealthy and some dependent drug users, it has now become part of the menu of psychoactive substances that young people use to enhance their leisure time. It may have come into fashion among these people as ecstasy reduced in perceived quality.[2]

By the turn of the millennium, Manchester's drug of choice began to change. What was once seen as a drug for celebrities and yuppies was bandied around our backstreet boozers. The working man had found cocaine. This was a strange phenomenon: the average Mancunian's wages didn't seem to equate the cost of this champagne drug. Yet it was everywhere. The chemical generation that raved at the Haçienda would spend just £8 to get high on ecstasy for six hours; now people were spending £50 for a gram of coke that roughly gave you thirty minutes per line.

> I worked in a call centre doing telesales, and there was an office with 30 of us and every single one of us did sniff. I mean there wasn't

> one person who didn't do it – everyone did it! We used to get paid by cheque. This is so fucking grim; what was my life about? We'd get paid by cheque, right? And rather than put it in the bank, we'd all go to Cash Generator in town to get paid. They take ten per cent and we can cash the cheque immediately. So that means if you had a good week you have like 340 quid, or whatever, so they'd take thirty-four quid, right? Who gives a shit – you have £300! Then you'd just be straight on the phone, get a load of that, and you're away on a Friday – sometimes I've done that and woke up on someone's couch on a Sunday afternoon with £4 in my pocket. This was what it was like.
>
> – Jay Motty[3]

Did people turn to coke because pills were more of a risk? In some cases, perhaps. Although it wasn't just a swapping of one drug for another that explained cocaine's rise, it was a change in the market and economics. With the rave scene moving to the outskirts of the city and beyond, ecstasy demand was on the wane. Dealers had to follow their custom, or push something else to stay in business. Cocaine, unlike compressed tablets, is easier to cut with other products. This meant that local dealers could massively increase their profit margins by mixing their drug with local anaesthetics such as benzocaine, which gave the same numbing sensation when rubbed on your gums. Ecstasy use was confined to nightclubs. This meant dealers would largely only operate at weekends. People tended to only score pills for a night out, not because they were heading down the pub. Cocaine on the other hand is highly addictive, users were more likely to become hooked, generating longer working hours and consistent custom. In every business aspect cocaine trumps ecstasy. Dealers had a product to supply that would make them a lot of money and all they needed was the demand. At the start of the century there was a shift in culture that would help create it.

MANCHESTER is Britain's capital for binge drinking

– *Manchester Evening News* headline, 2007[4]

British youth culture has changed since the high tide of dance culture in the late 1980s and early 1990s. As fashions change, it is possible that drugs such as ecstasy, amphetamines and LSD are losing out in competition with other attractions … [B]inge drinking has recently increased, as the alcohol industry and local authorities have promoted the night-time economy, in which the development of new alcohol brands, venues and later drinking hours have drawn more young people and their money into city centres. … [T]he co-occurrence of alcohol with illicit drug use [is] one of the dangers attendant to the normalisation of recreational drug use. Among this 'illegal leisure' study sample at age 22, 78% were drinking alcohol when they last took an illegal drug.[5]

The common line is that weed is the gateway to harder drugs. I've never believed that. The majority of stoners I knew/know have kept to marijuana as their drug of choice, and rarely strayed. From my own experience alcohol has always been the motivator to take drugs. The first time I've tried any drug there has always been an aperitif.

Legal consumption of alcohol and tobacco may directly increase the level of illicit drug use. However, the relationships are complex. Consuming one drug does appear to increase the consumption of another.[6]

Alcohol reduces inhibitions; any reluctance you may have had to take a drag, a pill, a line, reduces the more you drink. With binge drinking culture entrenched, combined with the increase in dealers, it was the perfect storm for cocaine use to thrive. The all-night raves were a thing of the past, it was the dawn of the all-day session. And if there's one drug that will enable you to keep on a drinking session, it is cocaine.

It says something about the effects and addictive qualities of coke as to why it took off. People on cocaine are not good adverts for cocaine: they talk at 100mph, have an inability to sit still, constantly sniffling, constantly running to the toilet, they repeat the same two questions all night 'Who's got the bag?' and 'Who wants a key?'. They engage in conversations harder to negotiate than Spaghetti Junction and always seem very, very tense … it's not the sexy man in an elevator Diet Coke advert, is it? You don't say to yourself, that looks like fun, I'll have a bit of that. People on ecstasy look happy, blissful, they radiate good energy; from the outside it has an appeal. Cocaine makes people look uncomfortable, which is why I believe alcohol was the instigator to its rise in use.

> It was the original Red Bull, albeit more fucking expensive, and leaves you, in my case, addicted, but it was pretty ferocious the way it moved through a pub. One, two of your mates had some sniff and about six pints in, they'd still look as sober as they did when they started, whilst you're close to calling a cab. They offer you a bit of that, and whether it's because you're steaming, inquisitive, or both, you bang a key under your hooter and you're off. Once you realise that it makes you feel like God with the ability to stay on the session, it becomes as normalised as buying some fags … when everyone else is doing it around you, you think nowt of it.
>
> – , former drug dealer 1[7]

In 2003, the Licensing Act was brought in to crack down on binge drinking culture. This seemed like a reasonable pursuit with an illogical approach: increase the drinking hours to curtail the amount people drank. Drinkers have a natural cut-off point; there's a limit to how much alcohol they can consume. This isn't the case with people that drink and use cocaine. Cocaine masks alcohol impairment and alcohol takes the edge off cocaine. They are the worst of bedfellows.[8] Theoretically, with the new laws, the amount of people using cocaine could now find somewhere across Manchester to drink twenty-four hours a day.

Recreational use of cocaine was rising but when dealers mixed it with baking soda to turn it into crack the problem soared 'to epidemic levels, particularly among 14- to 18-year-olds, fuelling the recent dramatic rise in violent street crime and driving the price down to a record low'.[9]

> Ecstasy was more of a dance thing, and probably taken recreationally by students or people who came in from Manchester to party. The main base of the gangs in South Manchester was crack and heroin. Ecstasy would be more Salford, in the other areas it was mostly heroin, then cocaine, and then people started to freebase crack.
>
> – [redacted], former drug dealer 2[10]

> A government crack conference in June this year [2002] revealed that trafficking and possession of crack cocaine in Britain has risen by more than 200 per cent over the past three years.[11]

The first time I saw someone freebase crack was on the 192, the main bus route from Manchester city centre to Stockport. It was an early afternoon and a couple of friends and I were heading home, sitting upstairs at the back. There is an unwritten rule amongst teens that if anyone is sat at the back then that is their territory for the journey and you don't sit amongst them – particularly if you have an entire empty upstairs to choose from. So when a young man got on at the Manchester Apollo stop and opted to join us our reaction was 'What's this dickhead up to?'. The usual fear was it was someone older trying to tax us. Not long after the bus starts rolling again we're sat to the left and him to the right of the back-seat. He then casually pulls out some foil and starts burning the bottom of it with a clipper lighter. It gave off this strong rancid metallic fish smell. We knew what he was doing but were unsure how we were to react. Crackheads came with a reputation of being erratic, fearless, and best avoided. In my mind they were pasty, mal-nourished, gaunt figures that were creatures of the night. This guy was clean-cut, decently dressed, and only a few years older than us. As he put the pipe to his lips he caught our eyes staring at him with intrigue. Before he took a hit, he reassured us:

- *Don't worry, it won't harm you.*

We were all enamoured with the hood movies coming out of America. Films such as *Menace 2 Society* and *Boyz in the Hood* that depicted violence, gang rivalries, murder, flagrant drug dealers, and abusers. We would religiously watch them. Young adults attracted to the danger, amazed that people led those lives, that tried to survive those circumstances – it felt a world away from where we found ourselves. We were never conscious that it was a lot closer to home than we realised. This stranger freebased next to us at the back of a bus, on a Saturday afternoon, and not an alarm went off about the type of fishbowl we were swimming in. We got off the bus in Levenshulme and never thought about it again.

> I was originally a salesman, so I was just taking cocaine at weekends. I took cocaine, I drank, I smoked weed, but I was working so I didn't really have all the time to give to it. I think the alcohol had got a bit played out and it wasn't fun anymore and I remember playing cards and a friend of mine brought this stuff out – and this first time I got experience of it, I didn't know what it was. He put it on the foil. No one at the table even looked at him because they didn't know what he was doing and I remember having some of it, you know, and I had not felt anything like that before. It was more potent than alcohol or weed. And not only that, it kind of stayed with me all day and it felt like, wow, this is great. You know you can take a couple of hits of this, and you don't have to worry all day about using anything else and I think there was a bit left on the foil and he scrunched it up and threw it in the bin. The strange thing was, a few days later, I found myself going back to the same bin for this foil. I was really naive, and had no idea what I thought, but I just knew I wanted some more. Then I got back in touch again, and connected to some people and I started to use it …

> I used to go to this house, I think it was one of the first crack houses in the area and it was the first time I saw people freebasing and it was curiosity, mixed in with stupidity. It's kind of dangerous as well, so that there's an attraction with that. I didn't realise that what was taking place was that I was getting hooked. And people did all sorts for that stuff, you know, all the criminals, all the shoplifters, all the burglars, everyone kind of seemed to be on it and seemed to be in a crackhouse to sell their wares and buy their drugs. The other side for me is having been a salesman, I saw the potential to sell and make money, so I started out selling it. But that soon went to hell. So there's two sides, there was the fact that I enjoyed taking it, but I also had the potential to make money. I mean the first three years, I didn't really have to pay for it 'cause I always had it, and sold it.
>
> – [redacted], former drug dealer 1[12]

On 2 January 1993, fourteen-year-old Benji Stanley was queuing at Alvino's Pattie and Dumplin Shop in Moss Side when 'a man in a balaclava and combat overalls shot him with a pump action shotgun. The first two bullets caught him in the leg and as he fell the gunman shot him a third time in the chest'.[13] He was the youngest person to be shot dead in Manchester. Benji was a pupil at Ellen Wilkinson High School where I had been given an option to attend, albeit Spurley High School was closer. When he was murdered it was my first year in high school, and it would be the first time I'd heard of the Doddington and Gooch gangs. His killing 'shocked the country, fuelling the city's reputation as "Gunchester". At that time Moss Side was being dubbed "the Bronx of Britain" as gun crime rocketed in an intense rivalry'.[14] This period of the early nineties was seen as the height of the drug wars between the Gooch and Doddington gangs. The understanding was that to stay away from Moss Side was to stay away from any gang trouble. By the time I'd leave school in 1997 it was unavoidable.

> In the beginning I would say if you wanted to buy drugs at this time, you'd go to Moss Side because they basically had an open market at the precinct – once the territories were marked they were openly selling it on the street, you know. So people from all over Manchester came there 'cause it was readily available, and it was good quality. What then happened is other dealers would appear in other areas so less people came into Moss Side to score so the gangs were making less money and decided to turn on each other. Probably their thinking was, well, the reason I'm not making as much money as last week is this guy here is taking my customers. And really, it was more that dealers were springing up all over Manchester.
>
> – ■■■■■[15]

> I mean it just exploded. It started like an underground thing and I think at the time when I started you could recognise five main dealers in the whole of Manchester who were probably in their forties or late thirties at the time, but once it exploded the whole game changed. And that's when the gangs came who were mostly teenagers who grouped together for protection, but it also gave them the leverage to take out all the main dealers by the sheer numbers and they started to mark their territory – so it just started organically like that.
>
> – ■■■■■, former drug dealer 1[16]

A Home Office report found that 'two well-established Manchester gangs, "Doddington" and "Gooch" formed about 1988, are now rivalled by two younger groups, known as the "Pitbull Crew" and the "Longsight Crew" '.[17]

> The Pitbull Crew emerged following a conflict and fatal shooting within Doddington. After the split the Pitbull Crew became a distinct entity, whose initial core members were related to the dead Doddington member and whose raison d'être was in part to take revenge. The Longsight Crew also crystallised as a group following the (unintended and misdirected) fatal shooting of the brother of a main player by a member of Gooch. As with the Pitbull Crew, its members too had previously been associated with Doddington.[18]

> A lot of those gangs kind of ran on revenge – driven more about someone's murder. Because they'd made money, it wasn't about the money. What made it dangerous was they wanted revenge, so was willing to just go out and kill people.
>
> – [redacted], former drug dealer 4[19]

> The 'Pit Bull Crew's business was the very regular retail supply of controlled drugs, including heroin, crack cocaine and cocaine, to customers within the gang's territory in Longsight in south east Manchester. Members of the gang would carry loaded firearms ostensibly for their own protection which were stored in safe houses ready and available for them to use. The safe houses would also be locations used by the gang to cut and prepare drugs for distribution. The firearms were an integral part of the drug-supply network. Members of the gang would not only carry them for their own protection but also to enforce the gang's territorial claims against rival gangs. On the occasions when the gang carried loaded weapons for use against their rivals, they dressed in dark clothing and wore balaclavas to conceal their identity, and they wore bullet-proof vests for self-protection. Also members of the gang would customarily wear golf-type gloves on their gun hand in order to prevent the transfer of fingerprints.[20]

> It was probably one of the most vicious eras. You had to actually be there to believe what was happening. The change was the amount of money they made, these kids, and then how organised they got. The police had actually found a military grade scorpion submachine gun, which was a massive eye opener for them, because even the police didn't believe it. You know these were sophisticated gangs. And trust me, these were an organised group. They were tactical. Don't ask me where they learned all this structure but they were just as deadly as you can get, and you wouldn't cross them because then you were gone, they wouldn't think twice about killing you.
>
> – [redacted], former drug dealer 1[21]

In just three years between my leaving school in 1997 and the turn of the millennium, there were 270 shootings across Manchester.

'People in Longsight and Greenheys were 140 times more likely to be shot than other residents of Greater Manchester.'[22]

> When I'd got back off the run it was like a war zone. I just walked back into it, absolute war zone, people killing each other, people that had grown up together were now enemies. And it was like, what am I involved in here? I should've known better but I had a massive habit. I was generally friendly with most of them. You know, I wasn't affiliated, I associated, but having known most of them in the past I've made money with them by credit cards; because you know their customers would give them credit cards for drugs that come to me and I'd work them. So I was kind of cool with them, I wasn't a threat to anyone. I would introduce people and sometimes get them customers from out of town.
>
> – ██████, former drug dealer 3[23]

> I wasn't affiliated but I was associated with ██████ [gang name] because my working partner at this time who I made money with, his brother kind of ran the gang. So I was associated but I wasn't really directly involved in their conflicts, but then again, there was a lot of other conflicts, the Yardies started arriving and there's a lot of conflict with them. Mainly trying to rip them off, and it all started changing around that point. So the Yardies were based around Old Trafford so that was a different ball game all together. So skirmishes with them, skirmishes with other people, with other users, but not directly involved in the wars, because I was like ten years older than most of them, and probably a bit more sensible. And it was more the teenagers that were really pushing things.
>
> – ██████, former drug dealer 4[24]

It was only when I saw the Christmas lights reflect off the body bag that I realised the true extent of the damage the gangs could cause. Prior to that selling £10 bags of weed for local dealers in my eyes was no different to starting a Youth Training Scheme with British Telecom. Two different jobs, but both jobs all the same. It wasn't seen as dangerous. It wasn't glamorised. There was no big gold chains, no fancy cars at that point. It was just a job, at a time where '40% of children in Manchester lived in a household where nobody had one'.[25]

School leavers weren't well-formed pupils primed for further education but wet putty to be moulded by whatever the outside world offered us: the dole office, the army, the factory, minimum wage, family business, fast food outlets. A few of us managed to get to college and others would sell drugs.

> You have to remember that before Thatcher stopped it, at sixteen you could get benefits, get your own flat, and do something. That gap for two years had all these sixteen-year-olds finishing school, and they can't claim any benefit, they didn't have jobs. So it was a ready market for any dealer looking for runners. The estate was awash with them. I think that was a key thing really, because all of a sudden, for two years between sixteen and eighteen, they didn't have any work, and they had time on their hands, and they saw people making money, so before you know it dealers started finding more customers.
>
> – Miss Greene, social worker[26]

My first job after I left school was to wait tables at Fatty Arbuckles, in Gorton – an American-themed diner that I fucking hated and saw no end in sight of – and would smoke cheap weed in bad joints to escape the monotony. My friends that chose selling drugs as a vocation would be the ones to supply me the weed. I, like many others, had had a paper round and this was seen as the same gig but delivering a different product for better money. If anything, posting copies of *The Sun* is much more toxic than dealing marijuana. It wasn't like there was an abundance of employers driving round the streets of South Manchester rallying up all the tearaways with no GCSEs or career prospects to give them a job. Hungry mouths need food, so when someone gives you a job that you know how to do for a decent wage and you have no other option, why would you not? It's not that difficult a job role to fulfil: collect weed, deliver weed, collect money, deliver money back to the boss, and collect a wage. The hours were good, no early starts, no tax, no shitty uniform, no being covered in tomato relish and singing happy birthday to crying brats every evening. There was never any talk of patches, rivalries, fights, guns, nor that your P45 may come in the shape of a prison sentence, or a pistol. It was hard not to be envious. It was hard not to be attracted to it. But then Kelvin died.

We moved from Longsight to Levenshulme when I was ten and Kelvin was one of the first friends I made in the new area. My new corner terrace faced down the street where he lived, less than 100 yards away. From my bedroom window one day I saw him and his younger brother banging a ball against a wall and went out to join in. Friendships at that age are forged in minutes and for a few years Kelvin, his brother, and my best mate Greg would be as tight as the headlocks we'd put each other in. The next five years together we would dismantle the innocence of our youth. We would go from playing football, climbing trees, scaling roofs, and playing street games to drinking, finding girls, stealing from the shop, riding motorbikes, and smoking weed.

Kelvin was a year older than me and went to Burnage High School, and as our teen years would advance our friendship would drift. There were different parts of Manchester I wanted to discover, different friends I wanted to hang out with, different interests I wanted to develop. He was probably the same and by the time I had finished high school he was already immersed in the adult world. I'd usually only see him in passing as he finished a shift working 'on the roads' laying pipes for water/gas/electric. It looked like the hard work had already had an impact on him, he cut a contrasted figure of high-vis jacket and the blackened skin from the dirt he'd spent the day digging.

One December, out of the blue, there was a knock at the door. It was Kelvin:

- Do you want to buy my Spider, Dave?
- No mate. What you selling it for?
- Christmas coming up innit, and could do with the extra cash for presents.
- Nah, I'm broke pal – plus my mam won't have owt like that in the house.
- No worries. Catch you soon mate. Laters.

And off he went. This wasn't particularly unusual for us to try and shift some unwanted gear to get more money for Christmas. Not with the intent of buying presents but for the cider, weed, and clothes for the upcoming festive parties. The following week my Mum pulls me up:

- Kelvin knocked on last night.
- Oh right. Did he want me?
- No, he was trying to sell some DVDs.
- Did you buy any?
- No.

Christmas finally came, and as was our family tradition we would spend a lot of time at my Mum's parents' in Longsight. One evening we were in a taxi back home and came down Stockport Road which required us to turn up the street where Kelvin lived to get to our house at the top. The taxi came to an abrupt stop shortly after taking the corner; an ambulance had blocked the road. A mass of people were out on the streets. My Mum and the taxi driver were speculating what it could be – festivities gone wrong, a bad accident. It was only when I saw the inconsolable faces did I realise whose house the emergency team were at. Then the taxi fell silent. The paramedics wheeled a trolley out of Kelvin's front door. The Christmas lights from his front window reflected gold and red on the black plastic of the body bag it carried. Our taxi was directed to reverse back to give them room to put it on to the ambulance. From the centre of the back passenger seat I watched them. Fictional scenarios played in my head – his Dad had been ill, he may have had a heart attack; maybe they had a grandparent over and they'd took a turn. These scenes played through my head as the taxi morosely followed the ambulance up towards my house. I looked out the side window as I passed, looking for any of the family, for some clues as to what had happened. I caught the eye of Michelle – a friend that also lived on the street – she saw me and ran up alongside the car to meet us. I got out of the car. Her eyes told me before she'd said a word. Kelvin was dead.

Somewhere, somehow, much to the obliviousness of his family, to his old friends, Kelvin had got hooked on crack. His habit had reached a level where his body craved what his pocket could not afford. It got so bad that he had run up such a debt that dealers were now threatening to hurt his parents if he did not pay up. The calls to my house were the act of a desperate teen trying to raise funds that never came. In his attic bedroom, his emotional state presented dangerous realities from which he could see no escape. He will have fought with the guilt of becoming an addict, the embarrassment too much to confide in his parents, the fear that their lives were in danger, the distrust he had with authorities. With paranoia as his only companion in the darkness Kelvin saw only one way to end his torment, and to protect his parents. He hung himself. He was eighteen.

Following Kelvin's suicide, death and violence surrounded me for years. Another friend committed suicide because of drugs on a street parallel to Kelvin's. Lee Fielding, who I would play football in school with, was bundled into a stolen car, took to the back of the Farmers Arms on Stockport Road, Levenshulme, shot with a sawn-off shotgun, doused in petrol, and set alight. Two of the people charged with that crime went to my school. There was an execution on Greenbank Fields where I played Sunday football, where one gang member was tied to a tree and his friend was forced to shoot him in the face. Ucal Chin, whose sister Racquel was in my year at school, was gunned down and murdered on Plymouth Grove in a revenge shooting. Stephen Roberts, whose sister Sharon we lived next door to, was shot four times inside the Farmers Arms. The shooter was the next-door neighbour of, and friend to, Kelvin. These were my peers. These were people that went to the same schools as I did. That ran the same streets. That played the same games. How did it get to this point?

> My experience of it was that these kids didn't have a lot, and the one thing they did have was respect. That's what it was all about, you know? 'You had to respect me.' Because that's all they had, that was their way out. If they felt disrespected, in order to protect their respect they had to be seen to do something about it. Because if they didn't, they were finished. That runs true from the cartels to your drug runner on the street – they can't be seen to let anyone disrespect you. They have nothing. So what they're gonna do is they're gonna go out and be the same things, because they're young and are susceptible to dreams, aren't they?
>
> – ████, former drug dealer 1[27]

I knew some of them personally and they're really smart kids, and there's some of them now who have moved around who are running businesses. The prime example I remember, the first lot of police that tried to turn up to catch these kids, I don't know if you remember Alexandra Park estate, it had a lot of back warrens and the police would come and could never catch them because they're younger, faster, and the police were bigger with all the stuff they had to carry on their body, so they could never catch them. So they started coming with Alsatians. And I'm watching this stuff from my window. So as soon as they get out the van, somebody runs, and they set the Alsatian on them. Within a couple of weeks the gang bought pit bulls. So when the police would arrive and release these Alsatians, they would set the pit bulls on the Alsatian. They just fucking found a way around it. They weren't just dumb people. They were smart kids, you know, they understood the business they were in, you know, and they came up with tactical things. They were not going to give up their territory, even to the police, this was their turf. So when you spoke to them, sometimes they'd say well, what's this fucking government ever given us? It was more than just dealing drugs. They wanted their piece of whatever they could get out of life and weren't going to wait for opportunities that were never coming. It was a trade off, and it was worth it.

– ███, former drug dealer 4[28]

It was getting to the point where it was more dealers robbing other dealers. So you basically had gangs who couldn't be bothered selling drugs, who'd say, 'Let's just wait for other dealers to get some in and just rob them.' You know, and kidnap them. Because some people knew how to use a gun but they weren't very good dealers. It's like they had a taste of money for so many years, then they spent their life chasing it.

– ███[29]

The *Daily Mail* said that Manchester was 'a great city gripped by gangsterism'.[30] This wasn't the case. Gangsterism didn't grip Didsbury, there was no trouble in Reddish, no shootings in Heaton Moor. It was the poorest suburbs that were affected by it, just like it had been in the eighties, just like it had been in the early nineties, just like it is in any major city across the globe where gang problems arise. The problem is never solved, because a solution is never sought.

Don't forget back then, people got into the game because they saw others getting away with it. And then once we start to see that no one gets away with it, then it's a matter of deterrence. And don't forget, the police got more sophisticated as well, their tactics and how they went about conviction. Then the learning of how the gang units in America

> operated. You know, this is what you need to do to take these people down. The use of old copper tactics, it just doesn't work.
>
> – ████, former drug dealer 1[31]

The approach was to cut out the tumour and to not cure the cancer. A quick fix. A botch job. Nullify the problem and ignore the root cause. Those in power didn't want to ask the difficult questions because it would have resulted in answers they didn't want to hear. If you create an environment where the education and social system causes a vacuum of poverty and unemployment, then whose responsibility is it when it breeds a generation that lacks guidance or a moral code? If you're responsible for a society where kids from the age of fifteen are willing to risk their life, willing to ruin the lives of others, that see murderous crime as a viable career option, then what portion of the blame lies at your feet when the bodies pile up? The crimes are wholly indefensible, but the cause lies beyond the kid with a gun. One of my best mates growing up was Michael Gordon. We both went to Crowcroft Park Primary School and would spend most of our free time round each other's houses, playing football, swimming, camping in back yards, and genuinely doing the normal things kids do at that age. We would go on to different high schools and different paths and our friendship naturally drifted. Michael would eventually go on to follow in his half-brothers' footsteps into gangs and become part of the Pitbull Crew. He was given a twelve-year sentence for 'conspiracy to possess firearms and ammunition with intent to endanger life and conspiracy to supply controlled drugs of class A and B, namely heroin, crack cocaine and cannabis'.[32] For the twelve years I knew him, and knew him well, there were no signposts he would head down this road. There were no signposts for any of the kids I knew who would go on to become gang members, drug addicts, or innocent bystanders killed in crossfire. At some point, all these people were innocent young children, but life choices, lack of support, or terrible luck sealed their fate.

In 2009, a decade after the period I focus on in this book, the then Shadow Home Secretary Chris Grayling said Manchester's streets were like a real-life version of the violent cop show *The Wire*.[33] Had he said this ten years prior, he may not been ridiculed, but as it was, political commentators responded with 'Chris Grayling is daft',[34] and Greater Manchester Police called his words 'really sensationalist', because from the start of the millennium, gang-related shootings in Manchester had declined. By 2009, 'they had plummeted to 82 per cent on the previous year's figures'.[35] The comparison to David Simon's masterpiece is a curious comparison given that the poverty and subsequent gang problems that affect the streets of Baltimore were a by-product of decisions made by politicians. If we are to believe that Manchester was like *The Wire*, what does that say about those in office? The kids that left high school to shoot guns on the streets of Manchester were born out of a society built by the Conservatives over the past eighteen years.

> What was brilliant about *The Wire* is that they showed the politicians, they showed the cops, and they showed the criminals. Then allowed you to see that each were just the same operators in different uniforms. And so they all affect each other. The whole thing that starts in Manchester, starts from politics, doesn't it? It's all linked and that was the brilliance of *The Wire* – they showed that they are the same people, but just in different businesses. Those who get to the top are just as worthless as the other guys. There is no difference. It was interesting that the people who wrote *The Wire* were a reporter and a police. People who understood the game – not these meaningless films about this horrible evil drug dealer without a backstory. Because nobody just becomes that. There are good sides and bad sides to dealers, police, and politicians depending on the pressures they were under.

> They all want power, leverage, money whatever trade they're in. It's all the same.
>
> – [redacted], recovering addict/rehab occupational therapist[36]

Authorities employed academic research to find a strategy to better understand gang culture with a view to ending the bloodshed. Operation Chrome, the first project into Manchester's gangs, saw a small group of researchers travel to Boston to study the effectiveness of Operation Ceasefire which had reduced homicides by an impressive rate. It was the hope that Chrome could apply this effective approach in Manchester. As well as the policing procedures learned, it was also understood that Ceasefire was successful due to the interventions and provisions Boston had in place prior, many of which Manchester did not.

> Agency personnel believe these to have been crucial to the sustained fall in shootings in Boston. Streetworkers (detached youth workers who engage with young people in or on the fringes of gangs); police-station based social workers providing support to families and young people in need coming to the attention of the police; a patrolling probation service working flexible hours alongside the police; prosecutors oriented to the local community needs; a police service committed to a philosophy of community policing; targeted employment services providing jobs to those otherwise drawn to gangs and gang life; and the involvement of a coalition of clergy were all highlighted. In Manchester, specific gang-focused youth provision had not been made, social workers are not attached to police stations, and differing probation and police service traditions operate.[37]

The arrests of the Pitbull Crew were seen as the first success of the multi-agency approach applied by Operation Chrome, although an off-the-record conversation I've had with a former police officer suggested it was down to hard work by those in uniform and recklessness by those in gangs which led to their downfall. In 2002, 'Thomas Pitt was given a life sentence for murder and 20 years for three attempted assassinations, racketeering and drug charges. In total, 13 members of the Pit Bull crew [were] sentenced to more than 170 years' imprisonment, plus three life sentences.'[38] Having the main perpetrators off the street was seen as a success by authorities, yet the shootings only decreased, they didn't stop; the gangs were abated, but not abolished. The killings continued long after the period this book discusses.

As Greater Manchester Police got to grips with the gang problem, they were now facing operational problems of their own. Government decisions were being made that would result in corruption.

> In 2002, when David Blunkett was Home Secretary, the Police Reform Act received Royal Assent. In many ways that Act, followed by others, laid the foundations and determined the culture of policing since. It was intended to allow the police to use its resources more effectively in the face of increased demand, to focus on the 'big picture' and make new provision for supervision, management, and administration. Many of the reforms were controversial, particularly increased powers for the Home Secretary. In my personal view it introduced what has probably been one of the biggest retrograde steps for policing effectiveness – the financial rewarding of senior police officers for achieving Key Performance Indicators. KPIs that were set centrally by government, determined by political imperative. At that time, the focus was on acquisitive and low-level volume crime that impacted disproportionately on people. When aligned with other statutes it led to a warped (and corrupted) focus on fixed penalty 'tickets', fines for 'minor' crime, public disorder. Ticking boxes and numbers.
>
> What actually happened as a result of the application of the legislation was that very senior police officers were rewarded financially if they achieved the targets, targets often set by central government with an inevitable political bias. My view is that it is very, very dangerous when performance is judged by arrests (not convictions), or fixed penalty tickets, but that's what happened, and to a large

extent continues today, even with more vigour, when in reality safe conviction (or acquittal) is likely a better barometer of performance.

'Managers', ACPO [the Association of Chief Police Officers] at the time, became obsessed with performance set by central government. That performance financially rewarded the key decision makers in policing. The phrase of 'Going Green' developed. The organisation had to hit the targets that have been set to 'Go Green'. If they were in the 'Red' at month-end there was a process at that time called 'the Grip Process', when the senior leadership team would 'grip' middle-managers and challenge them for 'not going green'. Their job, position, or career prospects would literally be in jeopardy. I was vocal in opposition at the time, probably because I didn't have a career to worry about! But the potential financial rewards for hitting politically nominated targets were huge at the time, thousands of pounds!

Imagine what corrupt practices that opens up?

I'm not for a moment defending some of the well-documented corrupt practices of policing before this Act but there is a discussion to be had around proportionality and consequence. To me, as a career police officer, cash rewards for senior command for achieving targets set by politicians is the worst kind of corruption, destabilising the political neutrality of law enforcement and undermining the very fabric of British policing, and it has continued to do so ever since.

– Ian Hynes, Detective Constable (retired)[39]

In 2002, I was arrested for swearing at a police officer. Not in an abusive manner, but in the sort of casual, friendly way you would tell a friend to 'fuck off' when they say it's your turn at the bar knowing fine well it's their round. I was having a cigarette outside a pub, told to move on by a police officer in a van, I thought they were messing about, I swore, with a cordial smile and I was thrown in the back of a van for my Northern niceties. I ended up with an £80 fine for 'behaviour likely to cause a breach of the peace'. This is a minor example of how the Police Reform

Act and officers need to Go Green affected me. The extent of its impact is much worse.

> This is a cameo example, and there were many. Towards the end of my policing career, I was mentoring some younger in-service officers in what became known as 'The Prisoner Processing Unit' (PPU). Incidentally, myself and others were of the controversial view that you process meat, not people, by the way. On a late shift I was asked by a middle-manager to sanction a course of action that I didn't agree with, the offer of ('just') a caution to a suspect if he admitted an offence. That course of action would have criminalised a fourteen-year-old boy and potentially put him on the sex offenders register. I refused to do it. I refused to offer up a caution in exchange for a confession. But I could refuse to do it, confident in the position that, unlike the manager, I had little at stake. It led to a terrific row culminating in this individual, who will remain nameless, 'pleading' because it was the last day of the month and he had to 'Go Green'. If he didn't 'Go Green', he'd be 'gripped' by the then Chief Constable and his fellow ACPO team. He would have been 'gripped' and his career would have been in jeopardy. Others would, and have, called this bullying and harassment in the workplace.
>
> I was there at the beginning of it with the drug issues in Moss Side that spawned the gangs of the late eighties that ran things into the nineties. I took a career choice with an eye to the future, to get some training qualifications, so I trained investigation and a thing called investigative interviewing to a specialist level. But training wasn't my bag, I'd always been operational. It was a means to an end to get some qualifications and learn. In the early 2000s I took a conscious decision to go back to core, operational, policing. Because I was due to retire in 2006, I wanted to spend my last few years policing in the CID, so I went back to Manchester City CID, joined some of the best detectives in Manchester who had travelled a similar journey, career detectives. They (the bosses) loved it because we were 'dead straight' and reliable. We were 'grafters'. Yes, we liked to earn overtime, but we worked hard and understood 'the rules'. This takes us right to 2002. Then when Blunkett's Police Reform Act

came about, I just thought, having travelled the journey, it alarmed me. I went on record at the time and said, 'People think policing was corrupt in the seventies', and I said, 'That is nothing compared to the impact on policing that this will have.' I'm not talking about the stuff you see in the media about cops taking 'backhanders'. That's always gone on in some circles, is always wrong, but we'd be kidding ourselves if we didn't think that it went on. This became a systemic organisational corruption in the true sense of the word which has allowed criminality to flourish in the vacuum it created. I'm not saying everything was right back in the day. A lot of things weren't right by any stretch. Slowly, the robust principles of competent investigation started to get eroded. And as I said, I'm not denying there weren't issues and problems, but what actually happened was that there was a massive swing of power in policing. Traditionally, certainly in most city police forces, the CID were the 'go-to' people, troubleshooters. They'd often put things right for the uniform command, and that was understood and appreciated. Then what happened from the early 2000s, was that there was a shift of power and you've got some chief officers with, frankly, very little operational investigation intent on 'shift that power'. They didn't understand, or chose not to understand, how organised crime works and sustains itself. It works by chipping away, starting with the minor stuff, and as soon as the power vacuum's created, they're in there.

– Ian Hynes[40]

Not only did the Police Reform Act have an impact on unjust arrests, but also, when your focus and time is spent on hitting targets, what becomes of the more complex cases? If you can be seen to be doing your job by 'going green' for making arrests for minor crimes, where is your enthusiasm for solving major cases that require more work, and being under more scrutiny for not putting the numbers on the board?

Personally, I'm in no doubt that the reformation of British policing has created much of the malaise exposed, documented, and reported during the last decade. Rapes of children, serious sexual abuse, CSE

> [Child Sexual Exploitation], spiralling crime figures, disengagement of the public, forces in special measures … all can be tracked back to the actions of politicians and senior commanders since 2000.
>
> – Ian Hynes[41]

If Manchester's streets were indeed like the world of *The Wire*, then so was its police force and the political powers persuading it; anyone who has seen the series will recognise this 'numbers by any means' MO is straight out of Deputy Commissioner Rawls' playbook. Maybe Christopher Grayling was on to something?

By the time I had reached twenty-one the gangs that had ravaged through the streets I grew up on had been arrested, killed, or vanished into the ether. With the number of young lives lost to drugs and crime, and the amount of families torn apart in the process, there should have been preventative measures put in place so that future generations weren't drawn into that world. However, it wouldn't be long before what has become a cyclical problem for Manchester would start up again. But how much of a concern was it that these young Mancunians were being killed outside of the city centre? It was a different matter when the gangs were causing problems in town; only then were the Council quick to eradicate their operation, most notably with Manchester's most famous nightclub.

4

'He's going to have sex with that girl on stage!'

NIGHTLIFE

> Manchester has this reputation of the Haçienda blah-blah, and all this rave scene, *24 Hour Party People*, but from my perspective, as someone that grew up in the late nineties, Manchester's nightlife was rough and limited. For the stuff I was into, it was dead compared to what other cities were doing at the time. I ain't gonna say we didn't have a good time, because we did, but it was in spite of the circumstances, not because of them.
>
> – Nathan Miles[1]

On 28 June 1997, the Haçienda closed its doors for good. The legend will tell you that this was a devastating loss to Manchester, a cultural blast to match the destruction of the IRA's bomb twelve months prior. The truth is it wasn't. The average Mancunian didn't weep, mourn, or bat an eyelid. Those that weren't clubbers had only heard of the Haçienda through the negative press.

A Haçienda regular, who wished to remain anonymous, was surprised that the club remained open as long as it did. They had stopped going a long time ago because of the behaviour of the security people:

> They was punching some of my friends, girls were being punched in the queue. None of my mates would go in anymore after that because it wasn't the same place. It was not about music, it was violent, it was threatening, it was aggressive. [The change in conduct by the door staff was mirrored by those that were there to go clubbing.] I think part

> of the reason had been the pills, probably back in the early nineties, late eighties, everyone was on those Dove pills, everybody was happy and dancing, but that changed when people weren't getting the good pills. People weren't dancing. They were fighting more. They were drinking more; it just became more of a violent, aggressive place and not what the Haçienda used to be about. I didn't care about it anymore, it just wasn't the same.
>
> – [illegible], clubber[2]

Outside of the owners and staff, those who were most upset that the Haçienda closed were the people who had been its ruin. The Haçienda had been quite the cash cow for the bouncers-cum-drug dealers who were running the door. But nothing lasts forever … except the legacy of the Haçienda, which has only grown in myth since it closed. When people think of Manchester nightlife, they will think of the Haçienda. It closed the same month I finished high school; I never went but that doesn't mean Manchester was without a nightlife after it closed.

The areas in Manchester city centre today bleed into each other. You can turn any corner and find a restaurant or watering hole to whet your appetite. There is something of interest on every street. You can easily venture between Spinningfields and the Corn Exchange without ever noticing you are leaving or entering a different part of the city. This wasn't always the case. There were only pockets of nightlife sporadically positioned across town. To travel between was to pass barren terrain: closed shops, derelict buildings, badly lit streets, urban nothingness, trouble. To get between the Northern Quarter and Deansgate was 'a hike' or cost you a taxi fare, so most people, when positioned in a part of town, would stay there for their evening. To go between was to cut into part of your night or your drink tokens. The most curious of areas across the city centre was around Oldham Street, recognised today as the Northern Quarter. Among the derelict buildings, porn shops, and

Affleck's Palace was a contrast of dodgy backstreet boozers, with one diamond within the rough.

> The pubs around Oldham Street at the time were really dodgy ... The Castle wasn't somewhere I wanted to go to back then, neither was The Kings, but I remember going in there, once, because it was the only place in town that was showing the footy and there's this young girl walking round the pub saying, 'I'll show you me fanny if you give me four quid!' She's like fourteen – and I was thinking, I don't want to watch this game now. The Millstone is, well, that's another place. It's quite a nice little pub to go to now, but back in the day it was pretty moody.
>
> – Stan Chow, artist[3]

> Gulliver's is a really cool bar, great music venue. I went in there, ages ago, about '96 and there's a guy in there saying, 'Can you lend me 52 pence please for a pint of beer?' I asked him to repeat himself. 'Do you want to buy a pair of trousers for 52 pence?' And he was going to sell the trousers he was wearing to get another pint!
>
> – Tom Bloxham[4]

I haven't been offered a garment, or a genital flash, to fund someone's pint, but it was a common practice amongst those desperate to get drunk to find creative ways to do so. In The Blob Shop, in the same part of town, a mobile music man would go around selling cassette copies of The Who's Greatest Hits. He had a trench coat lined with Maxwell C60s and had designed the covers himself in biro. He was always pissed, so it must have been a successful operation. But nobody lived in town. I always wondered what situation the person found themselves in to be drinking there during the day, and not at their local, a pastime I only enjoyed en route to watching the match. The Northern Quarter also provided accessible places for underage drinkers with Idols where punters and bar staff would dance on bars and The Lazy Pig where topless barmaids served flat pints of Fosters as meatheads drenched in Joop aftershave ogled at them. Then there was Piccadilly 21s, which was an entry level nightclub. It was a breeze to get in; it was how you left where the danger lay. Set in the Woolworth Building, above a slot-machine arcade overlooking Piccadilly Gardens, the interior had a roaring twenties decor, plush seating, and chandeliers; the ground-level entrance had a grand opening introducing you to sweeping red-carpeted stairs which led you to the nightclub. This grandiose impression soon vanished as you risked being a human skittle walking up the same steps bouncers were bowling party-goers down. Inside it was the refuge of those refused entry – a sanctuary for every reprobate, student, dealer, and teenager that couldn't get in anywhere else. Whizz was doled out from VIP areas by dealers in rolled gold chains and Rockport boots, squeaky sixteen-year-olds nailed alcopops through straws, and cheesy pop blasted through the speakers. The only reason you couldn't get into 21s was that it was packed. On my final visit, I was treated to the flying stair exit after a mishap with a bottle of WKD. As I lay writhing in agony, the female clerk at the ropes told the person next in the queue, 'you can go up now'. My dismissal wasn't seen as a deterrent but as someone else's opportunity to dance.

Amongst the seed and squalor there was the Night & Day Café. Your author would regularly sneak in underage where I would feel both intimidated and inspired by the locals. The interior, the punters, the staff didn't represent anywhere else in Manchester that I recognised; it was a mirror of Affleck's Palace which I loved in my early teens, but served alcohol. To push through those doors was me walking through the wardrobe and right into fucking Narnia. All the places I'd been out drinking in town had been loud, competitive, laddish, 'lager, lager, white thing, mega mega' joints. Establishments I merrily enjoyed along with my peers, but the bravado and bollocks of trying not to get into it with some booze-fuelled bully did become a tiresome exercise. I needed some calm in the carnage and it was here. Night & Day was full of creative people embarking on careers that I had long aspired to do – poets, writers, musicians, designers. I'd never known anyone not work in an office, factory, or on the roads. In my young naivety I thought artists came from London, Paris, and New York; nobody told me of Manchester's steeped creative culture, and here was I stumbling into a bar housing our city's next generation after I'd been chased down Oldham Street by a panhead none too impressed at my kissing his girlfriend.

> It was a chip shop called Pisces and Jan Oldenburg was the person who bought it with the idea of turning into a music venue. It wasn't a big portfolio business coming in and going, 'Bring the decorators and designers and let's go shopping for vintage knick-knacks.' He bought it on a shoestring. He decorated it himself. He banged nails himself. He worked behind the bar himself. So when he bought it, he continued it as a chip shop for a while because it took a while for those ultimate plans to coalesce – that was him being smart and resourceful. One of the most shrewd, resourceful, and interesting people I've met. It stopped being Pisces and became Night & Day very quickly, but the transformation from it being a chip shop through to it being a music venue took a while.
>
> – Jay Taylor, Music Venue Trust/Greater Manchester Music Commission[5]

> They had chips and chicken they were serving – he's dead now so they can't sue him – but they were selling booze in teapots so they could serve alcohol without actually having a licence. There was a saxophone player that used to play in the window and you had regulars who would be drinking out of the teapots so the outside would come in out of interest. I think he saw that it could have that Amsterdam vibe, it could have that café vibe.
>
> – Tash Willcocks, artist and designer[6]

We got into Kerouac, and into Chet Baker – and we were into this kind of jazz thing. We weren't old enough, or confident enough, to drink. But we used to go to a place called the Filling Station, which was a little feeder cafe for the Haçienda and behind the counter was Luke Unabomber. That was the first time I remember seeing him, and they served this nuclear coffee – you had two cups and it was like you'd had some proper old school speed – and this led us to Night & Day. He was going for this Kerouac Jazz Bar thing and he was always wearing a cardigan. We used to just sit in there and we'd drink coffee. There was never anybody in. I remember the first conversation with Jan was him asking us to bring our friends down. I think he was just trying to run a youth club, and we were all comfortable there. I remember there was a drunk guy kicking off with Jan – I suppose Jan was about fifty then, but looked older – all I saw was a young guy kicking off with an old guy. So, I jumped up – and I've never thrown a punch in me life, I'm happy to say, but I talk a good scrap – I helped him throw this guy out and we became lifelong friends. Me and Pete Turner from Elbow hung around in the Night & Day, all day and all night, literally.

– Guy Garvey, musician[7]

Before I'd moved to Chorlton I would drive from Bolton on a Saturday to Piccadilly Records, to buy six or seven albums every time I had enough money saved, and then go to Night & Day with these albums and knew nobody. I knew absolutely nobody. I remember seeing Jan and being scared to death of him because he looked like he was an angry guy. Until I got to know him, and he's like the nicest guy. So I'd be going there on my own for a coffee after buying some records and that's when it started from. There was a sense that there was something there, it felt like you're in New York in that part of the Northern Quarter.

– Badly Drawn Boy, musician[8]

Jan, without overtly doing it, he just wanted us all to be there. He embraced us all being there, and there he just filled the place full of people like us, and all the bar staff were just – you probably remember – a bunch of really good looking, miserable horrible girls. I mean I married one of them eventually. Eventually. But yeah, I was always terrified of them – they all used to look at us with total disdain.

– Andy Hargreaves, musician[9]

I think most of the women that were there were massive music fans, but they also, like all of us, had Masters and degrees and we had our own things going on so it wasn't like we were getting the job in the bar just to be close to musicians. It wasn't like we were a group of wannabes. We were doing our own thing. I think there were moments where you kind of went, 'Shit, this is really important', but we were so in it, we couldn't see it, and we were just doing what we were doing, we were just a bunch of kids that all hung out together.

– Tash Willcocks[10]

We were very friendly with all sorts of people, there was loads of bands of course, and that was the great thing about the Night & Day. We met loads of creative people in bands and I really don't think there was ever any jealousy or any snideness towards anybody. Everybody just buzzed on the fact that anybody was doing something creative.

– Andy Hargreaves[11]

I think everyone who met there were all kind of misfits – you know, didn't fit in with any other proper Manchester dudes; we were all just people who were creative really. We were all striving for something. I think anyone who went there had a dream, because more and more of these kind of people were there, you were drawn to the place. For example, you'd see Johnny Marr in the corner and I think some people would be intimidated by the fact that he's there drinking all time. But then there were people who wanted to be there because they wanted to be part of where he was. I literally spent every single day there between '96 to 2007. I was in there every single day.

– Stan Chow[12]

Whilst best known as a bar and music venue, the Night & Day Café had the stage and space for innovative film nights and theatre productions.

> It could be whatever you want it to be. We had Howard Marks come in and do a talking heads piece. You know, it didn't have to be a music venue, the stage was like a space for whatever it needed to be. We did the same thing with Andy Votel and Twisted Nerve for their counter-culture nights, where they would show a film. One night Jan was like, we're gonna have a theatre piece and it's gonna be *Rita, Sue and Bob Too*. So it's really lovely, we pull the seats out and have it like a little theatre space. And then there's these two car seats on the stage and this guy comes on stage and he pulls his pants down, they actually pull his pants down. So he's got his cock out on stage and I'm like 'Oh no, what's gonna go on?! Oh my god, he's going to have sex with that girl on stage!' I'm looking at Jan, and Jan's looking at me. He's laughing and I'm going, 'No, we're gonna get shut down if this happens. There are people that shouldn't be watching this in the audience.' He's laughing until he goes, 'Oh no, I actually think it's going to happen', and I'm like, 'We're gonna get shut down, this is live porn!' To this day I do not know whether they did or didn't have sex on that stage; something happened and it happens because there's no way of stopping it. But it was brilliant. And actually it was a brilliant play. I think it's done really well, but that bit was hilarious. There was a lot of times where I would be looking at Jan saying, 'Oh my God, we could get shut down', because I was the Licensee at that point, so I was the one that was going to get in trouble.
>
> – Tash Willcocks[13]

But it wasn't all fun and games. Night & Day and many of the bars and nightclubs across Manchester were targets for gangs to rush their way inside to steal whatever they could get their hands on.

> It was a New Year's Eve and we found out they were going to rush the door. The doorman came over and said, 'What I want you to do is just get all of the punters behind that velvet curtain and turn the front lights on but not the back lights, let them just dance, turn the music up as loud as you can. They're circling, they're gonna rush us in any second. Then get all of the girls …' and I mean this, we were *all* women, '… get them behind the bar, get as many beer bottles as you can near you, but stay behind that bar because they're going to rush the door

> and when they do you come up and throw as many bottles as physically possible'. So they rushed the door and we popped up when he shouted 'Go!' and we're just lobbing bottles; the bouncer had a chair like a lion tamer pushing them back out of the door with us throwing bottles at the gangsters. And they went away! I think they just wondered what the hell is going on!? None of the punters even knew what had happened. They had no idea. Then we turned the lights back off, removed the curtain and just carried on for the evening.
>
> – Tash Willcocks[14]

> It was an age when everyone's at each other's buttons and zips, and were really supportive of one another, you know. Even if you didn't dig it, even if you didn't dig what someone was doing, you were into the fact that they were doing something. It was a really remarkable magic time. It felt like we never went home. And why the fuck would you?
>
> – Guy Garvey[15]

In 2018, Jan Oldenburg passed away at the age of seventy-one. His story almost typifies the spirit of the city. Here was someone from somewhere else that created a space for local creatives to express themselves. The Night & Day Café and Jan Oldenburg helped shape the Northern Quarter, and the lives of many of the unique artists to come out of Manchester.

The legacy of the Haçienda has concealed a lot of Manchester's club scene, the black and yellow paint which the club is famed for a metaphorical barricade tape to stop anyone looking past that club to see what else was going on. And at the end of the nineties, there was a lot. I opened the question on my Twitter account to see what memories people had of the period, asking 'the club nights in Manchester you miss, that weren't at the Haçienda'. As is the case when I often ask nostalgic Manchester questions, I was inundated with responses. Out of the 200+ replies there were multiple mentions for Holy City Zoo, Home on Ducie Street, Venus, The Love Train at Royales/The Ritz, Funkademia, Bugged Out, Bop at Jabez, and many, many more. There were two names that came out most frequently: Jilly's Rockworld and the Electric Chair at The Roadhouse.

> I have a particular bugbear about Manchester's dogged insistence on hyperfocusing on the Haçienda and that time period. Obviously it was all huge, and we should celebrate our cultural history with the best of them, but it feels like it's gone a bit far when you've got the branding on estate agents' windows with a slogan about 'Doing things differently here'. Other things have definitely been lost in the noise, such as Jilly's Rockworld. The main thing with Jilly's was that it split between rooms that were quite different. The main room was mixed, but you could go through a door at one end and emerge into a sweaty room full of goths, or go through the other side and find a load of emo types dancing to hardcore. I used to orbit around depending on what I fancied, or who I was with. It was fun, sweaty, and filled with a bunch of diverse and interesting shitfaced weirdos with quite different subcultures and interests, but united in their alternative status. Places like this felt like welcoming spaces to me, as a largely underage metalhead. The all-nighters in particular were really special, turning up as a skinny punk guy with a mohawk, and coming out with a load of cyber goths as new best pals ten hours later. There's something unbeatable about a sweaty club full of hairy dudes and weird chicks banging their heads to something loud and necking pints out of plastic cups.
>
> – Dan Hett, artist[16]

Of Electric Chair, *Decoded Magazine* said, 'When [they] first draped The Roadhouse in camouflage netting back in the summer of 1995, nobody knew it would go on to have the lasting impact it did in the city of Manchester and beyond. For almost 13 years it bubbled away, evolving into almost a culture within itself. It was home to the most beautiful melting pot of people, of which many attended religiously, no matter the venue, guest or many local-hero DJs who played there.'[17]

> When we started Electric Chair it was [a] monthly party in a grotty little rock club, a shit hole, shit toilets and a great sound system. Longevity comes when there is no ego and no financial game plan. The best things in Manchester have always happened when they are understated and they are not trying to be the next big thing and not about fashion or hype ... [Andy] Weatherall said a beautiful thing; he said for him the underground is just where he felt comfortable. That's it. It's not about holier than thou. There was always a sense of belonging at Electric Chair and that family aspect has always underpinned it, so even on a night where the guest DJ wasn't your thing there was always the social element of it.
>
> – Luke Unabomber, DJ/promoter[18]

Manchester's most-well known nightclub post-Haçienda was at the Beehive Mill, in an Ancoats where people seldom ventured at night unless they were headed to Sankeys. Sankeys Soap originally opened in 1994 but fell to the same problems as the Haçienda and closed in 1998. Business partners Sacha Lord and David Vincent faced an uphill task when they reopened Sankeys in 2000.

> People talk about Manchester being Gunchester but it was bad, and kind of goes under the radar because everyone references the Haçienda but between '94 and '98 there were guns going off in Sankeys. The police shut it down and said they never want it reopened. I, as a new operator, managed to convince them to let me do it. The old door team wanted the door and the police said specifically you're not having them on there. I was like fine – they say it's not happening, it's not happening. The week leading up to opening night we were literally painting the place ourselves – it's mad that we opened that club on thirty-eight grand – we only ever rented everything as we didn't know whether it would work. We rented the sound, the lights; that money included stocking the bar, having a cash flow for change and there was no use of credit card. We had to say no to this door firm, and obviously it was financially important to them. So we were knackered the night before the opening. Absolutely knackered, we'd worked for three days non-stop, and the night before opening I got a call from the GMP.

> At the car park of the Beehive Mill there was a generator – they don't install them the same these days – but it was surrounded by a metal fence. So the police called me up to say you've got a problem, you'd better come down. The old door team had turned up at 3am, shoved a mattress over the fencing, poured petrol on it and set it up. It blew up the whole generator with the thought it would take out Sankeys and kibosh our opening night. The generator took the whole of Ancoats out, except Sankeys! What they didn't realise was that Sankeys had its own generator so we were raving, going for it, whilst Ancoats didn't have any electricity for two days. But it was bad in them days. There was still an element that made it so difficult for everybody. I think the change, for me, the moment when it became more professional, was probably around 2002. The police got a grip on the gangs, and most were either banged up or dead.
>
> – Sacha Lord, Night Time Economy Adviser for Greater Manchester[19]

Sankeys would welcome global names during the years it was open such as The Chemical Brothers, Björk, and Moby, but it was also the place for would-be superstars to break through at the time.

> We had acts like Daft Punk play, but I like to remember the people who played who weren't well known at the time. I remember Sam, now my business partner, used to work for me at Sankeys, picking up an unknown artist from Manchester Airport. I think we paid him £400. And Sam had been flyposting the night before and there was glue and shit everywhere over the hired Fiat and it was David Guetta he was picking up! He still remembers it to this day. A lot of artists have come through. I think people forget that they have to start somewhere and we've had Calvin Harris to Florence and the Machine and Stormzy coming through on that journey.
>
> – Sacha Lord[20]

In the mid- to late 1980s Manchester was at the forefront of the British dance scene and became the catalyst for the all-nighters, outdoor parties, and warehouse raves shooting up all across the country. In 1990, the Thatcher government passed the Entertainment (Increased Penalties) Act which threatened organisers with penalties of £20,000 and/or six months in prison. This was the beginning of the end for rave culture as it was. At the turn of the millennium it was Manchester once more that put ravers in a warehouse.

> Thatcher stopped all the illegal raves, all the M25 raves. If you turned up with the sound system, or you created noise, you could be arrested. When *24 Hour Party People* was being filmed around the corner from Sankeys we were invited to go to the scene where everyone was dancing – they'd literally rebuilt the Haçienda brick by brick, but it was phenomenal the way they did it. There was never a proper leaving party at the Haçienda, because you didn't know it was going to close. It was random when you walked in there, because Ang, the old manageress stood where she used to stand, Bobby Langley was where he used to stand, and Mike Pickering the same … everyone gradually took their old positions and it was like a farewell. At the end of that night, I thought it'd be great to do another party in there but they'd dismantled it within two weeks and it was just this empty warehouse on Pollard Street so I went and asked the authorities if we could do a warehouse party. I didn't know at the time, but it was the first legal warehouse party since Thatcher stopped them all. It was August Bank Holiday 2003. The sound systems went in on the back of lorries. The bars were temporary, the bar staff were nicking off me left, right, and centre. I didn't have a clue what to do, I was that naive. We had booked security from the operating time, six in the afternoon till six in the morning. Come six in the morning, they'd all cleared off and I was left in this room of cash all by myself in Ancoats – which you probably remember wasn't the shiny Ancoats it is now! But that night actually planted the seed for what is The Warehouse Project now.
>
> – Sacha Lord[21]

Other parts of Manchester's nightlife were beginning to blossom. During the late nineties, Manchester's Gay Village on Canal Street came out from the shadows; once a place where people went to be discreet with their sexuality behind closed doors, it did a complete 180 and became the spot to showcase and celebrate it.

> To be at a gay bar, it absolutely blew my mind in the nineties and then I found all these other gay bars all around that whole area around Canal Street, I was just blown away and so excited that all these gay bars were right in the city centre, and all in one area, and it was called the Gay Village! Where I lived in Liverpool, we had nothing like that as far as I knew, nowhere had anything like that really, apart from London. It was hugely enticing, and I spent most of my time as a student in Liverpool on the M62 to Manchester. Even though there were quite a few bars in that area, it was all a bit seedy, it was all a bit spit and sawdust. You know? Bad wallpaper, sticky carpet, and blacked-out windows. It wasn't a cool place to be seen or go, it had a sort of undercurrent of being a bit dirty and a bit unsure about itself, so it really was the mid-nineties where it all exploded and the bars had a lot more investment in the area and looked nicer. Manto's was really, really significant because it was the first gay bar where if you walked past it you could see inside. That was hugely significant because before that, gay people were lurking behind closed doors with secret knocks and secret handshakes, and it was all a bit dirty and grimy. But those glass windows at Manto's, and it had really amazing decor and furniture … So gay people were starting to come out of the shadows and go look, we're here and we don't care if you walk past and see that we're in a gay bar. I was a young gay person in my twenties and I was like a kid in a candy shop 'cause I just could not believe that there were all these places where I could go out and meet other gay people and they felt like a really nice, safe, fun environment. It made me feel really empowered. It was hugely important to me. If you wanted to meet another gay person, if you wanted to, essentially, get your leg over you had to go to a gay bar, there was no two ways about it. That's where you were going to meet other people that were gonna become your friends, your lovers, and just people that you hung out with.
>
> – Emma Goswell, radio presenter[22]

There is the impression of the Gay Village solely being a place of hedonism, but it was also a hive of activity for the LGBTQ+ community to get together to discuss activism and plan protests.

> The New Union pub shows the village was more than just booze and partying. It was in this pub where campaigners and political meetings would happen. It began in the eighties but went on throughout the nineties. This was where they were planning the marches against Section 28, when they were planning a lot of the political stuff. People went there to plot marches, design leaflets, and discuss issues. Some would go out and do mad stuff like paint things like 'LESBIANS EVERYWHERE' on bridges. The funny part of that story is the girls who did it ended up tipping the paint can in their mum's car and got in trouble. But these are women that went on to start women's refuges and campaign about violence against women and housing rights. And all of this was going on. In the New Union, that's where people met and it wasn't just for drinking. Back in the day, it was for meeting and talking about the way that they were being treated by the establishment and plotting political agendas. That went on in the village as well.
>
> – Emma Goswell[23]

While the Gay Village boasted a city centre location, what still felt like another minority community at the turn of the millennium, those into Hip Hop, Soul, and R&B, had fewer places to go.

> There wasn't a lot of the places for us to go, and we're all brought up with the same music, we're all going to go to the same events, so it became a thing when you were going out, the likelihood is you were going to see somebody that you know because the black community is pretty small. Everyone knows everyone and going out, I've made so many friends. I see people today and I know them from a night out. Back when I was younger, it was a case of you all pull together. It was a community. You look at people and you go well, I remember you from when we used to go to them nights out. We were all going out having a good time in the limited places that we had. They were specific. It was a really concentrated type

of night where we went out. It was like Buzz FM in a club. There was nothing like that. Because when you were listening to Buzz FM you knew you were listening to an illegal station because that music wasn't allowed in the mainstream. So to find a spot in town that was playing it, and catering for black people, felt kind of sneaky and you go in and you're like 'Oh My God, this is amazing'. You can now dance and enjoy yourself. Have a drink, have fun, meet people, socialise, and go home at the end of the night, and you had that every week. And that's definitely what Havana started for me. It was seeing black culture that was alienated on legal radio stations given the opportunity to exist in the centre of town.

– Marsha Bell[24]

Manchester never had regular kind of events on for Garage and Hip Hop and stuff like that, not in the same way as London, so we used to go to Garage Nation a couple of times a month with a whole coach load of us – but there was bad shit happening down in Tottenham as well. I remember one night we'd leave Manchester about 9.30pm, get to Garage Nation at 1am to see it all kick off and them only serve water, and then at 2am say it was closing early because of more trouble so there was like thirty of us stuck in North London til our coach came back at 6am. Still, London and other cities still had those sort of Garage and Hip Hop nights on.

– Nathan Miles[25]

I got to the point where I was going out three times a week, and probably one of them would have been out of Manchester; again it was that whole collective thing, everyone went to Mr Smiths in Warrington for the first Wednesday of every month for an R&B night, it targeted us. You had people from as far as Birmingham and Nottingham went there. Everybody went to Mr Smiths – it's a place that if you were black at that time, you went Mr Smiths, or The Temple at Bolton. And that's where for those planned events there used to be coaches from Manchester. So there was a lot of that going on, taking you outside of Manchester for events because there wasn't that much in town.

– Marsha Bell[26]

> I think that was a big problem with clubbing, and I look back with sadness really 'cause every time I used to go out it was hard to go out and find a good R&B or Hip Hop night. I think it was probably linked to the worry in town of potential violence that would come with it from venue owners and police. There were a few good nights I went to with that music being played but unfortunately some did end up with bad shit happening. Like Club Havana on the millennium, that went off proper mental. So after that we would have to venture outside of Manchester for that music.
>
> – Nathan Miles[27]

If it wasn't the bouncers handing out punches to people, then you could just as easily find yourself in fights with someone who couldn't handle their drink. It was as much a success to go home without having a scrap as it was to find someone to share your bed. I've found myself in some ridiculous scrapes, such as one evening after being at 42s because someone felt I was pushing the queue at Allen's Fried Chicken and decided I needed a smack because he was hungrier than I. It was intimidating for men, so I can't imagine what the experience was like for women.

> So the first places I ever went in town was Discotheque Royales and 21s, and that would have been the end of Year 10 so I would be fifteen when I was going there. So me and my friend, we were laughing the other day 'cause today people would say it's sexual assault but it was just so on the regular, it was expected. You know if you go to 21s, or Royales, then someone was going to grab you; a hundred per cent you were going to get manhandled, like that was just standard, so you'd be dancing, and somebody would come behind and grab your boobs. That was pretty much standard. People would try and put their hand up your skirt, if you were wearing a short skirt, and Royales was full of stairs so people would just put their hand up your skirt if you were walking up or down, that's to be expected. I was very into Britpop at the time, so that was my kind of music, and I discovered 42s and stopped going to mainstream places, probably because it was a bit

> like 'this is not the vibe for me!' And it wasn't just the touching, it just became standard that people were going to shout stuff at you. There was very much a sort of continuum. I think to be honest it probably made me good at the job that I do now in terms of I've got very good at quickly de-escalating the situation, but there was a very fine line as a young woman between being nice enough to men to pacify them. But not too nice so that they think that you're interested, because it can turn quickly when they realise that you're not. If you're too dismissive straight away, they'll just start screaming and shouting, but if you're nice enough where they may see an 'in' then they wouldn't leave you alone for the night and just ruin the evening. Men just coming to plonk themselves in your group and sitting down and being 'alright ladies' – it can go either way of them getting aggressive or passive aggressive if you don't diffuse the situation correctly. 42nd Street, 5th Ave, The Venue, was where I would say you were less likely to get sexually assaulted. It was a lot more freeing. You were dressed differently, so you could go in your jeans and stuff. Like to get into 21s, and those mainstream places, you had to be dressed in a hyper-feminine kind of way in the first place so it was quite liberating in the Indie clubs where I could go in my jeans, t-shirt, and trainers but you know it was more students, and less regular people from Manchester that you would be with. Because it was based around a particular kind of music, there was a bit more of a mix of people I would say, and that was a lot nicer, like I did not feel sort of threatened in those places.
>
> – Steph Lonsdale[28]

There was also an influence from the 'Ladette' culture emerging at the time and how some well-known female celebrities were behaving in the media was being represented within the nightlife.

The term 'Ladette' came to refer to 'bolshie women who could out-party and out-gross any hardened lad. Sara Cox, Denise van Outen and Zoe Ball were the media favourites: often pictured binge-drinking and out on the town. Ladettes went hand-in-hand with nineties lad culture, where Britpop, banter, and sport collided in a blizzard of hedonism.[29]

> I tell you what was really prevalent at that time, which I think goes to show this because in some respects, that culture, I loved it in terms of being a fifteen, sixteen-year-old. Adele always says that thing about Zoe Ball being one of the heroes because she remembered when she got married to Fat Boy Slim. She's in the wedding dress with a bottle of Jack Daniels and all that kind of thing. So I enjoyed that. Because my grandparents didn't like women drinking a pint, it was not something that a woman should do – which to be fair, it probably isn't, I would probably fare better if I stuck to half – but there was that element to it, I enjoyed that sort of bravado, as in 'I'm going to order a pint and I'm going to do this, that, and the other'. But I think the other side of it, I remember it was a definite thing, in '99/2000, peak Britney time, and it was just girls snogging each other when they were out, not because they're gay or bi but as a way of attracting boys. I remember there was a Ladette culture in that 'I'll do what I like', but it was also that a lot of it was being done in quite a performative way. It was nice and it was freeing in the sense of 'I can do whatever a boy can do', but what it wasn't doing was celebrating anything that's good about femininity. It's not about making yourself as masculine as possible in your personality qualities, but it took me quite a long time to understand that. When you look back, what it's saying to you, that sort of culture, the lad culture and the ladette culture was neither good for men or women.
>
> – Steph Lonsdale[30]

Personally I felt they were just trying too hard to be something, like just do whatever you want to do. If you want a pint, have a pint, no one is bothered. I always drank pints, but every time I was out with our kid, he used to buy me a pint but get me a half glass because he thought I looked ridiculous because I only had little hands! There were people that were trying to emulate that Ladette culture but I don't think it's that easy in Manchester because I don't think we're good at trying too hard. I don't think we accept it very much – like personally one of the things that annoys me is when people say that they're 'wacky', like 'I'm crazy', and I'm like who cares? What are you trying so hard for? Just be, have a chat, and be yourself.

– Mary McGuigan[31]

The Ladette culture wasn't the only thing trying too hard to be something; the areas of Manchester that had been the first parts to be regenerated were now looking like something else completely. The ten railway arches known as 'The Locks' now housed the sort of upmarket bars and clubs you'd expect to see down south. Expensive, exclusive, and initially a pain in the arse to get past the bouncers unless you were a footballer or on *Coronation Street*. The really frustrating thing? They played the music that I was into.

Let's say between 1998 when I first started going out properly, and 2002, it had changed massively. I remember going out and we couldn't hear R&B anywhere, they wouldn't play it because there was always trouble on the door. We had Club Havana but there was no big nightclubs that would play R&B, so when we first started going out it was House music. But by 2002 we used to go Sugar Lounge, so we went Friday, Saturday, Sunday. We would be out there and it was R&B, Hip Hop and Soul, a bit of House and Garage but it had completely changed on its head. This was the place that footballers would go, musicians, actors, and look flash. The music was top, the nights were top, they had the best door staff. There was rarely any trouble, it'd be quickly locked off. And I remember someone saying to me, about 2000 or 2001, and they'd put some bollards up or something and the guy I was with said, 'It's gentrification', and I went 'What do you mean?' He said that the whole city is about to change and this area will be one of the first. But around the millennium, Manchester was bubbling, my mates from London, Birmingham, wherever, would start wanting to come to the city.

– Leon Mike, ex-pro footballer[32]

Nightclub owners recognised that there was a need for a change and emerged to offer different sounds which reflected the interests of those that lived in, and visited, Manchester. The outside impression was that Manchester's musicians needed to do the same thing. On the face of it, we had Oasis, we had a heritage of great guitar bands, there was the dance music culture of the 1980s, but when tasked to name a nineties musician that wasn't male or white that came from Manchester the names are minimal. They existed, they succeeded, but by and large they are seldom celebrated.

5

'A different success for Manchester'

MUSIC

We all have musical guides in our youth. Those who have gone ahead into the soundscape to report what our ears should be exposed to and steer us away from any dodgy terrain. These pioneers can come in the shape of an older sibling, a young auntie, a cool family friend; it is seldom your parents. It could never have been mine. I had no musical influence at home. The only time Mum would play CDs was when she was cleaning the house – the soundtrack to her domestic chores was Simply Red and The Lighthouse Family. Thank God for the noise of a hoover. To this day my Dad remains an enigma. Not because he had an eclectic taste but because he had none. I don't mean that as a jibe, he doesn't listen to music – something I still can't get my head around. If I was successful in any of my rebellion against my parents it's that I became a musicphile in a home where there was no music. The first person that got me into 'Manchester' music was my best friend Greg Marshall's older brother, Chris. When he would be off raving at Maximes or Wigan Pier, Greg and I would break into his room and invade his record collection. We would rifle through his CDs, playing them if the artwork caught our eye, or we sought out something that Greg had heard Chris play. It was through these escapades I found New Order's *Movement*, James' *Laid*, Happy Mondays' *Pills, Thrills and Bellyaches*, The Stone Roses' debut, rave mixtapes, and the staple of our nightly pillage would be Ratpack's *Searching for my Rizla*. Outside of who the records belonged to there was nothing to suggest they were linked. New Order and Happy Mondays might have been from different planets, let alone cities. I had no context. No origin stories. No history lesson on Factory Records, the Haçienda, nor that because these bands came from Manchester it made the music any more, or less, important.

Chris was older than us, so these songs and artists were the soundtracks to his generation. To me, it was an exposure that people from Manchester, without the surname Gallagher, also made guitar music. When I first heard Oasis I thought they were an exception in the city, the only ones to do it, and not the latest thing to come off the production line of successful bands from Manchester. To me the guitar music that you would hear on the TV and radio always seemed a bit too straight, a bit too safe, a bit too much like what adults listened to, so I came to the Indie stuff later on in life. I found the music that would speak to me when I was thirteen. I'd asked my auntie for the new Snoop Dogg debut album *Doggystyle* and, none the wiser to the Parental Advisory Warning, she came through. When I opened the artwork inlay at my birthday party my Mum was none too pleased to see the provocative and profane eight-frame X-rated homage to The Peanuts' Snoopy. To see the other parents' faces as they looked over my young shoulder to see a cartoon dog carrying bags of weed, toting guns and dropping more f-bombs ... Needless to say I was forced to return *Doggystyle* for the latest *Now* ... album (not before copying it on tape). But what the parents forbid makes the child's heart grow fonder. *Bow wow wow, yippee yo, yippee yay,* I'd found my first love: Hip Hop.

A lot of my peers were growing their hair, wearing the Burberry shirts, and buying into the whole Britpop thing. Oasis would be the Blue Nun that would get me into finer wines (more of which later), but I could never commit to Indie in the same way as some of my mates. That's not to knock it but I find it claustrophobic to stick to one genre. Perhaps because of Hip Hop culture, I prefer to sample music from everywhere, and where I find a greater interest in that sound, I'll dive deeper into it; the same way Hip Hop producers compose beats. This inherent desire to explore started with music, but it would become how I live my life. Whether physically, socially, creatively, or intellectually, I've always felt the need to move. I am not comfortable with being comfortable. Once I've discovered the basic pattern of how an entity works, or it becomes too predictable, I'll move on. What was predictable during this time was mainstream music. The problem was trying to find a place to listen to an alternative.

> I've done panels where the theme is 'Manchester Music Scene's Evolved, there's a lot more black music now', and I'm like, it's always been there – it just never really got a platform on that level where indie bands did on new music programmes like the Chart Show or whatever. With some exceptions, like A Guy called Gerald – which again, was still quite underground. But it's always been there in Manchester. A lot of it was on white label. It wasn't getting a platform anywhere else apart from on pirate radio.
>
> – Natalie-Eve Williams, BBC Music[1]

The radio stations in Manchester were a landfill of chart playlists and cheesy presenters. Not too dissimilar to their national counterparts. Aside from a few niche shows: Stu Allan on Key 103, or James Stannage's late-night show where he'd argue with drunks about the existence of God, but by and large commercial radio was absolute shite. Pirates such as Buzz FM and Sunset 102 fulfilled the cultural need these legal stations couldn't provide. Makeshift studios transmitting out of tower blocks from Hulme, Old Trafford, and Moss Side nurtured local talent, facilitated art, and curated the sounds of the streets. If you wanted to get into a scene, it was through pirate radio; if you wanted to discover local musicians, it was through pirate radio; if you were a local musician and you wanted a place that would play your music and find an audience, then it was through pirate radio. Local guitar bands had the benefit of doing the live music circuit as bands previously, but if you were doing something different, it wasn't as easy. Through these platforms, new music scenes emerged; they brought communities together and gave a free space for expression unavailable anywhere else. The authorities didn't understand the audience demand nor the desire to have pirate stations, especially as little money was to be made from the enterprises. The legal stations would push commercial, whereas the pirates would push the culture until record labels smell the money and turn it mainstream. Pick a genre, and it's the same old story – Grime, Garage, Hip Hop, Soul, House, Indie, Punk, Rock ... all scenes that came through the pirates. They are unsung heroes and vital cogs in the music industry; they are responsible for cultivating sounds and harvesting new talent that record labels take to sell at market and make money. If it weren't for Buzz FM, I wouldn't have found Hip Hop. I wouldn't have discovered the R&B and Reggae stars that scored my teen years. The police had been raiding the stations and confiscating equipment since pirate stations had started, but with the size of fines increasing and the new threats of jail time, more and more ceased to exist. At the beginning of the millennium, DJ Eric B, the man behind Buzz FM, had to forfeit his car, was ordered to pay £10,000 costs, and was given a two-year conditional discharge for running a pirate station. That's some cost for giving aspiring musicians a platform, huh?

If you weren't a manufactured pop artist then your chances of breaking into the music industry were slim, at best. The difficulties increase if you were a woman, and/or an artist of colour. As recently as 2021 both the Black Lives in Music[2] and BE THE

CHANGE: Women Making Music[3] reports outline that gender inequality and discrimination are still prevalent in the industry twenty years after the period this book discusses.

> There are so many reasons! 1. Being discouraged from pursuing an artist career. 2. Labels/management saying they can't/don't know how to market a Black female artist. 3. Focused into the 'RnB' genre even if your music isn't! 4. Little to no funding. 5. Being called an angry/difficult Black woman. 6. The complete absence of dark-skinned Black female artists and a preference for light-skinned Black women. The music is an absolute mess that breaks Black female artists down and discourages them from pursuing their dreams. The fact that there are very few Black female artists, namely Ray BLK, Nao, and even they don't have the mainstream attention/push, says it all really.[4]

An added problem for musicians coming from Manchester, a city steeped in heritage for guitar bands, is that you are also fighting against presumed traditions of how you are supposed to sound and look. If you don't fit the Manchester brand, the chances stack against you for labels looking in and locals looking around. There is a strong brand identity that exists to build on, it's easier for PR companies to take to market and journalists already have the reference points to write about. It's an easier exercise for people whose end game is to sell units and advertising space to add onto a narrative than it is to create a new one. While you're considering this, I'll give you until the end of the book to name me a Number 1 single to come from a Manchester artist who wasn't white and male (no googling).

> Manchester music will always struggle to shirk the image of four aggressive WHITE MEN with their elbows pointing outwards, it's hard to see past this and find out what's bubbling at the core. I practically lived on Oldham Street, I slept in the office a lot [the Twisted Nerve office was below Fat City Records] so I saw everything. It's took my wife [Jane Weaver] twenty years for her to gain the focus that all her then peers Damon, Doves, Elbow achieved. It's a smokescreen.

> There's a reason gentrified Manchester was built on such a vibrant playground and that was undeniably because of the music of black culture that came before.
>
> – Andy Votel, musician[5]

> From the Stone Roses trying to imitate Young MC's 'Know How' for 'Fools Gold' right down to Northern Soul, in Manchester there has always been a black influence.
>
> – Tunde Babalola, musician[6]

A well-known music industry figure in Manchester felt that A&R people were frightened of missing out on the next Oasis or The Stone Roses and were intent on signing artists that looked and sounded like the big bands of the past rather than looking for new sounds and diverse musicians. 'They were signing some shit … If you were a shit musician in Manchester around that time then you got a deal – a lot were dropped straight afterward – they didn't sign many girls, and they certainly didn't sign any black people, which is a real shame as there was so much talent.'[7]

This isn't a slight at the artists who fit the brand or the journalists that are in it to promote new and interesting music at the time – but if we can all put on our big pants we can all agree that it was somewhat easier to be a white man making music in Manchester band in the nineties and beforehand (is it still?). And before an onslaught of DM sliders hit me on the socials this isn't the only reason those bands make it, but it's certainly more of a help than it is a hindrance. And for those where it was a hurdle, they are often overlooked despite making cultural and commercial impacts in music.

The Moss Side singer Diane Charlemagne was a Jazz, Soul, Funk, and Electronic singer who had chart success in the 1990s and appeared as a vocalist on the Drum and Bass track that broke the genre to the masses. As part of Manchester's Urban Cookie Collective, Diane had two top ten hits reaching Number 2 with

'The Key, The Secret'. In the late nineties she toured the world extensively with Moby. During a performance on the *TFI Friday* Christmas Special Elton John sang the lead vocals on a performance of Moby's 'Why Does My Heart Feel So Bad?' It's almost comical to watch Elton try to compete with Diane on the high notes and at several points in the video he looks over to her with a wry smile of acceptance that he can't; she was too good, and looks effortless throughout. A similar thing happened when Moby headlined Glastonbury in 2003. Against a blacked-out Pyramid Stage, accompanied by a string section, she takes centre stage to deliver a heart-aching, stripped-back rendition of 'In This World'. The slower tempo minus electronics, this gospel take allows Diane to display the full range of her voice on the most prestigious slot on the UK festival circuit. The crowd is in awe. It is one of the best forgotten Glastonbury performances. Diane's legacy, perhaps, is being the vocalist on a record that was instrumental in taking Drum and Bass to the mainstream. It is her haunting vocals that you hear on Goldie's 'Inner City Life'. Although the single didn't receive much airplay on its first release (*Mixmag* included it on their Best Singles of 1996 list), as the nineties moved forward, its popularity grew, and it is now widely considered one of the best dance singles of all time. When Diane passed, Goldie said, 'I can't thank you enough for what you contributed and we will carry on your legacy.'[8] Has Manchester carried her legacy?

She had big chart hits, she performed on the biggest stage, she was the voice of one of the best dance records of all time; and yet, this woman from Moss Side is rarely celebrated as part of Manchester's musical heritage. Just because she wasn't the name on the records does not detract from her significance to music or our history. Unfortunately, this is a problem that other singers of colour face; their contributions are often wrongly overlooked.

One Manchester musician, who didn't want to be named, described the racist undertones that came with being a black female singer. They felt that the music press would devalue their involvement. Their contribution, whilst fundamental in the creation of music, would be demoted to that of a backing singer, regardless of their input. Is this slight positioned for white female singers in bands? Is Fergie of the Black Eyed Peas referred to as a backing singer? Or Scissor Sisters' Ana Matronic, or Tulisa in N-Dubz? Can this be seen for anything other than a racial prejudice? When black female singers are being labelled backing vocalists, may they well be saying 'blacking vocalist?' Manchester has had many successful black female musicians, yet their names are absent when the city celebrates its musical heritage.

Goldie's 'Inner City Life' marked a crossover from the Ragga and Dancehall-influenced Jungle to the more sophisticated Drum and Bass. Whatever you want to call the genres, it was massive on me. I could never get into the House music Manchester is famed for. In my mind it belonged to the previous generation; by the time I was fifteen it had crossed over into the mainstream, and when a scene becomes popular it loses its allure, especially to young ears. And while fans are within their rights to say what was in the charts wasn't 'proper House music', if that was your first introduction to it, it dilutes its impact. In my mind nothing compares to mining through obscure channels to discover the new. Whether you were digging crates in a record shop, listening to illegal radio, or being passed mixtapes, the exploration was a vital part in the process. You were like Indiana Jones hunting for gold. That you had to work at finding new music gave it more value. It gave you more attachment. You were invested. Now you can find all the music you want from the temple of your front room and it removes the joy of discovery.

- How did you find that new music you're listening to?
- Algorithm.
- Wow. Cool story...

I hope I'm wrong. A forty-year-old relic out of touch with how new music scenes are found offline. I would hate for my own children not to go on what were adventures for me. When I discovered Drum and Bass music it was to join a secret organisation where people talk in code, pass music through mixtapes, where the nights gave you an alternative identity against the one the outside world is presenting you as.

> That mix of European Techno, Detroit Techno mixed with Hip Hop and Breakbeat and Reggae ... I was that kid in the sweetshop but these were every sweet that I loved in one big pot. But that's what it was when Jungle came along ... it was like, 'Fuck me', it's got everything I wanted, it's got the breaks I wanted, Electronic Techno sound, it's got the Roots Dub Bass I wanted, all rolled up into one genre of music. And I suppose notwithstanding, drugs had to play a major part in it. Just the franticness and the fatness, of being fifteen, sixteen pilling your tits off. I just don't think that stuff at 90bpm was going to particularly work for me at that time.
>
> – Tunde Babalola[9]

Sneaking off to house parties at night and during the days we'd gone from stealing car signs to finding good car bonnets to rattling fast drum patterns on – and unlike Hip Hop it felt incredibly British. The parties, the MCs, the DJs, the producers all represented the communities and cultures which I lived amongst. If there was a Cool Britannia in the nineties then this was it – multicultured musicians creating art as expression, and not for commercial gain. London and Bristol are the two cities famed for creating the scene, but there's some debate whether Manchester needs more credit for our input.

> Coming from a Mancunian point of view, we always have a little chip on our shoulders, don't we? Like the second city of the UK is London, and Birmingham is third. Even from a Drum and Bass side, because Gerald was the godfather of Techno and he moved into Jungle really early. So that was our chip on our shoulder, like 'We were doing this fucking shit before you lot,' and then Goldie was from Wolverhampton, which if you squint and twist your head a bit sort of looks Mancunian … or Northern at least.
>
> – Tunde Babalola[10]

Jokes aside, the origins of Jungle/Drum and Bass is a long-contested debate and with A Guy Called Gerald's early foray into it certainly demonstrates Manchester were at the forefront, if not the originators. Coming out of the record shops in the Northern Quarter, the Jungle/Drum and Bass scene had to overcome obstacles southern cities didn't.

Originally from Burnley, the late Marcus Intalex was one of the stalwarts of the scene in Manchester. The record shop staff I spoke about in the opening chapter was a reference to Marcus. He manned the counter at Eastern Bloc Records and wouldn't be shy in telling punters what he thought about what they were picking up; especially to a lad from South Manchester that didn't know his arse from his elbow. As well as being a tastemaker for people like me, he was a Drum and Bass pioneer in production and helped put new artists on.

> I started with Marcus Intalex, Mark XTC, and Paul Walker from about fifteen, sixteen, when I used to start going to the record shops. I was like Paul Walker's bag-carrier and I used to carry his records to gigs, and was the goofball carrying boxes. That's how I got to know them all, you get to your middle–late teens and you start getting an idea of what you want to do and I remember going to Marcus saying, 'I'm gonna start making music', and he was like, 'OK, I'll give you a starter pack', and he gave me these 3.5 inch floppy discs full of beats and samples on them, and stuff like that. And they all became like my

champions, and the first record I made was the Fosters Ice Breaker and made it on to Kiss Radio and then I was off. Marcus used to take my records to London and I started.

– Tunde Babalola[11]

Pirate radio for me was huge and turned me onto Jungle/Drum and Bass massively, you could just tune in to all the pirate radio stations that were going on back then and that was like a huge opening up. I went to Manchester. At that point, I was actually working for a record company called Newtown Records, and I managed to get off them a load of promos to take up, really just to figure out who's who and what was what. So I went up there and pretty quickly realised that a lot of it revolved around Eastern Bloc. They were still going then and 'cause it's such a tight community, within a few weeks I'd basically met most of the people I ended up getting to know really well over the next ten years. It was really weird because it felt underground, but not in the sense that no one knew about it, because there were so many students it was pretty overt, but it didn't feel as overt as it did in London where you had the big Drum and Bass nights and Jungle raves. Obviously with the gang stuff going on in Manchester it was a lot more difficult.

– Darren Lewis, musician[12]

I mean in Manchester there's always been bits of trouble, so it's not one scene or one area; in fact, all cities across the UK have had problems – I think what we felt in those days was that whilst there was trouble in London, it was never reported on in the same way it was in Manchester. I presume it was because it was the capital and may damage the tourist industry but anything that happened in Manchester was frustrating to us artists up here. When we saw everywhere else still having nights and events [across the UK], but in Manchester if someone kicked a can it would be reported as gang violence. Don't get me wrong, it was bloody bad, but it was happening elsewhere. Then the promoters and club owners just stopped putting on anything with Jungle in its name, they said you can't put a party or rave in here. I suppose anyone who wasn't into the scene, their knee-jerk reaction was based on the media and not the real story, so we were without places to play. So we started disguising nights under Drum and Bass instead of Jungle because the owners of venues didn't know any link, and we were calling them sophisticated names such as Knowledge and IQ ... you know, whatever name could suggest sophistication and intelligence. And we started in bars, from the beginning again really, but that eventually led us to the clubs; Marcus Intalex was doing his night at Sankeys and I was doing my FutureSounds night at Music Box, and then Inky had a night at Band on the Wall. With the transition between Jungle and Drum and Bass more of a live Drum and Bass sound, I think there was a band called King Rim which I think went on to become Simian Mobile Disco, and their drummer was James Ford who went on to produce the Arctic Monkeys and form the Last Shadow Puppets with Alex Turner and Miles Kane. There were live nights at Dry Bar and that's where we met Jenna G, that's where there were open mics and free-form riffing. It was really interesting, because when something was forced underground, or forced to re-evaluate itself, you find some really great music, artists, and creativity that came out of it. So the 'No Jungle' was a bit of a fucker when it happened in Manchester but it was forced to re-evaluate itself, went a bit mellow, and starting again in a way. Before '95, the idea of having a live Drum and Bass with musicians would never have entered my head but it was sort of forced upon you, it makes people think of different ways of 'How can I still play this music?' when the club owners and police are banning us from everywhere. We'd ended up creating a scene of live musicians, singers, MCs, and things we'd never really thought about before. Some people say it's more intelligent and I really don't like that term, but it became a bit more technical, shall we say ... it was less aggy but more weird, trippy, cinematic, ethereal but with these beats underneath it.

– Tunde Babalola[13]

This influence would pave the way for the sound of the project that would bring Tunde and Darren, along with singer Jenna G, to major label attention as the band Un-Cut.

We had this song idea for a few years that would eventually go on to be 'Midnight', we had given it to Jenna but she never quite found the sweet spot and then all of a sudden she hit it and figured it out. We'd

> been working on some other bits and pieces, and we decided to finish it off and put it out. It created a bit of a buzz and was being played in mainstream Drum and Bass clubs as the last song of the night. It was just so unique and didn't sound like anything that was out and it was going off. So all these independent labels came to us with offers but we held our ground because we knew we had something, and then we did a Cargo gig where all the Majors came.
>
> – Darren Lewis[14]

> When we did our first ever gig at Cargo in London there was a proper major buzz about us in the industry and all the labels were down. Even though we came from a Drum and Bass scene we could still get decent capacity. I don't think any of the labels expected us to have that following. They sort of saw it as you could be big in Drum and Bass but you would need commercial success for people to really know who you were. So they were a bit shocked at how many people turned up for this new band that nobody had really heard of. As producers and DJs we were known, and Jenna was well known, but not us as a collective, but it was packed out. Diane Charlemagne was there, and also Normsky – the gig went off! We were all buzzing backstage and Normsky was saying to us, 'Respect! This is amazing. This is gonna be massive', and when Normsky bigs you up you are walking about twenty foot tall after that conversation. But the main thing about that night was Diane coming over to Jenna and taking off a metaphorical crown off her head and placing it on to Jenna's head and saying the baton is yours. I remember thinking 'Fuck me', when you think about what Diane Charlemagne had done up to that point. It was just something to see one Manchester singer that was the Queen of Drum and Bass passing the torch onto another Mancunian singer.
>
> – Tunde Babalola[15]

Following the Cargo gig Un-Cut were signed to EMI Publishing and Warner Records for the release of their debut album *The Un-Calculated Truth* and the single 'Midnight', which in my opinion deserves to be placed alongside the greatest records to come out of Manchester. Jenna G is still singing, and Tunde and Darren, as FutureCut, have worked with some of the biggest stars in the world, writing and producing songs for the likes of Rihanna, Shakira, Tom Jones, and Lily Allen. How often do you hear them celebrated as Manchester musicians?

Another place that I was able to find new music that they weren't playing in the mainstream was at the monthly under-eighteens club nights that happened across the city. In Levenshulme, the Palace Nightclub would host them – for a short time – and it would attract people from all over the city to come down to my neck of the woods to get pissed, pull, and party outside of the park. They were great nights. The DJ would play a set similar to what we would listen to on the pirate stations: Jungle, Dancehall, US R&B, Hip Hop and Reggae. There were no adults outside of the staff. Girls in biker shorts and scrunchies would gyrate on the sticky dance floor whilst young lads would drool at them from the sidelines. It was at one of these nights I would go with a girl for the first time. After catching each other's eyes all evening as the disco was coming towards an end, the alcohol had begun to take its toll and people were puking, and testosterone-fuelled lads were becoming more boisterous. The DJ shouted over that this is the last one and called everyone on the dance floor as he played his signature Reggae tune to sign off with, 'Special Way' by Sylvia Tella. Everyone charges on to stand close to someone that they may have a shot of getting off with. As the fates had it I 'mysteriously' ended up next to this girl and she nodded me to come closer and dance (step all over her feet). I found Dutch courage from the bottles of Hooch I'd necked earlier and went in for the kiss. As we're snogging away everyone around us began coughing and shouting, the lights went on, and the staff was shouting people to get out of the building. Someone had let off a CS gas canister in the venue. The staff pulled us apart and hurried us out the fire exit to see our peers in fits of tears and coughing their guts out. This was the last time they did the under-eighteens disco, I never saw the girl again, nor got her name, but 'Special Way' always transports me back to that time, every time. It wasn't until decades after I found out that the singer wasn't from the Caribbean, as I presumed all Reggae stars were, but around the corner from where I lived.

> Sylvia Tella is from Manchester. She's one of the biggest Reggae stars in the world … She's not mentioned by the London people. Manchester people kind of know her, but do they go shouting off, 'We've got a big Lovers Rock star from our city?'
>
> – Karen Gabay, producer and presenter[16]

Sylvia Tella, born Silafatu Morenikeji Wahab Tella to a Nigerian father from the Ilaro royal family and an English mother with Polish/Romanian heritage, grew up surrounded by musicians in Hulme. She first found fame as a backing vocalist for Boney M. She released her debut album in 1981 but it was when she opted to become an independent artist in the nineties that she hit her stride. She now has a huge worldwide audience and is known as 'The First Lady of UK Reggae'. Her 1993 single 'Special Way' was my first introduction to her work; I had no idea when I would constantly harass the DJ at our local under-eighteens night to play it that she was from Manchester. In the nineties she would become a true independent artist; and whilst she wasn't a name in the pop charts, her story shows that to be a successful Reggae artist you didn't need to be.

> The songs that I write, I'm not going to get a decent royalty, right? Because they don't play our tunes. And if they do play our tunes, it's [the work] not reflected in the royalties. It's only when we were running our ship did it reflect it because we we're putting our own stuff out. I'm seeing what I'm selling. I know what I've sold from the boot in my car. So that is why independence was our alternative. You had the Reggae industry and a real industry, but we were running along

> and we were selling tunes, we were making dents, we were influencing, and we had a strategy, right? Because I knew that I could tour with all these bands, and I control my money and it goes back into my music. And that's what all of us did, we all had labels.
>
> – Sylvia Tella, musician[17]

The transition from being a signed artist to working independently is a steep learning curve. What success looks like in the mainstream is not the same as it is when you're operating outside it.

> At first, I was rubbish … I remember I did two tunes, and I still feel like pressing another. And I didn't listen to my people. I wanted it to be a hit. So I pressed up a thousand. You're supposed to press up to two hundred and see how it goes, and then you press more, so I was left with that thousand for about two years because I never did the thing right, because there's a formula. Even the record companies have their formula, but we, as we're independent people collectively moving together, nobody teaches you how the shit goes. You just have to learn.
>
> – Sylvia Tella[18]

The knowledge Sylvia gained from her previous years in the industry, and what she learned from going independent, she passed onto new, and struggling, artists within the Reggae community. How to obtain equity, how to join a union, ways to press records on the cheap to increase profit.

> I'm a female and I was teaching them 'cause they would say to me, 'Where you getting your pressing from?' I was driving all the way down to Slough, I know this man called Johnny, he likes a little smoke, so I'd take him a little weed and he gives me the right deal where I know I can afford to pay. I was always like that, with the Musicians' Union and PRS and equity. I was a member of that from when I was fifteen in Manchester. By the nineties, I'm now working with all these boys, big groups, you know, black musicians in London, and they didn't even know about the union, right? I would send them to get applications from the Musicians' Union and it was because we were a

> community, our collective right, and because we were trying to make an industry.
>
> – Sylvia Tella[19]

It says something that Reggae artists had to not only exist outside of the mainstream but also had to create their own industry to make and sell music within the UK. The obstacles she had to overcome to reach her position is testament to Sylvia's resolve, love of singing, and sheer determination.

> I've been robbed every which way now. But it's life. That's the reason why for the last twenty-three years I've been pressing my own records.
>
> – Sylvia Tella[20]

Sylvia's road to independence has not been an easy one. Whilst in hospital after having a miscarriage, for a child she didn't know she was carrying, she was coerced into signing a record contract. Upon discharge she was then flown to Germany where that contract was sold for £10,000 (none of which she saw) to another label that would tie her up for years. She's faced legal battles with major labels that have used her vocals without paying a session fee or offering a royalty. Perversely, it is perhaps an incident that happened when she was thirteen years old that gave Sylvia an eye-opener of how immoral the record industry can be.

> With all this Me Too stuff, that is relevant now, but back in my day it was a regular thing. Me personally, I was streetwise, plus brought up by an African. So I thought *it* was just for peeing out of, you know? I mean there was no way I was thinking on any levels of that. I didn't even understand it, and I remember winning *Opportunity Knocks* with The Romantics, we won *Opportunity Knocks* and it was the last season of Hughie Green [English presenter, game show host and actor] and he asked us to do this programme called *Nation*, right? Listen to me, I was only twelve, going on thirteen, I'd never been touched by a doctor, let alone a man. And both Hughie Green was there, and this guy who was the Managing Director of a record company.

They had all of us at a restaurant telling us the opportunities that are gonna come for us and I was young, very naive, didn't know nothing.

So I'm sitting there with all the boys in The Romantics who were older than me. One was married and had a child and they were all brothers right, and they didn't know about business evil ... we're all light skinned with big afros. So it was like the Jackson 5 with a female. Anyway, their father managed the band and he would buy equipment and rent it to us. So we never made any money, that's part of the industry. You didn't even think about that, you didn't think about getting paid. It was just the thought of being on the stage in them days. So there I am in this restaurant with all these people and they say, 'Oh we wanna talk to Sylvia and we'll bring her back to the hotel so you guys can go ahead' – so they left me with the two men sitting at the table. I have brothers, so I don't fear male company, but I just found it strange. We carried on talking and they had this litre thing of wine, right? And then they were talking and they wanted to offer me wine, and I said no, I don't drink. So then they start talking to me about scratching backs ... I don't know, some crap ... I didn't understand, which I told them. 'Don't be naive,' they said, I didn't even know what naive meant, let alone don't be naive. So I don't know what they're talking about. Anyway, Hughie Green spells it out, basically you're gonna come back to the hotel with us and we are going to make you into a star. This man is talking to me deviously, and my subconscious thought what is he talking about so I asked him again: what are you on about? And he spelled it out ... Well, I lost my cool, I'm thirteen, I was very young and sobbing, and they were telling me to calm down. I just picked up the wine and put it over his head. Do you know, I got blacklisted from the age of thirteen.

– Sylvia Tella[21]

Sylvia Tella, from Hulme, blacklisted at the age of thirteen due to her refusal to be sexually exploited, and goes on to become the Queen of UK Reggae and revered the world over when she tours.

But yet again, why is her name never brought up when we showcase Manchester musicians?

There were also musicians of colour that were creating music within the soundscape the city was famed for. In 1998, Ian Brown released his highly anticipated debut album. Following a split that went on for as long as a John Squire guitar solo, two years after The Stone Roses broke up Ian Brown was to release his debut solo album *Unfinished Monkey Business*. I was working at an advertising agency at the time and I remember lots of the staff buzzing about it; these were too old to latch on to the current Oasis buzz, so to see Ian Brown return was like their own messiah having a resurrection (yes, that's a pun). During the time Tony Wilson had a show on Granada TV called *After Dark* where he'd interview local cultural icons, he had an extensive interview with Ian Brown about the new release. I can't recall much of what was said in the interview but what stuck out to me was that there were two Asian musicians in the video and they added intrigue as to what sound he may have been going for with the new album. In 1996 Kula Shaker's debut album *K* had reached number 1 and leant heavily on traditional Indian instruments, including the tabla; was the former Stone Roses singer heading down this path? The only other Asian musicians you would have seen on TV during that time were Tjinder Singh from Cornershop who had smashed the charts with 'Brimful of Asha' a year previous, and Talvin Singh who I knew from the Drum and Bass scene, and his work with Björk. There had been chart success with Apache Indian but the less said about his 1990 single 'Boom-Shack-A-Lak' is probably the better. The musicians of Asian heritage that Ian Brown was working with were tabla player Inder Goldfinger from Leeds and guitarist Aziz Ibrahim from Longsight, Manchester. Although he is much loved and respected within the music community, Aziz's talent, and his fight against stereotypes, does not get the recognition it deserves on a larger scale.

> It's a challenge, that's all, I just say, how far can I push it? You know, where can I go with it? Does it lead somewhere? There is that thing about being stereotyped as you're a Pakistani Muslim, they expect you to go play cricket, and that's all you lot do, be into badminton, and you've got to be a doctor, a lawyer, or something. The guitar was almost like a rebellious symbol, a form of rebellion, and also almost a white stronghold for me, or white and black stronghold maybe, and for me to do that and play in the main, let's call it mainstream, to play in their field, to play the guitar and hear people say, 'Yeah, you play just as good as if not better than me', was an achievement. From there, it just became being treated as an equal, just the quality of it we focused on. Which others don't look at as much, but maybe I do but that's only just because I know I have to struggle twice as hard for that recognition. I don't see myself any better or worse, I've been shoulder to shoulder with Clapton and Brian May … and then being at home, rubbing shoulders with the heroes of Manchester from the Johnny Marrs to the Squires today, whoever, and I don't see myself as any less because I've not had maybe as much success, you know. I just see myself as somebody who's got a God-given talent and if I get the opportunity, I'll show you what I can do. You know where it comes from? In the old days, I got to tell you this, because it was here in Longsight. What used to happen when I was younger, people used to come knock on my door, that played guitar, they'd just turn up, strangers that play guitar, come round for a jam. What they meant was, I've come to show you that I'm better than you are. So I go, 'Mum, it's another one. Can I use the front room so they can come in?' So in they come, they show me what they got, and I go, 'Yeah, but check this out? Can you do this?' And I send them out, you know, tail between the legs, so I kind of grew up playing the guitar like that, like rappers do rap challenges. It's a competitive edge to it where I've been challenged all my life by people knocking on the door and people calling you this and that or whatever.
>
> – Aziz Ibrahim, musician[22]

Aziz is best known as lead guitarist for Simply Red and for replacing John Squire in The Stone Roses, but that only skims the fretboard. He has worked with Reggae artists from Dennis Brown, Barrington Levy, and Freddie McGregor to Paul Weller, Rebel MC and Errol Brown. He worked extensively with Ian Brown on his solo output, co-writing on his early albums, including one of his biggest songs 'Corpses in their Mouths'. In 2000 he set out to make a concept project, *Lahore to Longsight*; the album details the story of his parents' journey from a partitioned Pakistan to Manchester where he was born.

> I looked at the music and the songs that I'd written and I thought, well what it's saying is, Thanks, Dad, for coming to Manchester, Thanks, Dad, for making that journey, for taking that chance, that dangerous journey coming over. You know you can't get a room, you know people won't even let you rent a place. Then you hook up with some other South Asian blokes and they rent a house, or one of them got enough money to take on a property and they all rent a place. I wanted tunes that reflected that heritage, I wouldn't be here if it wasn't for them. My Mum and Dad, when they came to Longsight and settled here, and how that was an influence on me.
>
> – Aziz Ibrahim[23]

At the time he was making *Lahore to Longsight* there were musicians with an Asian heritage who were experiencing commercial and critical success. The success of London's Talvin Singh and Leicester's Cornershop demonstrated there was a UK audience for music with a South Asian influence. Yet Aziz, despite his pedigree performing with successful bands and coming from a city famed for its music and migrant population, struggled to find a deal. It's all the more surprising when you find out who plays on the album.

> I set up a label called No Label Records. I saw it as no record labels will give me a deal, so I'm giving myself a deal and I'll call it No Label Records to put music out, but we didn't have any distribution so I

> had to release it via mail order, a couple of thousand copies, not very much. It's just such a collection of eclectic people and this cool album that nobody has ever heard – it's got Paul Weller, Mike Joyce, Andy Rourke, Denise Johnson, Steve White, Inder Goldfinger, some of the Roses were on there.
>
> – Aziz Ibrahim[24]

How does an album that features the rhythm section of the Smiths, The Stone Roses' bass player and boasts appearances from Steve White and vocals by Paul Weller not get picked up by *any* record label? The line-up of musicians alone would have made this of interest to the contributors' own fans. The minimal reviews it found were encouraging, with *All Music* giving it a 3/5 with comparisons to Arthur Lee, The Wonder Stuff and The Housemartins.

> I look at my contributions, that's all I do ... and then come back to music and Manchester. I look at what is my contribution? And OK, so it's not always recognised, you don't see it on that big wall that says Manchester Music and Manchester Artists. And then I look at my contribution and go, well, would there be any 'Corpses in Their Mouths', or 'My Star'? Would there be these tracks I've written for Paul Weller, or would there be the collaborations that I've done outside of that as well? They wouldn't exist. Does that make a difference to musical history in Manchester? I think the answer is a resounding yes. So after answering that question myself, I move on without addressing these kind of imbalances and lack of recognition. I think that's probably more to do with the ego than it is to do with actually addressing the inequalities. I'm just looking for that gig, looking for the next release, or the opportunity to play, and that's just been the story of my life. I cannot stop to think on it because the thought processes always end up as negative, or it's like self-pity in a way, you know? I've just not got time for it. That's fine. I've had success in terms of output. I don't look at success in terms of fame, I look at in terms of output, so I've had the opportunity to release music to contribute to be a part of music in Manchester. But then you see polls go up about the Manchester music scene and you're omitted from that. But I've got

> no time for that, because it's not just me. You know, it'll be a load of musicians of part of Manchester music history, gender as well, never mind culturally. But if you're busy making or creating, let's call it art. You haven't got time to ponder over the rest.
>
> – Aziz Ibrahim[25]

Actually being from Manchester seemingly isn't of all that much importance as long as you have a tenuous link to the city. Whether they studied here, moved here, or are one of the multitude that come from the satellite towns in Greater Manchester, to have the Manchester prefix gave a certain gravitas. Even if half of the most celebrated bands from 'Manchester' are from Salford. It demonstrates the weight of the location to both artists, and to the outside world. That it means something to belong to the sonography of the city. What I find curious about this is if we aren't going to play hard and fast with the rules of location, then is this same luxury afforded to those that exist outside of Manchester's brand of musicians? A former pupil from the same high school I went to wasn't born in the city yet spent his formative years here and would write the songs around the corner from where I lived that would turn him into a household name.

The nomadic Finley Quaye was born in Edinburgh but following the tragic death of his mother when he was just eleven, he moved to his aunt's house in South Manchester. Here he would also go to the same high school as me before attending Arden Music College, collaborate with A Guy Called Gerald (who appeared on 'Finley's Rainbow' in 1995) and then pursue his solo music ambition:

> *Maverick a Strike*, 'I Need a Lover', 'Your Love Gets Sweeter', 'It's Great When We're Together', 'Even After All' and 'Sunday Shining' were all written and recorded by me at Osbourne Road, Levenshulme which was my Aunt Sal's house and our family house until she moved to Wales. I lived there between the ages of eleven and nineteen when

> I did a music course called Pop Music & Sound Recording at Arden Music College.[26]

Released in 1997, *Maverick a Strike* reached Number 3 in the album charts, had a Top 10 single with 'Even After All', it sold double-platinum, and he would beat Robbie Williams, Elton John, and Paul Weller for a BRIT Award. He was born in Scotland, yet Manchester unquestionably has an intrinsic link to his life story and musical success.

Here we have a Reggae star who has had a global following for decades; a vocalist who broke a genre to the mainstream and appeared on the biggest stage; a singer who worked alongside some of Manchester's biggest bands and sang on one of the UK's most critically acclaimed albums; a guitarist who had to fight against stereotypes to forge a career; a commercially successful musician who wrote his biggest hits in Levenshulme. Given their achievements, why are they consigned to footnotes in Manchester's musical history? Each was of huge significance to the music they made, the culture they represented, yet they aren't largely recognised in the city that made them. There is also the immeasurable loss of influence that these artists could have had on the generation of Mancunians that followed; how important would it have been for children of colour with dreams of being a musician to know they had people like Diane Charlemagne, Tunde Babalola, Jenna G, Sylvia Tella, Aziz Ibrahim, and Finley Quaye that came from the same place as them, that had made waves before them? Sadly, we will never know the true impact they could've had.

We often talk about Manchester for its musical exports, but don't look at the city's pull for touring and international musicians. Not long after I had turned eighteen, my friend Mark Dolan had taken me under his wing and shown me some of the unknown drinking dens in Manchester and also a few tricks that would allow you to keep on drinking past 2am when the nightclubs would shut. One in particular allowed me to meet many of the touring musicians who had come to the city for gigs. Like many things in life, the key is in the confidence. If you look like you know what you're talking about the person you're talking to will often believe you … even if it's a half-cut young lad proclaiming he is 'with the band'. At the time there were two prominent hotels in Manchester, The Palace and The Midland. Our blag was to venture into either (sometimes both) of the hotels, look all flustered and confused, explain to the concierge that we were roadies with whichever band and we'd lost our keycards, but were meeting the rest of the group in the bar area. And off we'd go. Very little persuasion needed. Then we'd sit and order drinks, food, and cigars to any given room number until 6am, and then leave to grab a £2 butty from the Spar store across the road for breakfast and get the Stagecoach home. The more we got away with it the more elaborate the stories got; we'd take on foreign accents, exaggerate our roles in the band, at one point my friend Nathan got that engrossed in his role he spent an hour explaining how he made his own drum kits out of bike parts and leather coats and began doing drum patterns on the bar table like some drug-crazed Tony Allen. We did this for years, not every weekend, as it would be too obvious, but every two to three months when a decent name was in town we would try our arm and very rarely fail. Here I drank Budweisers with The Offspring before being kicked out, talked football with Morten Harket and the rest of the A-Ha band – I think two of them professed to inexplicably be Stoke fans – and met DJ Muggs from Cypress Hill. Whilst the music coming out of Manchester wasn't seen as diverse, the range of artists coming into the city was massive.

> The Haçienda did have iconic gigs, it's not people fabricating it, but the point is how many other iconic gigs haven't been discussed?

Maxwell came to Manchester, a lot of people say he did some of the most iconic gigs. He had Alan Leeds [the drummer in Prince's band], and when Maxwell did the date at the Boardwalk it was with Marvin Gaye's guitarist! Every time I share a Maxwell ticket for the Boardwalk, everyone goes nuts on Twitter. It's really interesting that that's a really strong memory for people. But I think '98/'99 was really exciting musically, a lot of interesting stuff happened. It seemed at the time that maybe things happened over a one- to two-year period. But actually, when you look back now, it was over six months. A lot of US artists came to Manchester, so there's a lot of interactions with great gigs. There was a lot of new-soul was happening. Fugees, and even later, Lauryn Hill, Maxwell … the US artists that came loved Manchester. Artists really knew about Manchester because of the IRA bomb. They knew about Manchester because of *the* football team. They knew about Manchester because it had a musical heritage – not just Oasis. They thought it was quite an exciting place. Yeah, obviously they knew about the Haçienda, but it wasn't just that – they knew if they came there was a lot going on.

For example, Jazzy Jeff came, and he was really quite quiet, and he was with Jill Scott's boyfriend. He'd been gone a whole afternoon and he'd spent it in Eastern Bloc buying some tunes and he wanted to go back. There was a BBC bar upstairs and he was like, 'Can I have a pound to play pool?' I'd borrow him a quid, he played pool, then he'd go off to buy loads more records. So he was into that side of the city. Snoop Dogg came and, after the gig, loads of people were trying to ramrod the arena so we couldn't get out, and Snoop said to me: Alright then, tell me about Manchester. Tell me about the gang rivalry.

So you had these conversations with artists with a real interest in Manchester's culture. Like being asked to be taken to the football, and can I get a tour of the ground? They always did have this attraction to football. We didn't even realise then, but they would watch football on their stations. It was exported a lot more, but people didn't talk about it then.

I remember Jade who sang 'Don't Walk Away' coming, and I asked them what they were doing now and they were off to the

> Odeon. I went to meet these people in London, like Mary J. Blige, but it was interesting that they would come to Manchester as well and they would always be doing something, like going to, obviously the really good record shops. And Amp Fiddler would always go to Afflecks and said it was the best place to buy clothes. Debbie Harry says the same thing, that she gets her Christmas presents from there. So you know Manchester had an appeal to international artists in that era.
>
> – Karen Gabay[27]

The two notable gigs that I went to in Manchester (that wasn't Oasis at Maine Road) was Eminem at Manchester Academy, where I got into a fight with some sweaty student because I was stood in a mosh pit (I didn't know what a mosh pit was at the time), and The Fugees at Manchester Apollo. The Fugees gig was a huge event for Manchester, they were the biggest group on the planet with *The Score* album being Number 1 around the world and their singles were on every channel, pirate and mainstream. It was bedlam inside, and out.

> The Fugees gig at Manchester Apollo – so many people from Manchester will say that, for so many reasons, was such an incredible gig. The police turned up because it was a Hip Hop gig – and this is the other thing, around the country with Hip Hop gigs, there's a thing that they have to have a policing presence. So the police were outside of that gig and I went with four people, all journalists, and one of them was white. The police officer pulled her to the side and asked, 'Are you alright, love?' as if to say, I'm going to pull you out and she went, 'Pardon?' because she'd never seen that sort of thing before. There was dogs and everything. And on that night, because we covered it on the station the next day, I think a couple of girls got attacked on the way home from the concert. So it was this historic night for many reasons. The Fugees were speaking to everyone from the stage saying, 'Don't fight when you get outside', because the police were outside. And that's happened at quite

a few Hip Hop gigs where the police were. But anyway, the gig itself, for many, was a massive musical night in Manchester. It was iconic and therefore should be talked about as much as we talk about the Haçienda. I didn't go to the Public Enemy gig but people say that was one of the most historic gigs in Manchester's history.

Public Enemy loved Manchester, they've turned up and done tours in Moss Side. More than once. And it's an incredible night, the same as when Madonna came to the Haçienda. Shouldn't people be saying the same thing about these nights? The Fugees didn't last very long yet *we* got to see them live in Manchester! These stories need to be elevated in Manchester's discourse, in the discussion of our history. We need to talk about it because we've had them gigs, but people who live in Sheffield have been saying to me more recently that they didn't get any of those gigs, so they can't talk about that experience. Those people didn't come to their city. So Mancunians, in a way, take it a little bit for granted. My view is that just because the band aren't from Manchester doesn't mean that it's not part of our heritage.

– Karen Gabay[28]

The 'New Acoustic Movement'

The guitar bands that followed Oasis out of Manchester either fell into their slipstream and mimicked the Gallagher brothers' haircuts, clothes, personality, and became quickly forgotten; or they were the innovators that became part of a collective that pushed back against their predecessors, creating their own sound and style.

There was a growing number of guitar bands in Manchester that were expressing something different than Oasis had been. There was definitely, I'd like to say, some creative cells of activity. Because I always think of the cell as the defining feature of what makes culture happen, because you have people who are scattered around who are doing their thing or have their vision: making their music, doing the

> poetry, writing, or designing, or whatever they're doing. They have the vision. But they're young, they don't have money, they know there's no shortcut. They may feel quite alienated from what is then the music establishment. Part of all this is always the music establishment which you revolt against, or you rebel against. After all, if the music that was being given to you, or the culture that was being given to you, spoke very forcefully to you, you wouldn't get involved in making your own. You only get involved making your own because you're thinking, am I alone in this? Am I the only person who feels how I feel? So you have these scattered individuals, but then they begin to meet each other. That's why bricks and mortar are important – why those smaller venues are important, because that's where they might meet each other. There might be something that happens, there might be a band in town, for example, or a cinema may open or a quirky bar that has a certain kind of identity and draws a certain kind of person. And suddenly you're sat next to, or you meet up with, somebody and you start putting the world to rights and you suddenly meet another person who feels like you and so starts a community. Then they become your allies. And so a cell grows, and it only takes, ten to fifteen people. Okay, let's do a night. Let's do a club night. What should we call it, right? Let's call it that, you put the bands on, and I'll find the venue, I'll do the publicity. I know someone who does the flyers. In Manchester, that was happening at the end of the nineties.
>
> – Dave Haslam, writer and DJ[29]

In the year 2000, I was working at an ad agency on Blackfriars Bridge, facing the Ramada Hotel that firefighter John Moss had parked underneath when the bomb went off. It was a creative industry to work in, but my role was in the Production Department. My role was to contact newspapers, magazines, and local press to get specifications of how they wanted to receive the advertisements. It was easy but menial work. I wanted to work in the studio and art departments that enabled me to be creative, but it was made clear early on that a kid of my background wasn't getting that gig, nor would I get trained in how to use it. So I got creative in other ways; with access to unlimited fast internet (then still in its infancy), bosses unaware of Napster or Limewire, and facilities such as CD burners, Photoshop, and colour printers at hand, if one was inclined to start a bootlegging production line, then one would have everything needed to do so. This hypothetical venture could have started at the third-floor EasyJet Internet Café in St Ann's Square, where you had to take a ticket, wait for a computer like you would for a doctor's appointment, and when your number was called you could download what music you wanted, burn it, and own the new album for the price of a CD-ROM. This practice was so common that EasyJet Internet Café was found liable for copyright infringement occurring from customers using its service for that exact practice.

When I was at the agency I *could* have ripped as many as I wanted, *could* have billed it as overtime, and *could* have sold them on for a lot more money than my monthly salary brought in. I knew my way around the peer-to-peer sharing software like no one else and, as such, I unlocked access to what felt like limitless records. Through early chatrooms I'd become part of a global network, and we could have been passing around all the latest music, films, games through an obscure P2P software called DL Hotline. I'd smoke weed out the back of the agency when everyone had gone home, and spend the night in the office talking to people I'd never met. This doesn't sound as impressive now with the age of social media, but at a time when no one was doing this sort of thing it was pioneering. The lads in the studio would also rip CDs, but they were more into copying the original disc, the old-school method I'd got banned from HMV for. We had a communal stereo, so the office used to have a wild mix of differing tastes playing from whatever music people were burning. Some stuff I got into, some of it was awful and some was mad as fuck

(Mr Bungle?! WTF?). One afternoon I was sat in the studio for lunch when I heard 'We fuck and we fight, someone else does the dishes' come from the stereo:

- *Who's this?*
- *I Am Kloot.*
- *I am what?! Are they Dutch?*
- *No, Dickhead, they're from Manchester.*

Manchester's Northern Quarter at the turn of the millennium was a golden period for music. The bands that came out of Night & Day and The Roadhouse would win three Mercury Awards and countless nominations, and release several critically acclaimed albums. The music industry would soon irrevocably change with the internet. Elbow, Doves, I Am Kloot, and Badly Drawn Boy would be the last analogue scene of Manchester before the music world became digital. These musicians may have looked how a Manchester band should, but they sounded and carried themselves differently. This proved a problem for the music press as they couldn't easily fit them into the same box as Oasis, but the interest in the bands was becoming such that they needed something to label their sound so they created a new phrase: the New Acoustic Movement [insert sick emoji here].

> You've great bands making good music all the time in the background and so the New Acoustic Movement was a bit … You have to accept the way people perceive you. I mean, I stand on stage with an acoustic guitar a lot, and those are the photographs that circulate from gigs that I've done over the years, so you get classed as an Indie Troubadour. But if you listen to my records, there's a lot more going on musically in layers and textures and string arrangements and electronic stuff. It's hardly just acoustic records. So it wasn't really accurate for me, and a lot of the other bands, to say that we were all just polite guitar strummers.
>
> – Badly Drawn Boy[30]

I think the *NME* tried to lump us into a thing. The New Acoustic Movement. And of course we just kicked against it all hugely because scenes are dangerous, aren't they? As soon as that dies, you die with it. They tried lumping us in with the likes of Turin Brakes, and Kings of Convenience, there was a few. And so we just immediately legged it the other way, as much as you could do.

– Andy Hargreaves[31]

I know exactly who came up with it, it wasn't the *NME*, it was Ra Page [AKA Rampage]. He was a journalist in Manchester. I think it was the front cover in *CityLife* and he was trying to put a bracket around the whole thing. Kloot were particularly pissed off about that. I remember we were on Tib Street once, I was with Johnny [Bramwell] and Andy, and we see Tony Wilson getting into his car – and we still quote it to this day:

Johnny: Alright, Tony, how are you doing mate?
Tony: Loving it Johnny! Loads of it! Loads of it! Loads of it!

As Tony got into his car he turned around and said: *Loving this New Acoustic Movement lads.*

To which Johnny shouted: *Fuck off!*
Tony laughed: *I didn't think you'd like that!*

And 'Loads of it' became a bit of saying amongst us. How you doing? *Loads of it! Loads of it! Loads of it!*

– Guy Garvey[32]

The bands recognised the importance of Manchester; to belong to the list of names that had come out of the city was something to aspire to, but they were intent on doing it on their own terms by remaining true to themselves rather than aping what had gone before them.

I always wanted to be a Manchester band. I can remember it being really quite important to ever be spoken of in the same breath as these legendary bands. But there was a constant death toll conscious decision not to do anything that would ever sound like a baggy band. Of course, a lot of it all stems from the way Johnny writes his songs, but instrumental to all this is Guy Garvey. Because he was a friend of ours from the Night & Day, and it was just really innocent. We were rehearsing in Pete's house in Withington, Guy came down in the cellar with his little digital eight-track, and we were playing really quietly because of the neighbours next door. So I started playing with plastic brushes, and we played delicately and we loved that sound, so that's how I Am Kloot evolved to be a little bit delicate. Because they're watching *Coronation Street* upstairs and we don't want them to tell us to stop playing – that was like almost like the mother of invention that made us sound like that. Then Guy came down and was like, 'Right, this sounds great as we're doing it in here. We're going to record this.'

– Andy Hargreaves[33]

It was like that old ethos of the Summer of Love of Doing Your Thing. What's he doing? He's doing his own thing? Cool. How can I help him? When I was recording Kloot, I was helping mates out. It was only when I started recording them that I knew how good the songs were. And there was a thing then happening to bands – there was an amazing band called Subaqua – and they were really fucking fierce, really angular. The lead singer used a megaphone – it was proper ground-breaking stuff, and they got picked up and they had a little deal. The record came back and it had just been blanded out, it sounded like Coldplay – they were very popular at the time and it sounded like every band were put through the same mangle. As soon as a band had a deal, then the producer would make them sound like something that already existed. I knew because of John's essentially folk-writing, I thought, if they go through this mangle they're going to bland this shit out. And what you get when you go to see a Kloot gig is a punk gig – it's weird, sort of Red Wedge meets Beatles, burlesque punk but, nevertheless, the attitude on this is amazing. I thought, they sort of need anti-producing, they need recording warts and all. And I thought, well I have the lack of skills to help make that happen. It's like one of the worst recordings of some of the best music ever, but it got the vibe, it got the vibe.

– Guy Garvey[34]

We were very lucky to have met another Guy, Guy Lovelady. And he had a retail record label, it wasn't really doing anything, called Ugly Man Records, and he basically gave us £1,000 to put out our own 7 inches out. I think 'Twist' was the first one. Czechoslovakian vinyl – it was so thick and it was just amazing picking it up, it felt really impressive. Peter was working at a screen printers at the time, he screen printed load of brown paper bags, that you'd have sweeties in. And it just looked killer – got a little distribution deal, and then that record managed to find its way into Rough Trade Records in London, amongst other places. And then Wall of Sound just started up a little offshoot label called We Love You. Joe, the A&R man, who was a proper A&R man who gives a shit about music, went to a guy at Rough Trade and says, 'Listen to this.' Then Wall of Sound eventually offered this record deal and that was when I was able to quit my job, so it was really simple. And then we still kept Guy Garvey on board, with his little digital eight-track. And we went up to the Isle of Mull, Guy knew a woman who had a church there, a converted church, and we recorded *Natural History* over a couple of weeks; but we had no idea whether it was really going to ever see the light of day. There is no motivation of taking over the world, making loads of money, we just wanted to do this, and you can hear it – it's just so beautifully innocent I think, it's warmth and it's really not a high fly sounding record, but that's given it such a character. I had a girlfriend that worked at Granada and she borrowed loads of Neumann microphones – really top mics – that we took with us in the back of the Salford Van Hire. And we never used them, 'cause Guy didn't know what to do with them! So it was all recorded on little shitty PZM mics from Tandy, and you know it just gave it a beautiful quality and they put out the record and it started the ball rolling, really. 2001 for us was just brilliant – that was when *Natural History* came out – because we'd go to London, hanging out at Wall of Sound in their little offshoot office with Joe the A&R man, and Joe at that time was sharing an industrial unit. We've got a desk. And he shared it with Banksy!! Banksy is there with all his fucking stencils. Which is like my biggest claim to fame: I know who Banksy is! If only I bought some, though. What a dickhead!

– Andy Hargreaves[35]

What you got with Kloot was – John already had scene experience, he'd already been around and he'd seen the bullshit and seen the glitzy side of it and come out the other side with fewer teeth and a bad taste in his mouth. And when he met Pete, Pete saw the value in John's songs, and with Brian and Andy in The Mouth, it's like they all encouraged one another. They were an absolute unique cocktail, no one will ever sound like that band again. And I'm so massively proud to be anything to do with them, because them songs have endured, they've stood up. Not because I was involved in them – I'm not blowing my own trumpet – John is like a maelstrom, a difficult man to live with, to work with. At once my brother, and at times my mortal enemy – but a genius. Facilitated by another couple of geniuses. Kloot were very much anti-everything, you know, they weren't having the scene, they weren't having the label of New Acoustic Movement. They existed on their own terms, in their own parallel, in their own burrow.

– Guy Garvey[36]

Manchester band was something that we wanted. It was like earning your stripes. You know, we were within the borders really, so I think we had more of a chance to go, 'We're a Manchester band' rather than we're a Bury band, but I think anywhere outside of the metropolis they wanna kind of, make you their own. You know, you get into the *Bury Times* and it's like, 'Fucking hell it's the *Bury Times*' and then you get the *Radcliffe Times*, and it's, 'Oh my God' you know, and then we made this move into town. Garvey was the point man. Sort of the way an army sends out like a Pathfinder on a recce, all camouflaged up and shit: 'Well, you do it 'cause, you know, you're the singer.' You go in, and then you, Pete, and we'll follow up, but I think it was part of Garvey's steely resolve to not sit back as the Kings of Bury, you know, we need to keep on here. I think we were all of the same ilk but I think Garvey was like, 'Right, fuck it, I'm going in.'

– Richard Jupp, musician[37]

And we lived together and Pete got a job at The Roadhouse. We played there, and he chanced his arm and asked Katie Mountain, again my friend to this day, for a job. And she gave him a job behind the bar. And I said, 'Pete, can you get me a job at The Roadhouse?' and he said, 'Yeah'. And a week later, I asked him again, because she knew who I was because Soft [Elbow's original band name] had played there:

- *You asked her yet?*
- *Oh yeah, but she said there's no vacancies.*
- *You lying fucker, you've not asked her, have you?*
- *Aw don't, I'm trying to do my own thing…*
- *I was like, Fuck you.*

So I asked her for a job, and to cut a long story short, four of the five band members ended up working there. And then we built from there. This is when we changed to Elbow. Which was purely because the music had changed so much, we knew that in those days demo tapes with Mr Soft written on it were just getting binned, I don't blame them, because what it was, wasn't good. I think as is so often the case when a band connect, we were absolutely shit until the moment we weren't, you know, and you kind of pinpoint it really accurately. We had three of the songs of the first album *Asleep in the Back*. We had 'Powder Blue', we had 'Red', we had 'Newborn'. We put a set together but we were no good at bouncing our sound live, we never had a sound engineer. We were still very nervous about performance and stuff, and on the first show we did as Elbow, for many years I remembered it as this glorious moment because Katie, and Natasha Young, and everybody in the Night & Day, helped us fill the place. We went from six people at The Roadhouse in June '96 under the name Soft to 400 people, which is above its capacity, later as Elbow. And it was purely down to the enthusiasm of friends that owned and ran joints around there, and also mates that wrote for *CityLife*, and the *Evening News*. And once we had something it felt that the whole city were happy to get behind us. So the average day was dragging yourself to rehearsal at Sankeys Soap, having to leave about tea time to go set up at The Roadhouse, because I ended up at the door at The Roadhouse. I was a doorman, I was in charge of security and looking after the bands, and I'd sit there writing poetry.

– Guy Garvey[38]

I think that was the real cement for us, working at The Roadhouse. It was 250, but I think we got 400 in there one night but before we even played there we got to see how a venue operates. We got to see Muse on their first run, Coldplay on their first run. All these fucking massive bands. Yeah, and those two we ended up supporting – I don't know whether it was the shared history, I don't know. I don't know what it was, fucking stars and fate and all that but then it was the club night The Electric Chair. I mean they were fucking amazing nights. You'd go in with the light, and come out with the light, and then go Koffee Pot and just have your breakfast – unless you were too fucked from the night before – then you'd go home, couple of spliffs, sleep for a couple of hours, and then come back in and do another shift, because you wanted to.

– Richard Jupp[39]

Because what that place was all about was, we got two nights a month that made the money; there was Tropical Hot Dog Payday, which was run by Pip, and there was Unabombers' Electric Chair. The club nights paid the bills, and The Electric Chair put us in the black. It was really such a gratifying thing. The reason all those nights existed was to fund the ongoing local bands – three bands a night, four nights a week. In all that time, I saw maybe three things I liked in the four years I was working there. But that wasn't the point. It was like giving local bands a chance and giving lads that had been rehearsing their arse off a bit of platform to play to their friends and girlfriends. It's the way every band starts, and it was a nice thing to be part of. Then there were the touring bands, and the first time I met Muse I remember giving them some sandwiches, some coffee, and I remember getting drunk after hours. Because they were fucking ace! And then you know, come two years later we were supporting them on an arena tour, so it was this real cusp, you know? And all the people who were there was sound, especially Katie as a boss. The first thing she said to me is: 'Listen to me, this is essential, the customer is always a cunt. If you don't want to serve someone because of the way their nose is, you don't have to. You are the boss.

– Guy Garvey[40]

If Oasis were the soundtrack to a Saturday night, then the new bands that followed them scored the other six days of the week. The whole gamut of emotions run through Elbow's *Asleep in the Back*, Doves' *Lost Souls*, Kloot's *Natural History*, and Badly Drawn Boy's *The Hour of The Bewilderbeast*. There wasn't a similarity in sound but in what they were making songs about; in the past I had been enamoured by the 'stick out your chest and fuck the world' attitude, now I saw this as courageous, to put it all out there on record, warts and all. It was honesty on record from people who looked and lived like me, at the same time as me, in the same city as me. I find them fearless records; they aren't maudlin. If there's one trait that Mancunians despise, it is self-pity. These artists were bearing emotional scars like army veterans do war wounds:

> It's that comedown thing, sort of squaring stuff away, do you know what I mean? When you're asking yourself, 'What have I done?' We used to call it The Bad Thing, you know? I mean, when you wake up and think, 'Oh, I'm alright actually … oh fuck?!' You know, we had this sort of sensitive side. You know when you've had a shit day, right? And you put a tune on, whatever it is, and bam, you're back in the room. We wanted to do that. But before the 'Newborn' EP came out we said, wouldn't it be good if somebody said that to us – as a songwriter, lyricist, that you've communicated directly with somebody? That was our aim. And then we had this letter come off a woman who'd unfortunately had a stillbirth. So her and her husband are just fucking devastated, you know. I mean THE worst thing, but she said the track 'Newborn' had somehow kind of helped the grieving process and it was like fucking hell … we've done the one thing that you would hope for as any kind of creative, to have that connection.
>
> – Richard Jupp[41]

When you start out on a music career then you make no money, for a long time. It's an arduous road and trying to work full-time jobs and rehearse, and gig, and work will take its toll soon enough. If it wasn't for the dole, then I wonder how many musicians would have come out of Manchester.

> Johnny and Pete was signing on. And lots of my friends prior to the group – actually, the government was quite understanding of people signing on when they were trying to be creative. You were sent on restart courses where you'd meet like-minded people who were also trying to make music and they got a little bit of grace instead of having to go and get a shit job.
>
> – Andy Hargreaves[42]

> It's plainly not easy to be in a band. I know what Andy's getting at, people signed on – essentially pretended they were looking for work which treated the dole as an Arts Grant. I did that, right? So I was one of those people who went, sure, I'm going for the jobs, but yeah, I was treating it as the Arts Grant that the grassroots music never got, because at that point it wasn't there. There wasn't a version where I got money to develop artistically? Because the Arts Council probably would have laughed in my face at that point. So I was one of those people. I suspect if you'd walked into any DHSS and gone:
>
> - *Oh, okay Mr Taylor, what are you qualified to do?'*
> - *Gonna be in a band, me!*
>
> They probably weren't gonna go, *'Fine, sign here!'*
>
> – Jay Taylor[43]

Having dole money as support will pay your rent and allow you a few fun coupons for rehearsals and rum but musicians also needed a way to press and promote their records. What they need is a label. Manchester is famous for having one but we don't talk about the others. The fog that came from Factory Records is so dense it is difficult to see through. The bands, figures, and songs that came out of Tony Wilson's Charles Street headquarters created an opacity that allowed little space for any other light to permeate. It has become synonymous with Manchester and its culture.

It has become the barometer by which all things Mancunian are compared. Whether this is something to celebrate, or a cause for chagrin, differs depending on which Mancunian you speak to. But what of those labels hidden in the mist? The stories of labels such as Grand Central, Blood and Fire, Skam, Fat City, Ruf Beats, Paper Recordings, and many more, could fill a book, but due to limited space I'll focus on one. Twisted Nerve Records was formed from friendship, with limited resources and hope. It defied the stereotypical representation of Mancunian labels in the media. The label and artists were unassuming, self-deprecating, purposely made unpolished records, they were almost esoteric in their pursuit and completely independent in how they operated.

> I was at Generation X at this event that my housemates were putting on and I was just helping out. That's when I first met Andy Votel. He was booked as a DJ in the basement, and I'd never really heard a DJ play the music he was playing – I was just bowled over. That's what first impressed me with Andy. The stuff he was playing, like Jeremy Steig, which was the flute loop that the Beastie Boys had sampled, I wasn't aware of many people doing that – maybe I was quite out of the loop, but Andy was like the first guy I've ever come across that was digging out stuff like that and playing it and you are were like, 'Wow, how has he got that record that the Beastie Boys used on their album?' 'Cause Andy's knowledge and his Hip Hop background … he knew so much more than anyone I knew, his record collection was just constantly exciting. Andy didn't drive then so I used to be everybody's chauffeur. So I'd drive Andy back to Marple Bridge and I'd often stay for an hour at his Dad's place and then he'd just play me records that I'd never heard before. Just all sorts of stuff, so that was the first thing for me and Andy. Slowly I got the confidence to play him some of my demos in the car with a cassette, play him a few of my ideas, and Andy was surprisingly enthusiastic. I didn't think it would be his bag from his hip hop background. He was like, 'Wow, this your stuff? This is brilliant and let's do something with it.' So, because he'd done the artwork for Grand Central he had a bit of a handle on how a label operated,

he was doing their graphics, but we didn't really know what we were doing. My dream was to have a few of my demos that I'd done on a four-track on vinyl, that tied in nicely with Andy having this kind of a loose dream to have a label. So I want my music on vinyl, he wanted a label so we said, let's start a label. I think one of the things I'm proudest of is that we were just two, I'd say kids, having a go, taking on the world, with not much knowledge and not much help.

– Badly Drawn Boy[44]

I had no intentions. The best way to describe it would have been an 'imaginary label'. We had something that resembled music, I was a designer, and the format was available, so I literally made the name up and drew the logo right at the very end while sat at a table in Night & Day. I was so disenfranchised with the idea that record labels in the mid-1990s were the result of successful club nights that I was quite interested in the concept of a label that was born out of unsuccessful club nights (I ran many), so if there was anything that resembled a statement of intent then that was it. The fact that vinyl was cheaper than cassettes, and most certainly cheaper than beer, was an impetus, any other weekend we might have gone to the cinema or bowling.

– Andy Votel[45]

I think why we did so well with Twisted Nerve was because we really did do it ourselves. We were just astonished at the amount of interest we got almost immediately. Just because we had the courage, the balls to make a record with my first EP at the end of '97. Me and Andy just paid for it ourselves. Found a record pressing plant in America that was cheaper than here, we just found this place in Nashville. It was like half a dollar or a dollar per single … just way cheaper with the exchange rate as well, as the dollar was weak against us at that point. And it did turn it into a romantic thing as the records were sent back. We had 500 copies of the first EP flown in to Manchester Airport. We drove to pick them up, got the box of records, took them to my house in Chorlton, and then opened the box together. It's just so exciting, to take up the first copy of what was my first record and Twisted Nerve's first release and we put the needle on together, literally like held it together. It was symbolic, like the first time. I still do get goosebumps when I think of that first EP and how connected you are to it. When you're doing it yourself and listening to it was one thing and it sounded great, the vinyl of the pressing was good. Then we just said, what do we do with these? ...We took ten copies to Piccadilly Records asked if they would put them on the shelves and they did. A day or two later they called us to say they'd sold them all!

We seriously couldn't believe it as there'd been no press, nothing ... To this day, I'd still love to find out who those ten people were and I actually asked the guys at Piccadilly Records, who bought 'em? What did they look like? I wanted to know who they were ... Who bought this when they know nothing about it? They just saw the cover. It said by the Badly Drawn Boy EP1, and Andy's artwork was nice. It struck a chord somehow.

– Badly Drawn Boy[46]

I think a certain type of Mancunian wanted something more, and the answer was to actually create something less. Music on Twisted Nerve was achievable, affordable, and approachable which was directly at odds with Manchester's self-celebratory goals at the time. It was absolutely a rebellion, but strangely an unintentional one really, because we didn't have a target of any description.

– Andy Votel[47]

So it was a fluke, but there's gotta be something that captures people's imaginations that was actually on the record. It set me out as this artist that was kind of Lo Fi, 'cause the records were Lo Fi recordings from four-track demos. I was like putting out my demos really before I'd finished the songs and the gigs were similarly under-rehearsed ... I excited quite a few people that thought, well this is different. Somebody's daring to do something that's not polished and finished in high production ... There's something about that moment that you can never, really, ever repeat or get back – it's like a proper primal connection, somebody else likes it and bought it, and so that was a thrill. Then I think Piccadilly asked for fifty more copies. Then

Rough Trade, and a few other shops around the country. So within two months we've pretty much sold those 500 through word of mouth. So we did the second EP with 1,000 copies. Within that period of time, between those three EPs, I was getting loads of record companies calling me up. I still worked at my Mum and Dad's in Bolton at a sign printers and my Mum was answering the phone and saying that X, Y, and Z from a record label wants me. I didn't know what the hell to do – these weird gigs that we put on as well, like the famous one at the Boardwalk, where all the A&R people turned up. I think it shaped the kind of artist I became because I just found it all so funny, exciting as well, but just ultimately hilarious, that we were just having a laugh and doing what we wanted to do and it seemed to get attention.

– Badly Drawn Boy[48]

I think the mid-1990s was the epitome of the music industry at its most sheep-like. When what felt like the entire music industry came to the Boardwalk to try and steal Badly Drawn Boy from his own label you had a prime example of everyone chasing the same tip-offs. Labels were always battling to sign the same bands and outbid each other, it was grotesque. I think Damon just wanted to make as much music as possible and hold off the pressures of releasing an actual album for as long as possible. Our original intentions hadn't extended to things like album campaigns, so when Damon took money from XL he had to start piecing things together, which is why *HOB* resembled an incredible mix-tape as opposed to what was the common conception of an album (herein lies its allure).

– Andy Votel[49]

On 12 September 2000, Badly Drawn Boy's debut album *The Hour of the Bewilderbeast* was up for the Mercury Prize. An award long considered the UK's most prestigious, he faced competition from the likes of Coldplay, Richard Ashcroft, Death in Vegas, and fellow Mancunians Doves.

I had no interest in music competitions. To join over 1,000 other bands paying 200 quid to enter a glorified corporate 'battle of the bands' competition was stomach turning. At the time that money could have pressed another 45 in my opinion. But XL were keen to enter, and lo and behold Damon, and my friends Doves, got nominated, alongside eight other bands that meant nothing to me. Twisted Nerve then erroneously got a phone call asking us if we'd like to book a £2,000 dinner table at the ceremony and we laughed and said 'no thanks'. They then told us that they strongly recommend that we attend because we would be happy with the winning result, wink wink.

– Andy Votel[50]

Everybody bumping into me was saying, 'I reckon it's nailed on, this, for you, Damon.' Everybody kept saying it, and then there was Jeff Barrett from Heavenly Records with Doves, he was there with Doves manager Dave Rofe. Everyone was just, 'You deserve this, you', and I said why me? But they're all good records. I said I'd be happy to win it, but I doubt it and then we got to the Grosvenor itself, the big hotel. And there's some kid running around with a big homemade flag with Badly Drawn Boy on it – like he turned up just to support me and I was like wow, that's nice of him! It just seemed everybody I met was going, 'There's something about your album, that everybody wants this to do well.' So, it was a really nice humbling thing but, you know, back then I was a bit shy and socially awkward, even though I've overcome those feelings over the years, but it's a hard set of emotions to keep together. But even to the point of the end of the night, and Jools Holland announcing the winner I was sat with the Doves and I distinctly remember the Doves guys jumping up and cheering – and I thought they'd won it because they were jumping up cheering, but they were cheering for me! Bless them. I was sat there chatting to Claire, my girlfriend at the time that was heavily pregnant, I was kind of distracted by Doves cheering and I didn't hear him say Badly Drawn Boy, I just sort of heard this cheer go up, then I slowly realised I'd won it …

– Badly Drawn Boy

Without being cynical, to me, Damon winning the Mercury Music Prize signified a time when neither myself nor Manchester could do any more for him. The positive repercussions meant that Damon's music began to influence a new kind of artist and Manchester successfully lost its bad swagger, but at the same time virtually everybody who came to TN genuinely thought they could win the next Mercury Prize, which did very little for experimental pop music. People did take TN more seriously from this point, until they got a whiff of our empty bank account. By association it did open a lot of doors for me, on a global scale, which helped with my next label Finders Keepers. I was truly heartbroken when Damon did his speech, but six months later I was his sidekick and tour DJ travelling to Australia and Japan.

– Andy Votel[51]

Over the years I've had the opportunity to thank Andy and not done so. Like when I won the Mercury Prize. He was pissed off that I didn't thank him:

- *I'm sure I did, you were the first person I mentioned!*
- *You didn't!*
- *Oh fuck… I'm sorry!*

But it was Andy that gave me that confidence. You need someone in your life that's going to say, 'We're going to do this. We CAN do this!' Andy was that to me. I couldn't do it on my own, and he probably couldn't have done it without me. We needed each other to say we can do this, we can take it on, we can start a label, and put some music out. Without Andy saying it, I wouldn't done it, and without him having me to say go on, okay … You know, that's what the spirit of Manchester had in those days in Night & Day, the other bands that you bump into and talk about what they were doing, it made it all feel easier because everyone was doing it, so there is that thing about it. And it's not just music, it's everything, it's getting on in life, and having that support system.

– Badly Drawn Boy[52]

It was talented young people with a necessary chip on the shoulder, that's what it was. And in a nutshell, when Damon won the Mercury in 2000, he came home and there's a big party at Night

> & Day. We were so fucking proud of him for what he'd done, and I remember getting hold of him, and hugging him and saying:
>
> *- Fucking hell mate! You've done it!*
>
> And I swear to God, this is true, this is not nostalgia. He said:
>
> *'Well, it's good for* all *of us, isn't it, Guy?*
>
> – Guy Garvey[53]

> I was sharing it with everyone, because we all kind of come through those years for one of us to do well out of that pack of people. Perhaps I was the first one, and Elbow went on to get their own Mercury Prize. I suppose I was the first for a while that had done something that wasn't just Oasis's success, it was a different strand of success for the Manchester music community.
>
> – Badly Drawn Boy[54]

Manchester music doesn't exist. At least, not in the way you think. The city has undoubtedly created some of the greatest songs of all time, yet there is nothing sonically that ties them all together. For Manchester music to exist you would be able to identify a shared set of conventions across the musical output unique to the city. You can't. The instruments, the themes, the genres, the sounds can all be found in different cities. Whilst you're trying to disprove my argument consider this; let's say you feel Liam Gallagher's exaggerated singing-snarl in a Mancunian accent typifies Manchester music; then by proxy those singers that don't do it aren't Manchester music. The term is a fallacy, a construct, a brand. The success of the guitar bands that came out of the Northern Quarter were successful because they tried to be different, they pushed against what was expected.

6

'Did horse semen lead to their downfall?'

FOOTBALL

I was a promising footballer. At fourteen, I had been flitting between teams across Manchester doing a bit with Gorton Eagles and training with Fletcher Moss before beginning with a new side, Red Star, that had started in Levenshulme. Whereas the other teams had structure and training facilities, this was shambolic at best as a new outfit. Half our team were talented street footballers, and the rest of the squad were the sort of kids that would get picked last for a kickabout in school. The manager was a foul-mouthed, red-faced sadist who enjoyed berating and bullying his players as much as he did kicking off with the opposing team's manager. We had no cones, punctured footballs, a charity shop kit, football nets with no holes, and when we couldn't make it to a game through lack of transport the manager crammed us into his car like beans in a tin; one game he turned up with lads, in full kit, sat on the roof of his car.

Our first season was a catastrophe. Every team annihilated us; our keeper was the only person we could find to go in net, which would go some way to explain how many goals we shipped, but he also had a hidden medical condition. In one match, the opposition striker was one-on-one, and rather than slide out to meet him, our goalkeeper walked off to his post, put his head on it, and the striker rolled the ball into an empty net. The players were looking back as confused as we were cross; the manager legged it from the sidelines to the goalkeeper, who was now rattling on a badly painted pole.

- *What's fuckin' wrong with you, you dickhead?! What are you doing!!*
- *Sorry … I've got epilepsy.*
- *That's no fuckin' excuse. Get off the pitch.*

The poor lad had an epileptic seizure and was substituted with no sympathy; he never returned to play for us. If we could have got relegated that year, we would have. Any team that could string a few passes together would beat us; we won a couple of games but were clutching at draws not to finish bottom of the league. The following season we were a total contrast. Kids who couldn't stand the manager left; we roped in a couple of better players, and, through fear of embarrassment, we took that summer to train and discipline ourselves, spending eight hours a day on Greenbank Fields. The other important aspect of this change was the parents. In our first season, as it was a new outfit, they would come along to the odd game, but after seeing how much it meant to us when the new season started, they were there every single game; and by parents, I mean the mums. Not really with an interest or understanding in football, they would stand on the sidelines through all sorts of weather to watch their sons hoof a ball about mud baths for pitches. The army of mothers seemingly quelled the aggression of the manager, and he was not the same man he was the previous season; not a chance would he call any of the players the names he had when they were around. My Mum was gold with me and football; she'd take me all around Greater Manchester to play games in her battered Mini Metro, consoling us when we lost, celebrating our victories, and buying us a chippy tea after every game.

We were unbeatable that season; David Graham had joined in centre-midfield and ran the team like a general, creating some much-needed organisation for those around him. I was up front alongside Martin Chambers; after years of playing on the street together, we knew each other's game so well we never needed to look where the other one was to pass the ball, which resulted in us being nicknamed Bebeto and Romario. If he didn't score a hat-trick one week, it was me. The biggest game was against the best team in the league, Stalybridge Celtic; last season they spanked us 9–0 and were full of confidence from doing so. We battered them! Coincidentally, this game was the odd occasion that my Dad wasn't working and had come to watch. My Dad had a unique approach to me and sport; never wanting me to get ahead of myself, he replaced praise with criticism with the belief it would fuel me to improve. I scored the first goal, 'That was a fluke'; the second goal, 'You didn't mean that!'; I bagged a hat-trick, 'That was a mis-hit.' I scored eight goals in that game against the best team in the league; afterward he rubbed my head, 'You had a decent game.' Twisted logic worked; I wanted nothing more than to perform because he was watching, and every goal was my giving him two fingers. Thanks, Dad!

In 1997, I was forced to leave Red Star due to league age restrictions. The next time I saw my former manager, Darren Vickers, was on national TV and in the tabloids. His actions were not limited to bullying from the sidelines. On 5 May, he abducted and murdered eight-year-old Jamie Lavis, a local schoolboy, after he boarded the bus driven by Vickers. During the police investigation, Vickers cunningly portrayed himself as the last person to see the boy, fronting media appeals, and even went as far as befriending the Lavis family, moving into their home to help search for the child he had murdered.

> In 1999, he was sentenced to life in prison for murder with Mr Justice Forbes sentencing: 'Jamie's brief life was cruelly and prematurely brought to an end because he had the tragic misfortune of boarding your bus at around 10.30am on Ashton Old Road on May 5 1997. Thereafter you carefully groomed this little boy so he stayed on your

> bus for the rest of the day. You did this for your own base motives and intended to, and did, sexually abuse this little boy and then killed him and abandoned his body in Reddish Vale. You unclothed his body and left it naked on the ground.'[1]

My dreams of becoming a footballer were dashed at Bolton Wanderers, who deemed my physicality insufficient to make it. I was gutted. My academic ability wasn't promising, my artistic interests were mere hobbies, and now the only door I felt I could walk through and make something of myself slammed shut because I wasn't as tall as some of the less gifted players. I had opportunities to go to Oldham and a few other lower league clubs, but I'd lost all interest in how I was let go and proceeded to throw myself into the sort of antics you read about in Chapter 2. Football for me, from then on, would be something I'd enjoy in the stands. And what a time it was to be a fan of Manchester United.

The moment I exited my mother and entered Manchester, I was a United fan. Much like the decision to have me baptised a Catholic, I had no choice in either my football team or religion. But, as my faith in an Almighty waned as the years passed, my devotion toward Manchester United only grew more zealous. It is easier to leave Jesus than it is your football club. This was the same modus operandi for all my friends that were into football, they didn't decide who they supported as much as they inherited it. My Dad is a Red; therefore, I am a Red.

At the turn of the millennium, Manchester's football clubs faced polarised fates. The culmination of the 1995/96 season saw United lift a Premier League and FA Cup double at the same time as their civic rivals were relegated on the final day of the season. United would reach their zenith within a few years by completing an unprecedented treble, while Manchester City plummeted to their lowest ever league position in the Second Division. If I'd known then what I do now, I would have felt more inclined to rub salt into the wounds of City fans, but back there and then, it felt like picking at roadkill. Liverpool was then, as they are now, our biggest rival; Manchester City was a mere afterthought.

> Liverpool were always our main rivals, I mean City were a yo-yo club, and not even that, they were in the third tier at one point. There is a deeper hatred than just football in the rivalry with Liverpool fans, because you're probably mates with more City fans. I remember when City got promoted at the play-off final and I mean it was comical. Looking back, you know, things might have turned out different if they hadn't won that game. But they were so far down below us it was punching down, really, because I barely ever thought of Man City.
>
> – Jay Motty[2]

> I remember being distraught absolutely, being relegated from the Premier League. It was devastating for the club. I remember the game against Liverpool where Alan Ball thought that he was playing for the draw so we kept playing to keep ball in the corner, and you look back and you think how idiotic is that, how painful is it looking back. It just kind of summed the club up at that point. That kind of calamity, City should have been going all-out, gung ho for the winner; it was so painful seeing Kinkladze walking down the tunnel at Maine Road; the rot had already set in at that point, but that was the start of the real decline in the real dark days.
>
> – Emily Brobyn, journalist[3]

> You won the league as well, the same day, didn't you, like, you bastards, man! I think that was like the first time I'd seen them relegated – I went to my first game in '88, we were in the Second Division but it was the first time I'd seen them relegated and it was like, you dirty bastards, of all the times, it was when you were good! It was a kick in the teeth, but it had been coming all season 'cause we had such a shit start, I think we got one point in the first ten games, but, you know, it weren't that bad. I was seventeen at the time, so I was just going getting pissed

> anyway, going to away games and enjoying ourselves. That's the way it was. It was obviously gutting, but also knowing that we can go to different grounds, see different shit, and enjoy it. United fans have an arrogance that they're expected to win, and that still comes across now. United fans always had that 'Nah, we'll smash them' confidence. I always go to the game and still don't have that attitude.
>
> – JP Dolan, author's friend[4]

There is a theory that this 'arrogance' stems from a masterplan from Sir Alex Ferguson. There was an 'us against the world' philosophy drummed into the players which was also adopted by the fans.

> Everyone was out to get us, it felt like everyone hated us. It really did. It felt as a United fan you was literally against almost the entire Football League, or the entire country at times. For example, how Beckham was treated after '98, how Ferguson was often treated, how some of our players were treated. We were hated because of our success and in the stands at the time it felt like you were part of that, it sort of pulls us all together, as United fans against everyone else. I know most fans will think they've the same thing, that camaraderie was against everyone else, but I don't think most clubs have that level of hatred towards them. Everyone would be either jealous or angry towards Manchester United throughout the nineties and being a fan, you did feel like it was something you could buy into. It was something you were almost proud of, the fact that United were hated.
>
> – Jay Motty[5]

As United was closing ranks against the rest of the footballing world, City opted for Manchester's famed black humour with how they dealt with their demise.

> Self-deprecating humour was what we're known for, and we used it as a coping mechanism. When I went to Maine Road for the first time, I fell in love with Manchester City. I got bullied at school for my personal imperfections and I went to Maine Road and all I saw was imperfections. I was really happy that one could be perfectly imperfect. This was this club that had a plastic seagull hanging on a piece

> of string from the Kippax Stand which more often than not I'd watch during a game because, believe it, it was more interesting than the football. We had plastic garden furniture for our substitutes bench, had a scoreboard that never worked, it always gave the wrong scores. We had the Gene Kelly stands in the corner. None of our stands matched and all these little imperfections added up, and I felt right at home in this football club because I felt like I belonged, they had little quirks, waving these daft yellow bananas around, and I just absolutely fell head over heels in love with it and I could identify with it. And once that happened there was just no going back in. And, yeah, it was kind of like let's just poke fun at ourselves and because the times were so bad on the pitch, we'd just sit singing to other different stands. The rivalry at school is something that stays with me and haunts me now, and it's something that drives my rivalry with United fans today, because I got dog's abuse at high school, I remember the 5–0 game when Kanchelskis scored the hat-trick and I wanted the day off school. I tried to fake being ill but my Mum was having none of it. She knew it was because of the football – you've got to remember that it was just on the cusp of Helen Chamberlain doing *Soccer AM*, so women in football was a reasonably new entity, a rare breed. I was one of two City fans in my year. I remember I was walking in the corridor going in that day to school and I could hear them, all the lads banging on the table and when I walked in, they were all there winding me up. The contrast between the two clubs' fortunes made it worse. United doing so well winning silverware, winning trophies, and City getting relegated. We had no stick we could beat you with. So we threw whatever we could at United fans. Glory fans from London, I remember singing. We'd grab any stick that we could to beat you guys with and looking back it is really petty, but it's all we had. We didn't have much, clutching at straws at best.
>
> – Emily Brobyn[6]

'Glory Supporter' and 'We have proper fans!' are the only two insults I can recall Man City fans having; a misguided notion that Man United's fanbase was from outside Manchester and only supported them for the trophies. A laughable insult that never landed on me, having negated the two parameters that made up what was a weak jibe. Although there was some truth in the straws City fans were clutching. Man United has always had a global fanbase, but with how voraciously they were hoovering up trophies in the nineties, more and more fans followed the club.

> It became a kind of joke for Manc-based United fans. Although I do remember going to the Stretford End and talking to this guy who was there with his dad and I was just talking away when his dad suddenly turned on me and goes – in clearly not a Manc accent – 'Where do you live, son?' and I said, I live like twenty minutes away and he says, 'Well that's not proper commitment, we live in Plymouth and it takes us five hours to get here. That's proper commitment, lad.' So my commitment is minor because I'm just coming up the road. They had to spend the whole weekend getting there and back. When we were growing up, your identity was forged on going to the game. It's what you wore to the game. The game was central. You couldn't really identify as a United fan unless you went to the game. I would differentiate the gap between fan and supporter being whether you actually went to the game. When I was a kid there were plenty of people who had an emotional feeling towards United, but they weren't fans 'cause they didn't go to the game. And then, of course, you're a *proper* fan if you went to away games, so there was differentials even within that. Then you'd always meet someone who was a better fan than you were; you'd meet someone at some bizarre friendly away game at the beginning of the season, and there'd be someone who hadn't missed the game for thirty years, saying, 'Oh well, you know you're not a proper fan unless you were at Luton Away in 1925.' You know there were gradations of it, but effectively, fans went to the game, supporters just had a kind of vague emotional attachment. That I think has changed with the television coverage.
>
> –Jim White, journalist[7]

The demographics of the fanbase definitely changed, the bus from Urmston in the eighties was full of local people and now it's empty. A generation of working-class kids were basically alienated because the minute you couldn't turn up at Old Trafford and pay on the day, when you couldn't decide on a Saturday morning and go to the match, combine that with ticket prices rising, and it massively affected the demographic of the match-going fans in the nineties. I protested strongly against the ticket price rises, it damaged the match-going culture. I was still going with my mates, we were all young lads, but to a more casual fan who didn't necessarily want to go to all the away matches, it became really difficult to get tickets. That said, I still saw the same people coming and buying *United We Stand*, but it changed. I can remember one of the lads involved in *Red Issue* standing week after week, saying, 'It's going to shit, it's going to shit! You can see before your own eyes, look at him. Look at this fucking idiot, he's never been to a game before!' So it changed. Now the increased capacity also allowed it to change because if you go from 44 to 68 there's far more scope there for more types of fans to come to the game. In the sixties and seventies United started attracting fans from Wales and Scotland and all around England for various reasons, it wasn't all about success. I know people from Doncaster who became United fans because of Munich, or because of the love of the hooliganism in the seventies. It grew and grew and became far more international, United now have fans in places like India, Nigeria, West Africa which is brilliant. But they don't know the nuances, if they're not at the matches; there's nothing wrong with that, you can't expect them to be going to matches. But they're seeing YouTubers who've never been to a game come in and talk to these young fans in these far-off lands and they don't know that this guy isn't from Manchester, or not been to the game; they just see an Englishman and presume it has some authenticity. They're not bothered that he doesn't go to matches or uses a false name. I just find it a bit weird because if you go to the matches you know who's who. A lot of the main characters at United did earn their real stripes by the time they were twenty years old. And that's all changed now.

– Andy Mitten, journalist[8]

The distance beginning to creep in between United fans was also happening between the players and supporters. It once felt like they were working-class heroes, everymen with cool jobs, approachable and accessible in the eighties and early nineties, but by the decade's end they existed on another plain. I remember the exact date it all changed.

On 18 May 1997, I first felt heartbreak. It wasn't at the hands of Joanne, my mate's sister I was besotted with; it wasn't Nicola, nor was it Lisa (or her sister Brenda), who I'd been seeing intermittently over the past year, no. A barrel-chested, mono-browed Gaul from Marseille crushed my young world. And I wasn't alone. The day Eric Cantona announced his retirement from football brought watery eyes to every United fan. It wasn't just the success he orchestrated on the pitch that struck a chord in the hearts of Reds, but the way he conducted himself, and the man's character. He was synonymous with what not only what the club stood for but the city.

Eric Cantona was one of Us. Someone that came from elsewhere to make his name in this city; he was an artist, a poet, and a philosopher; he fought injustice, he was flawed, outspoken, enigmatic, and courageous. Eric Cantona was a Mancunian. Even the most hard-nosed ardent City fans held him highly regarded as a person, if not a player. He transcended the game. No player who followed Eric Cantona has come close to having the affinity with United fans. It was a watershed moment when the curtain fell on Cantona's career. The players who followed him would achieve more impressive accolades but did so as superstars, not as the cult figures I saw in Eric Cantona and his generation.

> I'm in love with Eric Cantona, as a human, as a player. I was in the museum the day he signed, didn't know who he was … and you know the shirt that they come and give you on the pitch? Which had Cantona with no number on? I got that shirt! My Mum sewed a number on to it, a black one by the way – it should be in the museum! But

they came and gave us that shirt, because I was having my birthday at the museum and they had to cut it short because Eric was signing. My Dad came out holding this shirt, it was an XL men's and I'm 9 … so obviously I wore it. It's short-sleeved but it's literally down to my wrist! And I asked him, 'Who is Cantona?' And he didn't know either, other than United had signed him. But it all changed with Eric, going to the match was something that we did, and it was like it was a black and white experience but Eric Cantona coloured it in – that's the only way I can describe what he did. Your teen years, you're struggling somewhat with your own identity, as a man, or whatever, as a Mancunian Man, and you see this guy giving zero fucks about what everyone else thinks and we'd never seen anything or anyone like him. He was part of that transition from the eighties thuggery type of football to the modern era in the Premier League we have today.

– Ste Howson, British Army veteran[9]

One of my favourite things as a kid was go down to The Cliff. This was around '95, and I'd sit on the training pitch whilst United were training. One of my mates nicked a training top – I think the statute of limitations is gone now – and I apologise to Mark Hughes, who I think it belonged to. But the accessibility was there, you could chat to them at training, and after the training you'd be in the car park. You'd get photos, autographs. I've got a lot of photos with players from then, Bryan Robson, Paul Ince, and a few others. They did seem like they were very accessible. And it changed. Then you started getting the players on front pages. David Beckham wears a sarong, he's on the front page of every paper, not just back pages. Eric Cantona was a front-page story all the time. You know when he, in my opinion, rightly kung-fu kicked Matthew Simmons. Footballers were becoming bigger stories than just the football, David Beckham is a great example. He wasn't just advertising football boots, advertising Brylcreem, and things like that. And I know footballers in the past have done advertising, you know, George Best or Ryan Giggs, but it did feel like these players were going into a sort of a stratosphere. And for me, I always look at Beckham as being the one of the pioneers of that, or one of the biggest ones because he almost ticked every box. He married the pop star. He had the great storyline: hated by everyone except United fans after '98, fully redeems himself, wins his treble, scores the winner against Argentina in 2002. It's just a massive great story arc, but with the attention that players were getting on a larger scale it did feel like from a fan point of view that you did lose that connection. That familiarity. I mean it wasn't just United, but we were the most successful club, so it was more apparent.

– Jay Motty[10]

This would never happen now but there's Cheetham Hill Cricket Club – I don't know if it still exists – and they had a charity match and basically the teams would be a load of United and City players, and afterwards they were just there hanging about, sat around having beers and stuff, and you could just go right up to them get autographs and chat with them. You had Bryan Robson, you had Gary Pallister, Lee Sharpe – it's such a weird scenario to imagine it today. First of all, that they'd be so accessible; secondly, that they'd be playing cricket. It's such a random thing. It's not as if this is happening at Lancashire Cricket Club, it's happening in Cheetham Hill! It just wouldn't happen today.

– Nooruddean Choudry[11]

City players were still pretty close-knit with the fans. You'd still see some of them in The Palace in Levenshulme, like Mark Kennedy. They were in your local nightclub. I remember meeting Andy Morrison in Long Legs where he bought me a lap dance. There was a night I was out in Bramhall and I met Kevin Horlock. I was on the piss with Kevin Horlock all night and getting him to leave messages on Chadwick's phone giving him a load of shit and calling him a Red Bastard and all that. But with us, we weren't that far away from them. Obviously, now you see the difference between fans and footballers.

– JP Dolan[12]

As new players from the Continent arrived to live in Manchester during its early regeneration phase, they were less than impressed by what the city had to offer.

> New players moving to the city had a shock; in '96 Jordi Cruyff moved to Manchester and he hated it. This is a twenty-two-year-old lad who lived in Barcelona and they put him in a house in Bramhall. He had to walk like a mile to the local shop and he said it was full of old people and he hated it. Had he come here ten years later, he could have lived happily in the city centre. By '99 you had people like Fabien Barthez living in the centre with Linda Evangelista, his supermodel wife, and she didn't like it. I remember the Real Madrid team being in Manchester looking out the window on the way to the ground and being horrified by what they saw. And I'd be gutted when I hear stuff like that now. They were probably being taken the back way through Trafford Park and maybe it isn't quite as glamorous as the middle of Madrid.
>
> – Andy Mitten[13]

The young players that had come through both clubs' academies during this time had markedly different experiences. The success of Manchester United's Class of '92 is well documented, but less is said of Manchester City's Class of '93. This is former City player Ged Tarpey on how life was for a young player coming through the ranks at Maine Road:

> There's obviously the famous class of '92 at United, and there's the less famous class of '93 at Man City whose career didn't quite pan out like the others. But you know, I got to play against most of those boys which was brilliant. And I wouldn't change any of it for the world. But City was an absolute shambles at the time. I was there for four seasons, and I think probably in that time I can't even tell you how many managers there were. There was some season where you'd have three or four managers. Steve Coppell was a manager for a couple of weeks. Niall Quinn was one of the nicest people you'd ever meet; I was really lucky that I was his boot-boy because he kind of took me under his wing a little bit, he helped me with lots of questions about getting an agent and things like that. He brought me over to his house and he just sat me down and talked through all the pros and cons. Like don't waste your money, it's not worth it. Like if you need help, I'll come in

with you. I don't know if you'd get footballers doing that these days. I mean, football has moved on a lot in the last thirty years, of course, but a there was a lot of just really really good people.

– Ged Tarpey, ex-pro footballer[14]

Tarpey excelled in the youth team and was offered a two-year professional contract and had his sights on challenging for a place on the biggest stage with the club. However, his strong progress came to an abrupt halt during a Lancashire Youth Cup semi-final against Manchester United at Maine Road; a bad tackle left Tarpey with a snapped medial ligament and a torn anterior cruciate ligament … It was an injury that he never fully recovered from and it effectively ended his chances of a career in professional football.

– The PFA[15]

It was the Lancashire Youth Cup semi-final at Maine Road. Playing against United and David Johnson in the last minute of the game, we were beating them and he two-footed me and got sent off immediately. I'd already signed a professional contract – thank God – because at the time, you know what would have happened. I spent two-thirds of the next season trying to get back, and back then, a knee injury, you didn't come back as often as today. But I'd lost pace and that was that. I knew my time was up and then I was probably, for the first time in my life – it's come out recently with football – but I got a little bit depressed. My mates are going back in pre-season and I was just at home and had offers to go on trials at a few other places. I'd fallen out of love with it because I felt I'd been treated badly. The *Manchester Evening News* did an article on me. There was an embargo on City players from talking to the press at the time, so Paul Haynes, who was the chief writer back then, was like gold, he was like, do you want to do an interview? I was like, absolutely, so they did a double-page spread about Ged's battle. City did nothing. It's like, 'Yeah, you've done your knee; I'm sorry we're not giving you another contract. All the best.' You know, good luck, and you're just thrown out on the on the scrap heap, and I had a period where I felt really depressed for probably six months. I was lucky, I had my brother, I was academically inclined, and he inspired

> me to go back to school. But there was a lack of understanding, and I think what makes it even worse, is the majority of lads are working class and this is your way out, right? This is your chance to be the local hero, to make some money, to make your family proud, and all of a sudden that's just ripped away from you and you've got to start from scratch again. I think people were afraid to talk about it [mental health] in general. Maybe there's an element of you that wants to keep your masculinity; that's a critical part of who you are, so you don't talk about mental health. People just didn't raise that stuff up. Now I'd like to think the PFA would do a really good job of helping players, you know, certainly when kids are released. I mean, what's the percentage of kids who make it to be Marcus Rashford? It's minuscule. You've got all these lads that have spent their entire life from seven years old to get into an academy at sixteen and then there's a massive drop off. All of a sudden your life can screech to a halt and it's horrific; you think your life is going in one direction, and it just completely ends and back then there was zero help.
>
> – Ged Tarpey[16]

Unlike the mental health support players like Ged lacked within the club's confines, it felt like it was there in abundance between fans. The match-going experience is about seeing friends and sharing time with like-minded people to let off steam and forget the ills of everyday life. Oh, how those afternoons spent singing, swearing, and swigging in the stands were a much-needed respite.

> We very famously used to go on the same coach with the same people to away games, The Monkey Bus, and it was named entirely appropriately because the behaviour of people while on there was a zoo. But it was that feeling of being amongst mates. The thing I loved about our community was not just the sense that we were going to games together. It was that feeling of a group with trust, mutual respect, and that your back was covered up as well as your front. It was that type of environment. But there's been other times where I've been in and around people who support the same club who I just wouldn't give the time of day. Within any huge tribe you can have these divisions, and

these factions, that want to consume things and do things in a different way. You know that culture exists as it does in any kind of mass gathering. But by and large it was a hundred per cent about being in that environment of trust, mutual respect, and support of other people, and it was a special period that coach, at the time. You talk of mental health. I've always been very conscious of it my whole life. I was in a job that was very demanding, high pressure, and having an environment where you could go and release some of that, match-going culture supported those kinds of things. This is when people talk about men's mental health; I've been pissed off, and fed up, down in the dumps like we all get, but I've never felt that I have a mental health problem. But every single one of us sometimes needs somewhere to go so you can get away from how your employers expect you to behave, get away from the expectations of what family expect you to be like, and just go and be a fucking knob and forget. Because I see this at football grounds all the time. I completely get why some football fans suddenly go from being forty-odd-year-old blokes and start acting like they're fifteen and throwing beer around and stuff – I don't like that it interferes with people who don't like that but I completely understand the need for people to have that exit from day-to-day stuff in an environment where they can go and be a bit childlike. In the same way, you know, a football fan is no different to someone going on a dance floor and getting everything out of their system, or going to a gig and having a good fling around at a club. It's a similar situation, but I think with football, sometimes your outgoing behaviour under the banner of being at the match or in a match environment, I think you've just got to be careful of how far your desire to have a day off from being serious about life impacts others. That was the special thing about the bus. We were all contained in this sixty-foot steel drum and all sorts of weird and wonderful things took place on there. It was a really special and really important part of my life. I had the best of times. There's been all sorts of things, people getting set alight for a laugh, you know that sort of stuff, we had one where two lads – I can't remember how it started but they were arguing who was the best dancer – neither of them having natural rhythm – so we decided to have a dance-off on the coach between the two of them. And it just became like a world

> heavyweight title fight. They'd do press conferences as if it was in public, you know where they were staring each other out, we were doing interviews, and then these guys start dancing. One of the lads in in the middle of his dance just basically let this big firework off on this coach and was waving it around – I mean there's a fuel pipe only just below him and the driver's looking in the mirror going mad. We've had some good laughs for sure.
>
> – Steve Armstrong[17]

It was a golden time for football fans in Manchester. Despite the two teams being leagues apart, both clubs had cause for celebration, with Reds and Blues revelling in their teams' achievements at the end of May 1999. With rumours that the club was due to face administration, Man City took on Gillingham in the Football League Second Division play-off final.

> It was absolutely batshit crazy. We went down there and everybody thought Gillingham had no chance, because Manchester City needed to get promoted, needed to get out of this division. But the Gillingham game was pretty boring for the vast majority. And then in the eighty-fifth minute, was it, Robert Taylor got the first goal and then Carl Asaba got their second, I think, or the other way around. And we were like, 'Wow, what is going on?' So we actually went down to the concourse, I was crying over my Dad's shoulder, and I was saying to him, you don't understand that United had just won the treble and we can't even get out of Division Two. You don't understand the grief I'm going to get when I go to college. When is it going to stop with this football club putting us through the ringer, time and time again, I said, I don't know how much more I can genuinely take of it. There were grown men crying all around me, sobbing their eyes out, tears streaming down their faces. And he looks at me, grabbed me and said, 'Do you just want to go now?' and I said yeah. So we're walking towards the turnstiles and then there was this roar, so we run to the steps through pandemonium and that was Kevin Horlock scoring the first goal, and

as we were in a squash of people in delirium trying to get up back up to our seats, we turn around the corner, that was Dickov's goal. You heard like the anticipation in the air, you know it's coming in the build-up and then the roar and the mayhem and the bedlam. It was crazy. I experienced every emotion I could that day. The reality was that who knows what would have happened to the club if we stayed in that division? Because we were on a precipice, and after doing interviews with people who were there at the time and we're falling off a cliff edge, it was unsustainable. Who knows what would have happened.

– Emily Brobyn[18]

Days earlier, Manchester United had reached 'The Promised Land' with Ole Gunnar Solskjær scoring an injury-time winner against Bayern Munich to crown the Red Devils European Champions and complete the treble alongside the FA Cup and Premier League titles.

I think that if you look back that would be the pinnacle being amongst United fans, it was, the greatest sort of couple of months, to be honest with you. Just the run-in from the last three months onwards, just phenomenal and when I look back to that, just nothing but fond memories. Some of the games that I went to, and the ones that I didn't, the celebrations and the whole of Manchester – it felt like the whole of Manchester anyway – although City fans will disagree, but all of Manchester coming together and obviously the celebration at the end of it. It was just an amazing time. It was a great feeling being a Manchester United fan and watching that history unfold, there was so many twists in that final few weeks as well. And it wasn't until the last game of the season we won the league. The semi-final against Arsenal in the FA Cup. The semi-finals in the Champions League, and then obviously the final as well. It was just non-stop drama and at the end of all that drama in every single game, in every single way, Manchester United came out on top.

– Jay Motty[19]

Manchester's tourist board, commercial businesses, and institutions saw United's success as a way to promote the city and gain foreign investment.

> United is Manchester's biggest cultural export. I'm sorry Gallagher brothers, but United is the thing that is most known around the world. There's the old joke about how you can get a taxi in Mexico City and the taxi driver knows two words of English: Bobby and Charlton. I mean it was ever thus, but I think that Manchester United certainly in the nineties became that engine of Manchester culturally, and that's what everybody knew the city for. In the mid-nineties – sort of '97, '98 – all four of Manchester's unis had a picture of Old Trafford in their glossy brochures that they would send out. It's actually done in a rather scary way in China to get overseas students. These kids are thinking of where they're going to go in England, and they actually have agents, so Coventry University or something will actually employ an agent to go out there to persuade kids to go to their university, and they get a cut of the fee. And, of course, Manchester was just the biggest and easiest sell because what's a comparative university? Bristol, Reading, Cardiff? What have they got to match Manchester? Well, they've got the academic things, they've got the architectural things, but what they haven't got is the football and Manchester ruthlessly used that to attract overseas students and tourists off the back of United. It became almost a joke, didn't it? The overseas visitors to Manchester coming to see United. They'd coming specifically for the weekend, go to a match, go to the museum, it's all part of the offer. United was at the centre of the experience; City just wasn't. I mean, it might be nowadays …
>
> – Jim White[20]

Indeed, as Manchester used United's success to bring money into the city, the club itself was as ruthlessly keen to profit. Using the team's triumphs on the pitch, Man United's marketing people cast their net far and wide to attract more fans, not because the team needed support but because of their financial opportunities. As a lifelong Man United fan and journalist, Jim White offers insight as both supporter and reporter:

> There was a guy called Edward Freedman who was the kind of marketing boss – the first presiding genius there marketing and pushing it. It all looks very quaint compared to what it is now. It was the Ryan Giggs duvet-cover era, but I remember talking to him and saying, what right have you got to target kids in Wolverhampton or kids in Oxford or Plymouth when they've a local club there? He said, 'The pound in every pocket is the same. As far as we're concerned, we're after the pound, wherever it is.' Which I thought was a really telling thing. As far as the club's concerned, as long as you're expressing your devotion through financial recourse, by buying things from the club shop, they didn't mind where you came from. So they had no moral obligation from the club side to local fans. Their driving force was that the pound in every pocket is equal to us, so we're after everybody financially. I think that was a really big engine in driving United commercially in the nineties. They were constant. I remember talking to somebody at United around the year 2000 when they were convinced that getting mobile phone goal alerts was a way of monetising support around the world. So if they could be in control of goal alerts to mobile phones, that they were going to somehow make a fortune. I don't think any anything came of that, but it was indicative of the fact that they thought they had possession of some technological content, as opposed to anything emotional. I think it's driven by two things. The assumption has long been at United that profitability leads to success: we make money and then we spend money on the pitch and then that becomes a benevolent circle. The more we spend on the pitch, the more we win, the bigger we become and the more of a saleable product we have. I don't think it was their priority to line their pockets, although having said that, I would imagine that marketing executive was on healthy bonuses. Martin Edwards didn't really realise what he had for a long time, you know? I mean, everybody talks about United being so good at seizing the moment of the Premier League

> and grabbing it. I think there's a bit of post-rationalisation in that I don't think United really realised what they had until, you know, the mid-nineties.
>
> – Jim White[21]

'BSkyB bid for Manchester United fails'

As Manchester United's dominance on the field continued, it became apparent to Martin Edwards just how lucrative the cash cow he sat on was. In 1989 he had tried to sell the club to Michael Knighton for £20 million, only for Edwards to realise his error in the final stages. With the rise of the Premier League and United's success within eleven years they had become a £1 billion business; when a new offer came along it was financially on another planet. In 1998, the beginning of what would become Manchester United's most successful season, the club accepted a £623.4m bid from Rupert Murdoch's television company, BSkyB. The news was met with visceral opposition from fans and Government, and a fortnight before United's famous semi-final FA Cup win against Arsenal in April 1999 the takeover was blocked by the Department of Trade and Industry. In 2000, Martin Edwards stood down as Chairman of the club.

> The arguments around the Sky takeover were very similar to the arguments around the Super League. It was about authenticity. The argument was if we're bought by a conglomerate, you know we'll be sold, there was lots of talk of 'Sky will move us to another place; you know they'll move Manchester United to London because they can.' I don't think they ever would have done that, but that was definitely an argument. It goes back to the differentiation in the board's mind of the locality of United. The authenticity, the fact the Mancunian identity is important for the fans, is vital for the match-going fans, it was vital and that really came out in the in the Sky takeover battle. What is the Mancunian authenticity of this institution if Sky take

> over? The interesting thing about Sky taking over was the Labour government had just come into power in '97 and had a huge majority in Parliament, and there were a lot of Labour MPs who residually loathed [Rupert] Murdoch because of the Wapping dispute and the destruction of the unions, and so that was at the forefront of the protests. They probably didn't have that when the Glazers came in. There was a lot of emotional power behind the anti-Sky campaign because a lot of these MPs weren't gonna let a Murdoch bid go through. They were going to fight against it all the way. At the time Labour was in a huge majority and basically they insisted to the DCMS [Department for Culture, Media and Sport] – or whoever it was in charge – that this takeover was anticompetitive and for all the shouting that we fans did, and for all the vociferous campaigning we did, and the excellence of the campaign that was organised by Andy Walsh (who then later went to FC United), I think it was the political power that stopped that takeover. You had local MPs in Manchester who both understood that this was a fight between authenticity and corporatisation, but also had a lingering loathing of Murdoch and this was an opportunity for revenge. I don't think you should underplay that, this was the absolute peak of New Labour. So, OK, Tony Blair needed Murdoch to get in, but now he was in Number 10, he probably thought that it's not so necessary anymore. So he was happy to wave it through, 'Yeah, I'll let this one go through because that will pacify the left in the party.' Pragmatically, it was the perfect time. I think you would have to accept having that political power was really important and we just didn't have it when the Glazers came in. It was a different group, and for all we love to hate the Glazers they didn't do anything illegal. It was quite hard to try and find a legal loophole, whereas with Sky there was a legal loophole because there was potentially the broadcaster of the Premier League also owning part of the biggest club in the league.
>
> –Jim White[22]

The Glazers may not have done anything illegal in their obtaining the club, but how they managed to get such a stake that would allow them to go on to buy the club is a bone of contention amongst United fans.

A horse! A horse! My kingdom for a horse!

Some Manchester United fans whisper that it all started with a horse. Sir Alex Ferguson believed he co-owned the champion stallion 'Rock of Gibraltar', but John Magnier and J.P. McManus held a different view. As members of the Coolmore racing conglomerate and United shareholders, their relationship with Ferguson had developed through their mutual love for horse racing. However, a disagreement over ownership led to a legal battle and the eventual sale of their shares to the Glazer family. The outcome for Manchester United may have been different if Sir Alex was not interested in horse racing.

In 2003, Malcolm Glazer bought 2.9% of Manchester United shares for $4.7 million, which grew to 30% by year-end. In 2004, the dispute between Alex Ferguson and owners John Magnier and J.P. McManus led to the sale of their 28.7% shares to Glazer, giving him control of 57% of the club, eventually increasing to 75%. With 30% ownership, Glazer was able to bid for complete control. He delisted the club from the stock exchange, acquired 98% of shares and forced the remaining 2% to sell, completing the £790 million takeover of Manchester United.

> There's a lot of variables. Did The Rock of Gibraltar lead to the Glazers? Did horse semen lead to the downfall of one of the world's greatest sporting institutions? There is an argument there, he fell out with the owners and they then wanted to sell their shares which ultimately gave the Glazers the opportunity. I always feel, though, that that opportunity could have arisen anyway. I think the Glazers became aware of how they could structure the deal and do the deal without much money, just on a leverage buyout. I think it's safe to say they would have attempted to do it anyway. The only question is, would they have been successful? I mean, it does seem like a quite an ironic storyline. The greatest ever manager helped to pull the rug from the club, but I'm not sure how accurate it is. I think

> there's so many ifs and buts and maybes that you can argue the case for and against. But you can't say definitively if Fergie didn't have his row with the owners that the Glazers wouldn't have come in. Because I always felt like if you look at ownership now, every club, every major club is owned by one rich owner, or one rich organisation, and I think it would have been either the Glazers or maybe a billionaire oil state or whatever. Someone would have come in for United eventually. There's no way it would have carried on. They almost sold to Michael Knighton. Then it was Rupert Murdoch. There was always someone sniffing around as you expect with what is a cash cow, and eventually, unfortunately for United, we end up with the Glazers.[23]

On 11 May 2003, Manchester City played their final ever game at Maine Road. The following season, after eighty years, they would be playing their home games at the vacant Commonwealth Stadium. The game ended in a dull 1–0 defeat to Southampton, with the final farewell seeing live pitch performances from some of the City's most famous musical supporters.

> It was top. It was a big difference moving from Maine Road. Just walking up the little terraced streets, and coming round to the lights at the Kippax, and the smell in the air and that old ground feel that you only get at a few places now. That feeling when you'd go to a night game; the atmosphere when you were all walking through the streets together. It was mint. Although you've got to move on, haven't you? Would we still have got the investment we've got now if we were still at Maine Road? It was mega, and it was sad when it came down … and I didn't even get to the last game because of your Uncle. He'd rang us on the Thursday, it was when he was 'away' in Marbella, shall we say; so he's rang us and gone are you coming over, so me and Shep and your Dad went over. I was like, 'Right, I've got a flight first thing Sunday morning, City have got a game', and he was like, 'Yeah, you'll be back, you'll be back', So obviously we had a good weekend, and we were at it all weekend, the Sunday morning arrives, and I've

woke up and your Uncle's still dancing around the gaff, off his face, and I've gone:

- *T, what time is it?*
- *It's half ten or something, man.*
- *What?! You know we've got flights, you dickhead!*

And he's just laughing, so me and Dave Shep end up getting a flight to fucking Birmingham, my sisters came to pick us up, got us to Maine Road and by the time I'd got there you could hear Badly Drawn Boy singing, and I was dying, I had to go home, man. I couldn't even go in the ground, I was that bad. But it was top at Maine Road, man; we'd go from St Alban's High School and there'd be like fifteen of us getting in the Kippax getting hammered two hours before the game.

– JP Dolan[24]

Yeah, it was Doves and Badly Drawn Boy. There's some music on and it was just really emotional, really sad. I went back in. I really miss Maine Road and I know that I do romanticise a lot about it because I have blue-tinted specs, but let's be honest, they were shit days for City, but I miss it because that's where I fell in love with the club. And that's where the identity side of it came in. And you go there now and we've only got a really small little plaque on the ground and it's a travesty because you go to that area, I do the walk sometimes. I'll go back and walk from where we used to park our car, and then walk past the pub which is now a nursery, walk all the way up, and as I turn the corner and expect to see Maine Road, it's a housing estate.

– Emily Brobyn[25]

The millennium was a kernel for what both Manchester clubs have become. City's promotion back into the Premier League and move to the Commonwealth Stadium made them a more attractive option for anyone in the market looking to buy a football club. United's dominance on the pitch, and their global commercial revenue opportunities off it, made them almost irresistible to any capitalist parasites wanting to cream off our success. Both teams' achievements, combined with the rise of the internet, garnered supporters far and wide; what constitutes being a fan has a capricious framework, depending on who you ask. So it's almost as impossible to decipher what makes a proper red or blue as it is to decide what is a proper Mancunian.

7

'And Tony Wilson didn't even say it!'

MEDIA

If Manchester's diverse sounds were struggling to find national recognition, then it wasn't the case for how Mancunians were being represented on the screen. The millennium would prove to be a golden age for the city on screen. Pockets of our population that had been overlooked for storylines and features were now the focus for new TV and film productions. During this period we would see Mancunians of different colours, sexuality, and class on screen and lifting major awards in the process. We would also see Manchester's working class reimagined in a series that would break the mould of British comedy.

> I remember being with my Mum down south once and she was saying, 'That's just like our home.' What was good about *The Royle Family* is that you could see that your life was being mined for comedy. It's inspirational in that what it does is make you realise that your life can be funny if you look at it in a funny way and that's what comedians do. It wasn't exaggerated. There's nothing that's happened in *The Royle Family* that's not happened in one of our families. There's nothing outlandish. There's nothing outrageous. It's just the comedy of how we talk and interact with each other and you wouldn't expect that, would you? And it's actually done with so much love.
>
> – Justin Moorhouse [1]

Nothing that has come out of Manchester has impacted me as much as *The Royle Family*. The success of United and our musical exports; they were escapism as much as celebration of where I am from. I could wrap myself up in a sense of belonging with other fans, experiencing matches and gigs but the Us was in the crowd, not those on the pitch or the stage. *The Royle Family* was Us. It was my front room, it was my friend's house, it was what home looked like to so many Mancunian working-class families. There were no crass caricatures, no exaggerated storylines but just a true representation of the warmth, wit, sarcasm, and love which was being shared behind the front doors of the terraced houses across the city. At the time I didn't think of how it was shot or the absence of a laughter track but was just in awe at seeing our lives on the telly, as well as creasing up at how funny it was. Only in hindsight did I appreciate how ground-breaking it was.

As the BBC described it in 2015, 'Nothing on television had been quite like *The Royle Family*. It eschewed a laughter track and the traditional three-camera set-up, and was shot on 16mm film, the resulting grain adding to the dowdy atmosphere. Not only that, but it seemed to take place in real time. It is unlikely this bold, unique and brilliant rewriting of what is possible in British comedy will be bettered.'[2]

The genius in the writing is equalled by the ability of creators Caroline Aherne and Craig Cash to get it made. How do you pitch the premise of *The Royle Family* to commissioners? 'I've got this show about a family that watches TV and rarely move out of their front room or couch.' It doesn't scream BAFTA from the script.

> She only got it commissioned because of the *Mrs Merton Show*. BBC had got it at that point and she said she wouldn't do any more shows unless they commission *The Royle Family* because that was her thing. Mrs Merton had won a lot of awards so she was in a good position, but they were hesitant on the concept and intention.
>
> – Phil Mealey, writer[3]

It was a game changer, *The Royle Family*, really. Caroline said we're writing a thing called The Royal Family and I went, oh right, and I thought … that's weird. But I thought The *Royal* Family, you know, Queen Mum and all that. And I thought, that is such a weird route to take. I saw a documentary recently about one of the unbelievably brilliantly written shows, *Modern Family*, and the writers sit around and they've got, say, the theme of a wedding and they go, 'I got these stories about weddings gone wrong' and a lot of the stuff that goes into *Modern Family* are actual things that they've heard, or been part of, so they're real things that have happened. And with Caroline and Craig and *The Royle Family* cast, a lot of what was written had been gleaned from real stuff. I mean, Caroline's mum is such a character – like the bit where Barbara says, 'I've not got enough potatoes,' and Denise says, 'Well, cut them in half,' to which Barbara says, 'But then I'll have too many.' … I just know that Caroline got a lot from her Irish mum. When I watched the first one, I didn't know what to make of it, really, because there's no canned laughter. And it was just a grower for me. I don't know about other people, but it was just so well defined. Such great humour and the angles they chose were absolutely perfect, so I loved it, I thought it was brilliant. And Caroline. I mean, it's like Steve Coogan. Caroline used to, and Steve still does, make me roar when they're talking about their family or just things that have happened to them.

– John Thomson, comedian and actor[4]

She was so confident about it. I remember seeing the first episode, I wasn't working on it then, but I was mates with Craig, and to be honest I was like 'fucking hell' because it was like watching a documentary, there was no laughter track on it, and when it came out everything had a laughter track on it, but she was absolutely confident about it and it being exactly how it is. They had to reshoot the first episode because it was shot like a conventional sitcom and Caroline is like, 'No, that's not right, it needs to be different,' and they shot again which must have cost them a few bob.

– Phil Mealey[5]

How avant-garde *The Royle Family* is was appreciated not only by UK critics but also found fans across the globe, with people such as *The Sopranos*' Michael Imperioli revealing himself as a huge fan:

> I think it took a lot of guts to make that show, it's very experimental if you think about it, because there's no real story. I've never seen a show like that, I thought it was one of the most creative things I've ever seen in my life.
>
> – Michael Imperioli, *Talking Sopranos* podcast[6]

> Caroline was just brilliant. I've known Caroline since she did some work on Signal Radio and then she came and started doing *Mrs Merton*. You know, I think everyone worked there, there was Terry Christian, Jon Ronson worked there, Craig Cash – so I'd known her from right back in the day. She was really lovely and funny. She just wanted to write, her favourite thing was writing.
>
> – Phil Mealey[7]

> One thing about Caroline was that she would suffer from terrible writer's block. We all have rotten days where you just can't write and think everything's shit and I could tell in an episode when that happened because they all do a singsong, like Lily Allen in a car or they'd just get Old Joe up to sing a sad Irish ballad. And I said to her, you were stuck there, weren't you? And she was like, 'Yeah, we couldn't think of anything.'
>
> –John Thomson[8]

> She was really funny. I mean we'd go round to her house, and this is typical of her, and I had these shoes at one time – they were like these Hush Puppy type things (I don't know what the fuck I was doing with them!) and she was like:
>
> - *Oh, you alright, Phil? Erm … what's Richard Briers doing if you've got his shoes on?*
>
> So I start laughing about it and then when I went to her house the following day, there was a note on the front door saying: If there is

anybody with Richard Briers' shoes, can you please take them off before you come in? It was just typical of her, she'd come at things from really odd angles. She was proper funny. Really quick. We did *Sunshine* with Steve Coogan and she came to the readthrough. We'd said, do you want to come, and she'd knew there would be a few drinks and there'd be a bit of a craic after it's finished. So we have the readthrough and there's usually a polite applause at the end and all that, and it's silent and she goes:

- *Hey, Steve, what's it like to be in something good?*

In front of everybody, you know what I mean, just taking the micky. She just really liked to throw you when you were in public. I remember being with a girlfriend and we'd met Caroline and I was like 'Oh, hi Caroline!' and she starts asking my girlfriend who she'd never met before:

- *So what do you think of Phil? Do you like him? Do you think you've got a future together? What do you think? Do you think he's nice?*

That's the first time she'd met her and she's asking her all this. I was used to it and I was saying, 'Oh, don't worry, it's just Caroline.' But that was just the way she was. She had a real childlike quality to her in many ways, but all about fun. She was great and she was different to me and Craig, we were closer, but she would always come in with things at left field.

– Phil Mealey[9]

During its three series and specials *The Royle Family* amassed twenty-three awards, including a BAFTA for Best Situation Comedy for the show's writers. The irony is that the 'Queen of Sheba' episode for which they lifted the award wasn't purely comedy. The one-off hour special was as tender and moving as it was funny. Despite my seeing it countless times, watching the Royles say farewell to Nana still leaves me with damp eyes on every single watch. My Nana passed away whilst writing this book and the moments my family spent with her before she died were a mirror image; we laughed, we cried, we bickered, and we loved, exactly as it was portrayed in that episode.

> [Before the 'Queen of Sheba' episode] Liz was knocking on a bit then and Caroline had just lost her Nan and we felt that we wanted to maybe try and tackle the subject but make it funny, warm, and moving. Representing that kind of family that is a bit dysfunctional but that doesn't mean to say that they don't all love each other. I mean it won the BAFTA for the hour special so you know it meant something to people and I don't think it had been done before – maybe *Only Fools* [*and Horses*] – but [Nana] was prevalent throughout the episode. It was like a celebration really, of her. She was stuck in the bed and one of my favourite scenes in that is the scene where Barbara is doing Nana's hair and she says at the end, 'I do love you, you know, Barbara.' It's like she's probably never said it to her. You know, I do that to my Mum now, I've gone soft, but about ten years ago I'd never tell my Mum I love her and I do, so I'm going to tell her – but it's difficult, because my Mum and Dad never said that sort of stuff, so even now on the phone I'll say, 'See ya Mum, love you,' and she'll say 'OK. OK.' You know, I never get it back. I know she does, but it's one of them things. I think they just find it hard to say, so that scene went from being funny, and then to her being a bit of a pain in the arse, and then telling her daughter how much she appreciated everything she'd done for her. And that's just in one scene – you know having the craic with the mum and then when they're doing her hair and she says, 'Bloody heck, Barbara, I look like Jeremy Clarkson with this hair,' and 'Can you make sure you wash these on their own; I don't want them in with Jim's Y-fronts,' and then saying she loves her and then them singing 'Que Sera, Sera' together. And what we wanted to do was, again, explore that thing when you've got family members like your Nana, and how we all deal with it and the warmth as well, and the fact that everybody wasn't going 'Narrrr! Me Nana's died ... Anyone got any Es? Nice one!' as is the stereotype.
>
> – Phil Mealey[10]

On 2 July 2016 Caroline Aherne died of lung cancer at her Timperley home at the age of fifty-two. Her passing created a collective mourning across Manchester. Caroline wasn't just one of Manchester's finest writers and comedians, she was one of the best in the world. *The Royle Family* brought an immeasurable amount of pride to Mancunians for how it represented us, and furthermore, her entire body of work is so critically acclaimed. Yet, despite all her success we still have failed to commemorate Caroline within Manchester city centre. It's not good enough.

> Caroline's passing was a massive shock 'cause I thought she was alright, she was gonna pull through, but it was a real shock when someone said they can't do anything this time. I wouldn't believe it. I'm an eternal optimist and I just thought, well, maybe there's a chance. I was told that information secretly, but didn't tell anybody that she was terminal, and I was doing a show with Craig and Caroline called *After Hours* about a pirate radio station on a canal barge. And mine and Caroline's characters had fallen out. Ironically, my character had just got over cancer. It never transpired what it was he'd done, but she was my wife and locked me out and I was living with Ardal O'Hanlon, and she was my wife, Sheila. I had to sing in a local *Britain's Got Talent* thing and I had to learn 'Sheila Take A Bow' on guitar and everything – it's the closest I've done to method acting – and I sang it to her. I was so glad that I'd done that last bit of work with her. I was OK at the time and then I did a documentary about Caroline, only for an hour, and then they showed *The Royle Family* and I thought it was too late. Too little, too late. I think she's worth a much better kind of tribute to be honest. I hadn't dealt with it – I was so used to seeing her character, or chatting on Parky – but it broke me and it was like four, five years after, this shock, delayed reaction which I'd sat on like a fucking pressure cooker and seeing her as her in the old footage, it really hit a nerve. I was really heartbroken.
>
> – John Thomson[11]

Whereas *The Royle Family* was Manchester's working class at home, *Early Doors* was them down their local, The Grapes. Written by Phil Mealey and Craig Cash, that series wasn't as easy to get off the ground, despite the success of *The Royle Family* with which it shared similar themes.

> Me and Craig had always chatted about doing a working-class sitcom because we didn't see anything else doing it right. Well, aside from *The Royle Family* obviously. The idea was we wanted to do something that we knew about. We knew a pub because, obviously, we've done a lot of research. So then it ended up being like a working-class *Cheers*, if you like. We felt the representation of working-class people was a lot of times seen through the eyes of southern commissioners. In many ways you got a stereotype, so you get scallies who was robbing their mates or selling drugs or knocking their mate's girlfriend off. That sort of thing seemed like the Channel 4 commissioners' idea of what The North was like. I'm working class, obviously, right? And I saw a bit of that, but in the main I saw a lot of people having the craic with each other, getting on with each other, taking the piss out of each other, but having a real affinity with each other. And I thought, and still think by the way, that's under-represented. I mean, it's almost like an identikit version of what The North is, like Scousers get it all the time. If you wrote a Scouse sitcom where one of the kids was a heroin addict, and someone was robbing this, that, and the other, I think you'd probably get it commissioned because it's an Oxbridge version of what they think it's like. When we sent out *Early Doors* it took eighteen months to get a commission, and everybody turned it down. BBC 2, BBC 1, Channel 4. Every comment we got back pretty much the same:
>
> - *Why don't these people like each other?*
> - *What do you mean, they do like each other.*
> - *They're always like taking the piss out of each other, and having a go at one another.*
> - *Well, like, no you are missing the whole thing there. It's not bullying, it's how people talk to each other. If they didn't care about each other then they wouldn't talk to one another. That banter (I hate that word) is them showing they care.*
>
> But they couldn't get their heads around it as culture. It's hard to get work in music, poetry, literature, and TV, to get stuff that's born

> out of a working-class background and a working-class sensibility, because what you have to do is get people who have no sense of what that world is like to commission it. You're dealing with people who are – certainly in the BBC, but in lots of those jobs – privately educated. I'm not knocking that but I'm just telling you how it is because they don't have an affinity or appreciation of us. They don't recognise that world. Whereas ninety per cent of us, even in the middle classes of Manchester, do. It's lazy commissioning because it's about pigeonholing people and their perception of it. I think sometimes commissioners feel more comfortable in reinforcing old tropes. We've had the comment before of, 'Oh, it's very Northern, isn't it?' But what does that mean? If you write something that is based in London does anyone go, 'Oh, it's a bit Southern.' Nobody said to Ricky Gervais when he wrote *The Office* that 'This is very Southern.' We always got it, this need to stamp it with a regional identity. Well, it was Northern in that it is based in the North, but we sold out the Hammersmith Odeon in London, so what does that tell you about the themes, characters, and stories? The culture of having some miserable tight git sat in a pub isn't unique to Manchester? Craig's character being in the pub when his missus is at home looking after the kids doesn't just exist in the North.
>
> – Phil Mealey[12]

If Manchester's working classes had a tradition of being misrepresented on television, then the middle classes were non-existent. At the end of the century this would change, and Manchester was showcased in a more affluent way. Starting in 1997, *Cold Feet* was a sharp contrast to how Manchester had been previously portrayed on screen.

> *Cold Feet* was a game changer for how the North, and Manchester particularly, was viewed. In the more recent series there's scenes I'm not in and there are locations that I've seen when I've gone, 'That's nice, where did they shoot that?' and they found some great places that I wouldn't know, but this did, style-wise, show more period of the time, architecture and design and everything about Manchester you hadn't seen on screen. It's very pleasant. You know there's something

> about it that will still stand the test of time. You know there's certain things from the past, sixties high-rise flats and they've got very tired. The thing about *Cold Feet* is we've been so used to the 'It's grim up north' tropes; those kitchen-sink films from the sixties, those Ken Loach-type films. And I think that's what people actually thought the North is like and it's so far from the truth. Everyone is a lot more aspirational. You can make things look nice on an aesthetic level cheaply. People take pride in their homes. There's always been a great pride in the North, like women cleaning their front step. You know, making their front step look immaculate. I was laughing with Jason Manford recently about mums who will put on a tabard in the morning, and they're not even a cleaner! You know, in their housecoats to clean, but it's that pride, I mean that lovely working-class pride. I remember one time we were filming and the things that locals used to do to get extra money was brilliant. Once there was this burglar alarm going off where we were filming and some of the crew went round to the house because it was disturbing filming, and they were doing it on purpose and they said, 'Fifty quid and I'll turn it off.' They were doing it on purpose. And another one was where they'd set a shed on fire for the same thing.
>
> – John Thomson[13]

Film sets being used as an alternative way to make money would become a bit of a trend. When *East is East* was being filmed in North Manchester the set would often be a source for light fingers. I was sat in the Prince of Wales when two lads came in trying to sell a boom mic from the set; with no buyers forthcoming it was soon reinvented as a pool cue.

If there was one minor criticism I would say about *The Royle Family* is that it didn't represent the different cultures I lived amongst. Not everyone that came through my front door was the same colour or creed. The more multi-cultural side of Manchester could be found in the 1999 film *East in East*. Set in 1971, this adaptation of Ayub Khan Din's biographical stage play was the first time an Asian family had been the focus of a feature film set in

Manchester (Salford). This story about a Pakistani Muslim father, George Khan, increasingly alienated from his children and quarrelling with his white British-born wife over how the family should live. It is a clash of cultures, and depicts the problems that first-generation Asian British people faced but also how families negotiate problems, regardless of their race. This is important because it demonstrated similarities between people and families regardless of their racial and religious differences. There is little to differentiate a George Khan and a Jim Royle – both are fathers that are the source of ridicule for the family they are head of, and in the same way *The Royle Family* did, *East is East* relies on comedy to tell a complex story but is wrapped up with the same moments of tenderness and affection between the characters. The film is rightly celebrated for its portrayal of Asian culture, but it is as Mancunian a film as it is British Asian.

> I was influenced by the bitter-sweet northern films of the 1960s, like *A Taste of Honey*, *Spring and Port Wine* and *This Sporting Life*. Although people try and marginalise films like *East is East* as 'Asian', for me it has always been a northern comedy in tradition.[14]

In total, *East is East* lifted seven awards, including Best British Film at the BAFTA Awards and the Best Comedy Film at the British Comedy Awards. Although more people from diverse backgrounds were getting represented on screen, the storylines they were being given would often centre around restrictive themes. To audiences it seemed people from minority backgrounds could only ever lead lives within the confines of their culture, and not fall foul of the same everyday problems the majority of British people do.

> It's become like a bit of a stereotype. Genuinely, when I was growing up, it was at the stage where if there was an Asian person on TV, you'd call your mom and say, 'Look, there's an Asian person on TV.' It was that weird. We had our own TV show called *Network East* that was on

BBC 2 and there was a couple of other shows like that, like daytime magazine shows for Asian people, but that's it – you could count them on one hand. And then it got to a stage where there started to be more Asians, but it was always like any storyline or anything about them was always about them being Asian. We didn't have a normal storyline, there wasn't a case of they were moving into the Queen Vic, or they were just moving into the street. It was always like they've got an Asian angle, like the dad won't let them go out, etc. Like an Asian person's life problems could only stem from their race or religion.

– Nooruddean Choudry[15]

Along with the people of colour being pigeonholed on screen, northern stereotypes have also long been a problem for our actors, artists, and comedians. Following on from the strong line-up of comics that came out of Greater Manchester in the early nineties, the end of the decade saw an equally hilarious comedic troupe arrive, from Peter Kay to Chris Addison to Justin Moorhouse.

So in comedy, you've always got a class, like in school you're like your year group. Caroline Aherne, Steve Coogan, and John Thomson were like the sixth formers and we were like fourth year. And she's come from where we come from. She'd come from the Frog and Bucket and doing characters and things like everybody else. I mean it when I say that everybody on the circuit loved her and she had all the time in the world for everybody. So my year was me, Alan Carr, Mick Ferry, John Bishop, and Jason Manford, and other people as well. We used to go to the Frog on a Monday every single week, we would get up and do an Open Mic night. And we used to get paid a fiver, and that fiver would get your packet of fags. So it was like, it was worth doing. It was great but my Mum couldn't get her head around it, some nights I wouldn't get paid when I would perform outside of Manchester, but that's the legwork that you have to do. The circuit had a very tight thing going on and then it was like little competitions you could do for the BBC and *CityLife* which I entered and I won that. And what came at a really good time for me was that The Comedy Store opened [in 2000]. I think suddenly it made comedy legitimate in many ways. The Frog

> and Bucket did, and still does, market itself as the home of original comedy but The Comedy Store came in and it was a bit more sleek and a bit more polish, but then it had that history as well. Everybody knows the history of The Comedy Store, so it was really good for giving us different opportunities.
>
> –Justin Moorhouse[16]

Many Northern artists will have fallen foul of the problematic prefix attached to their chosen medium. One is not simply a creative, one is a *Mancunian* creative. If you live north of Birmingham you are not just a comedian, you are a *Northern* comedian. Your reputation precedes you based on your place of origin.

> So Northern Comedian is the thing, rather than Mancunian, and I would get lumped in with Peter Kay all the time, which was, you know, fine, but it's kind of, it's a lazy, easy way to describe you, isn't it? I never see any London comedians described as a London comedian. It's almost like we have to wear a badge, and it's not even a badge of pride 'cause they're putting the badge on you, like saying this is your box, stay in your box. I definitely felt like, and I still feel like, in comedy there's still a prejudice for someone who's from the North or lives in Manchester who didn't go to Oxford or Cambridge, I don't know, it doesn't make any sense. I think my subject matter and the things I talk about is the same as everybody else from anywhere would talk about. I don't live in a cold-water flat, I mean this isn't Kes! But that's what they think, and if I'm being honest, when I was younger, naive, and inexperienced, I would play on that, you know, and do jokes about Greggs and unmarried mothers and I look back now, not with regret because you can't, but I can see how I've developed. We can't just blame everybody else all the time, you know, do you think that's because we do benefit from this idea of what the Mancunian stereotype or the northern kind of thing is? It does give us some identity and it does give us a leg up, sometimes straight away. Me, certainly for my voiceover work, I'm Northern. I don't mind that they're looking for a northern voice. I'll take that. There is a benefit to it.
>
> –Justin Moorhouse[17]

There is a definite benefit to having a strong Northern stereotype; it does give you a pedestal. There is a presumed brand of what a Mancunian/Northern artist is, despite the output often being universal. If you look at a lot of our successful artists and actors they have leaned on their Mancunian, or Northernness, as a way to get a foothold in the game at some point in their career. It's a paradox where you have to dip your toe in the pigeonhole, but it can become parody if not done delicately. This approach was used by many of the artists that came to prominence at the end of the century. In *The Royle Family*, Caroline Aherne gives the audience a relatable family but uses the trope to film in a ground-breaking style. She gives you the recognisable to do something unexpected. Female comics were seen as safe until the revolutionary Victoria Wood from Prestwich emerged. Using the device of a dim girl without a filter as a character enabled her to discuss sex, boring marriages, and ladies on the lash without seeming threatening to the male world of comedy. She accommodated the gender bias, the Northern stereotype, only to then challenge it in action, almost like a Trojan Horse. The people and characters may be of place but there is nothing inherently Mancunian/Northern in the subject matter; they discuss themes that are as relevant to the country's population as they are to a region.

> When you're doing a working-class parody, there's always a thing that you don't want to take the piss, you gotta try and make it real, like there's Paul Calfs, there's hundreds of Fat Bobs and Paulines, but there's got to be a warmth to them characters, you know? There has to be an essence of warmth and you have to be able to empathise with them, otherwise they're just grotesques. It's not enough. There's a really sweet scene in Paul Calf:
>
> *PAUL: Mam! I've got no pants left.*
> *MUM: Go and check in the drawer.*

> And he pulls out these big Y-fronts and says, 'I'm not wearing Dead Man's Pants.'
>
> It's really sweet, but it's very sad. The problem with London crews working, or writing, about Manchester and the North is they don't get it. I remember someone saying they were filming in Yorkshire and the London directors sent a runner to a local Co-op to get twenty Camel Lights. The women in the shop went, 'There's no call for anything like that round here.' It's those subtleties and they get missed in some shows because the performances are so heightened – if you look at something like *Shameless* it's almost like a graphic novel adaptation of Manchester. It was all comic book. Even if it's comedy, there has to be a desire to make it as truthful as possible.
>
> – John Thomson[18]

As graphic novel representations of Manchester go there was no film larger or louder that left a lasting impression of the city as much as *24 Hour Party People*. Michael Winterbottom's portrait of the Madchester scene was, for many of my generation, an introduction to the Haçienda and Factory Records for those of us that weren't there. A brilliant hyper-realised piece of cinema it was; a definitive narrative of the people and period it wasn't. But what did that matter?

> [Michael] Winterbottom and writer Frank Cottrell Boyce knowingly play fast and loose with the truth, preferring to 'print the legend'. Manchester musos will fume at the absences and the outright lies, but that's just fuel to the film's fire.[19]

What is fact and fiction in the film would only be known to those involved in the making of it, or those whose lives it depicted. As part of a young audience not au fait with the events, I took it as true depiction of what had happened when I first watched it. Even when Tony Wilson (played by Steve Coogan) breaks the fourth wall to tell the audience that his wife didn't sleep with Howard Devoto, I just presumed he was avoiding a lawsuit.

> I wasn't that excited about it, I'd had enough of the whole thing at that point. We're looking at five years after that and by then I'd moved so mentally away from that place, I didn't even have a nostalgic feeling for it. It's kind of like if you have an ex, you may have some nostalgia if it was ten years ago but certainly not one from five years ago and so I felt a bit like that. So when it came out and everyone was going to screenings and all that, I just wasn't bothered by any of it at all. So I didn't watch the film until it came out on DVD. Because I was in it, I did a bit of a filming for it because I got asked but I just wasn't that bothered about seeing it. But then watching on DVD I was like, actually this is fucking great! It is really well made and it really made me laugh. I just saw the whole thing as a comedy rather than any inkling of any truth in there whatsoever. I mean, progressively the order of how things happen in the film is about the only correct thing that happened. There's so many things that didn't, you know that bit about Rob Gretton threatening Tony Wilson over spending all that money on the table. You know, there were things that might have happened but now because of the film people are like, oh yeah, that really did happen. But it didn't, it's just a film. You know, Tony Wilson used to always be like, why let the truth get in the way of a good story? You know he was totally aware of that and loved it, and that's what the film's done. I wonder whether he was around long enough to see that that was happening. I don't know, but he certainly would have thought it was great that people take it now as fact.
>
> – Elliot Eastwick, DJ and label owner[20]

> You know my favourite thing about all that is that quote. And Tony Wilson didn't even fucking say it, it was Frank Cottrell-Boyce. But they have it on buildings and posters. It's everywhere.
>
> – Justin Moorhouse[21]

And so was born Manchester's unofficial slogan:

This is Manchester. We do things differently here.

A sentence attributed to Tony Wilson, which was written by scouser Frank Cottrell-Boyce, paraphrasing L.P. Hartley,[22] and said by actor Steve Coogan. A work of fiction that has become fact. It is EVERYWHERE in Manchester. T-shirts, posters, coffee mugs, office walls, billboards, even in my own work when I'm commissioned to write poems on the city I get asked if I can 'put in the Tony Wilson quote'.

The film *24 Hour Party People* breathed new life into all things Factory Records, Haçienda, and the Madchester scene. I'm not downplaying the significance of the musicians or people, but I do wonder if we would have seen the commodification of their work on such a level had it not been for the success of the film amplifying their work. Regardless of how factually correct the film is, it certainly shone a spotlight on the period for my generation. Another screen representation of Manchester resulted in a large migration of people that would move to the city after seeing how liberating life could be for those whose sexuality may not have been accepted in other UK cities.

Originally titled *Queer as Fuck* (which to my ears sounds more Mancunian), the landmark *Queer as Folk*, created by Russell T. Davies, celebrated Manchester's burgeoning Gay Village and homosexuality in a way that hadn't been seen on British TV before. It still remains the high point of representation of what LGBTQ+ life is like.

> Twenty years on, *Queer as Folk* remains a more radical and fearless tribute to gay life than many LGBT+ shows today … In 1999, the gay community was still reeling from the Aids crisis while continuing to navigate a hostile press. To many, gay sex was still synonymised with death, secrecy and shame. Yet Davies highlighted how important sex can be to both gay and urban male identities without shying away from when this can verge on unhealthy dependency. Twenty

years on, the fact that gay sex remains a taboo within the mainstream – with films like *Bohemian Rhapsody* and *Call Me By Your Name* facing criticism for 'airbrushing' it from the screen – only reinforces the show's path-breaker status. Even the use of the word 'queer' – originally an insult that, at this point, had not been fully reclaimed by the LGBT+ community in the way it has now – was bold and confronting.[23]

If you watch some of the scenes in *Queer as Folk*, there's some of them are pretty fucking graphic, yeah. They really do go for it in terms of gay sex, don't they? It put Manchester on the map, it made people realise that there were loads of gay people going out and living their best lives and enjoying themselves, and being totally unapologetic about it, and just you know, being fabulous and partying and having relationships and just getting on with it really, so it did make people a lot more aware about how gay people live their day-to-day lives, absolutely.

– Emma Goswell[24]

The emergence of Manchester's Gay Village at the turn of the millennium is one of the most culturally significant moments in the city's history. It represents our principles of liberation, diversity, and acceptance; that this is a place where people can live how they want. When *Queer as Folk* appeared on the screen it was a beacon to those LGBTQ+ people that felt alienated outside of the city. The influence would also see people moving from other gay communities to Manchester, because if you were LGBTQ+ this was the place to be.

Somebody needs to do a survey about how many people moved to Manchester because of *Queer as Folk* because it will be substantial. I mean, people were already flocking to Manchester because of the gay scene, because I've spoken to umpteen LGBT people from places like Blackpool, Lancashire, Cumbria, all over, who moved to Manchester because they didn't feel safe in their communities.

> They didn't feel welcomed by their own families even in the eighties or early nineties. It wasn't safe for them. They moved to a big city where they could sort of vanish, and they knew that there was a gay scene so that was already happening, and that already happens in all big cities. But *Queer as Folk* made it absolutely explode. People then started moving from London as well because, you know, Canal Street and the Gay Village was seen as even better than Soho. And that's where everyone wanted to be. It just looks so beautiful, doesn't it, like a party street by a river, on a sunny day, you could think you're somewhere really glamorous and not in actually what was once a really downtrodden, cheap, disused area of warehouses. *Queer as Folk* absolutely was responsible for people upping sticks and moving to Manchester, without a shadow of a doubt.
>
> – Emma Goswell[25]

Despite it being on TV didn't mean that it was as easily accessible for those who hadn't come out to watch, particularly if they still lived with their parents.

> There was still a lot of homophobia around, so there was still a lot of parents turning it off going, 'That's disgusting. Queers and gay men, they shouldn't be shown on television.' So there's still a lot of that going on. A lot of gay people who actually watched it in private or tried to secretly record it, 'cause in those days there was no OnDemand. If you didn't record it on your VHS and you couldn't watch it on the night, you missed it, didn't you? If you had unsupportive parents living at home, then you were fucked, or not. I think it's a mixture of making it more accepting, but also there was still a lot of homophobia around it.
>
> – Emma Goswell[26]

Some commentators felt that the characters in *Queer as Folk* embellished the lifestyle too heavily, whilst to others it was a perfect representation of what being gay in Manchester was really like.

> In this wonderful world, gaggles of glamorous gay men jump from party to party and bed to bed, barely stopping long enough to check their mascara and bulging bank balances. The packed bars of Soho and Canal Street may suggest otherwise but many gay men have moved beyond the ghetto and its enforced 'gay straitjacket' lifestyle. For us, the characters in *Queer as Folk* are little more than a comical reminder of the superficial lifestyle we left behind years ago. It makes you yearn for the 1980s and Brookside's Gay Gordon or Cuddly Colin of EastEnders, characters who, for all their exaggerated earnestness, at least had a role in the shows which went beyond their homosexuality.[27]

> It's still my favourite TV show to this day. I went to Shena Simon College when I was eighteen and their Performing Arts College is in the Gay Village and they were filming on site when I was there, and that was around the time I was about to come out and I was actually dating a girl at the time – and my mum is like, what are you doing, you're gay! – and I was like, I can't tell her as she'll be heartbroken but when I finally did, she said, 'It's fine, I'm gay too!' And I never guessed, like she's a really pretty lipstick lesbian – I never thought she would be gay, but we were both obviously drawn to *Queer as Folk* during that period. I've probably binge watched that series about, gosh, ten times at least. I still absolutely love it. I love the writing. I thought it was ground-breaking, I just thought it was brilliant. It was kind of a true depiction of what it was like being a gay man going out in Manchester at the time, getting drunk, drugs, threesomes, all that kind of thing. It was a brilliant show.
>
> – Kurtis-Lee Spittle, author's friend[28]

How Manchester was now being represented on screen was the beginning in shattering the stereotypes. The success of the TV and films of the time demonstrated that there is no archetypal Mancunian, and further still, that audiences were interested in storylines showcasing the multitudes that make up the population. The series *Cold Feet* was the most indicative of the direction Manchester was moving towards. A future of aspiration and affluence;

an ambition that was shared by both the city's football clubs who were also facing times of transition. This was when players went from cult heroes to front-page superstars, where decisions made in boardrooms would dictate the running of the clubs twenty years later.

8

'Proper Manc'

IDENTITY

> Maybe we blame Tony Warren, maybe we blame Lowry, maybe we blame some of the other Northern creatives, maybe there's an element of some truth in it, but it won't be *all* the truth, will it? And that's the point. Those people that try to put a through line in Mancunians should really recognise that they can't do that. There isn't one.
>
> – Jay Taylor[1]

If you spend any time in Manchester, you will hear the term 'Proper Manc', a label attributed to those Mancunians who have the personality traits of what it means to be from the city. The parameters which make up these traits are as easy to grasp as cigarette smoke. It is elusive. When you look at the stereotypes across the UK, there are stronger social categorisations made about people from northern cities than you would find placed on those that live in the south. Whether you are a Mancunian or a Scouser, if you live in Newcastle or Sheffield, your personality has perceived characteristics. Our cities' people are over-simplified to tropes and don't benefit from London's nuance, despite the diversity that exists in these places.

> Manchester certainly has got an identity that seems apart from other places. I think most places would argue that Sheffield's got its own identity, Birmingham has, Glasgow has, Cardiff has. I think those things all have identity. I've been quite lucky that my job, be it performing or

putting gigs on, has allowed me to travel around and places do have a sense of identity, some stronger than others. And that's brilliant, isn't it? When you think about how close those towns and cities are next to each other. You think how different Liverpool's sense of identity is compared to Manchester. You could drive from one to the other in less than an hour. They're really defined. And I just think that's positive because it adds an interesting dimension to the United Kingdom. The damage is that some of those things that are important and add a real diverse flavour to the city don't get scrutinised or supported as much as others. You know it made me think of how the Bayeux Tapestry isn't a true representation of that battle, but a representation of who made that tapestry's idea of what happened in that battle.

– Jay Taylor[2]

Researchers in *Psychological Science* write that 'the process of repeatedly passing social information from person to person can result in the unintentional and spontaneous formation of cultural stereotypes'.[3] But which information gets passed, how is it delivered, and how is it received? Manchester's cultural exports have been so successful and convincing that they have become factual portrayals rather than a fragment of a bigger picture. This impact of mistaken identity through mass media can be traced back to 1960s Weatherfield. Northern stereotypes go back to the Industrial Revolution and beyond, but nothing planted the impression of what life was like in Manchester on the nation's psyche as much as *Coronation Street*, a soap opera, set in Salford. When the revolutionary show began it was almost immediately met with backlash from the locals it represented. Outsiders from the city would flock to Archie Street (where it was originally filmed) to see the Manchester they were being shown on screen.

Though Corrie was supposed to capture the real lives of working-class people across industrial northern towns of the 1960s, its residents insisted they would never dare do certain things that happened on

> the show – they would never leave dirty milk bottles on doorsteps nor would they go outside wearing curling pins in their hair …[4]

The fictionalised lives, exaggerated characters, and embellished storylines for the following three decades were the outsider's portal into Manchester. The rise of gang culture and the use of recreational drugs in the nineties was more fuel to the 'Grim Up North' narrative. The city had produced multiple iconic bands with charismatic singers, but they were more cult figures than figureheads. Nothing, and no one, shone a light on what Mancunians were perceived to be like in the same way as *Coronation Street*; then, a lad from Burnage simian-strolled his way onto centre stage.

When Oasis became headline news, Liam Gallagher found himself on a pedestal as the archetypal Mancunian. His mannerisms, attitude, behaviour, and clothes were all considered totemic to Manchester. He was a 'Proper Manc'.

> They were just doing their own thing. I don't think it ever crossed their minds about carrying Manchester or a Mancunian identity, they were just part of the same timeline as Joy Division and Stone Roses. I don't think they ever considered any reputation of the city or their expectations. Aside from Bone they all left by '96/'97 because they couldn't walk down the street and it was almost impossible for them to live in Manchester. They'd either get someone trying to fight them – to prove they'd battered Liam Gallagher – or it was suffocating. Whereas in London they could just do what they wanted. Like our kid [Paul McGuigan] still gets it now, he used to just want to stay in for a takeaway when he came back, but we decided to go out and a seventeen-year-old in a restaurant asked his mum to approach us for a photo. He doesn't even look like the same person as he did in 1997 – like how do these people recognise him?
>
> – Mary McGuigan[5]

If his image as the representation of a city wasn't intentional, Liam Gallagher did become synonymous with being Mancunian. But which part is Manc? Which attributes of his are solely from this city and can't be found elsewhere? If we consider the confidence, that simian stroll and swagger, is that particularly from this place, or is that not the hallmark of a rockstar?

> It could be an attitude thing, but I think there's an attitude in some people from every society. You can say, 'He's a Proper Manc', but then you can go down to somewhere like Yorkshire. And then they go, 'He's Proper Yorkshire', and they've got the same sort of get-up-and-go attitude and are very confident.
>
> – Stan Chow[6]

> Not everybody is the same, but there are tropes and there are stereotypes and there are elements of character about people who are brought up around here. If you're told all the time that you're great, you start to believe it, and I think we do carry that around with us. And I do think that we need to be wary about having that arrogance. Confidence is a Mancunian trait, and I'll give you an example. Mancunians can't ask you a question without answering it. 'You been on holiday, yeah?' 'Have you had your dinner, no?' 'How are you, alright?' Give me a bleeding chance to answer!
>
> – Justin Moorhouse[7]

So, if it's not Liam Gallagher's confidence that is a solely Mancunian trait, is it the accent? Is his South Manchester twang 'Proper Manc'? And if so, what does that say for the rest of the city that talks with a different accent? Are they then pidgin Mancs?

> That would probably involve the whole Manchester area being classed as one single accent. But we know there's more. So what if I say there are ten in Greater Manchester? Then someone would point out that people in one part of Oldham speak differently from people in another. And they'd be right. Then what about Caribbean Mancunian, or Asian Mancunian? Or posh Mancunian?
>
> – Dr Rob Drummond, linguist[8]

> I've been sold the cliche, you know. When I was younger, I don't think the 'Proper Manc' thing even existed. It is definitely something that was propagated by the whole Manchester and Oasis thing. I mean it's kind of that South Manchester Irish thing, probably the best way to describe it. All those cliches do exist. You go out into town and you expect to see normal people. But then you'd see someone who's a little bit more gregarious than others. And who does the kind of monkey walk. But saying that, would I even consider them a Proper Manc, if they're the exception? I don't think you can really prescribe Proper Manc as being an actual thing.
>
> – Stan Chow[9]

Stan is correct. It doesn't exist. The more you unpack the identity of what a 'Proper Manc' is supposed to be, the more it becomes apparent that it draws influence and heritage from elsewhere. The haircuts are nods to the London mod scene, the parka coats are a Caribou Inuit creation, and the vocal style leans on John Lennon. It is an identity built upon influences and heritage from elsewhere. More Mancinstein than Mancunian. Could that not be said for all Mancunians? The irony in all of this is that we're not talking about Liam Gallagher; we're talking about the media's portrayal of who Liam Gallagher was. And they are two very different people.

> The press had an awful lot to do with Oasis's image and reputation. They found something and they held onto it and they were not going to let it go. They weren't angels by any stretch of the imagination and certainly at the beginning – 'cause they've been gigging for ever, like every day they get in the van. They drive down to London. They play the gig. They get back in the van. They drive back to Manchester because they were going to Newcastle the next morning, they work their arse off every single week. So they got signed and they got a bit of money, and suddenly they were travelling to Hamburg or Amsterdam. They just went a bit loopy, like any lads do when they're travelling to Hamburg or Amsterdam, so they'd get pissed up and obviously that gave fuel to the fire, but when the novelty wore off I never saw any bad behaviour, a couple of times maybe, but it was

> nothing other than I'd see my mates or people around town get up to. But the press used to set them up and this is what never, ever gets mentioned. Liam told me once that he hadn't done anything bad for a while and the press were getting bored of him so they used to ring his doorbell at 3am to wind him up and get him swearing at his front door and take photographs – who wouldn't react like that? Then there was one time he was walking down the street and someone jumped out from behind a bush and punched him in the face and there just so happened to be a cameraman across the road at the exact same time as Liam punched him back. The next day, it was all in the papers that Liam attacked someone in the street, but they didn't know, or print, the circumstances. But everyone was like, 'Oh, he's a dickhead', and I would get loads of abuse because I'd say I love Liam, he's such a sound guy. I think my description has always been excited Labrador puppy. He's very excited. He's always happy to see you, and he's got so much emotion. It's just he's like a Labrador puppy and nobody would believe me and nobody would get it. Even my Mum, my Mother loves Liam, too, because he's always been a very sweet boy. You know, he's always been very respectful. The public's view of him now has started to change. They would just sort of loosen it until, I'd say, the last couple of years or so. Suddenly people that I've not spoken to for years are sending text messages and saying, 'I now totally get it.' They don't like Noel now.
>
> – Mary McGuigan[10]

There has been a definite shift in how Liam Gallagher is seen today compared with the media representation when Oasis were in their pomp; social media has allowed him to control how his image is portrayed rather than it coming from sensationalist headlines and a manipulative press.

> I guess at the beginning they were having a ball and being dickheads, but also, at the beginning, no publicity was bad publicity. Then everyone knew their name – I think Alan McGee was loving all of that and I'm not sure Marcus Russell was quite as keen on some of it because he was having to do the press releases. Well, Alan could just kind of

> glory in it. The press fuelled their identity as bad boys [and as such enlarged the stereotype]. That whole Blur and Oasis thing – you know, this is what London is like, we're all pretty art students that behave ourselves, and this is what Manchester is like, we're all thugs – I always found it just ridiculous. The press did all sorts of stunts with Liam. They locked him in his house and stuff, just being dickheads. It's like poking a bear in a cage and that bear would roar – he's a bit older now and a bit older, more sensible, so you'd have to poke him for longer.
>
> – Mary McGuigan[11]

The cultural impact of Oasis on the young people of Manchester was immeasurable. The band had been toiling away for years but when they blew up it felt like overnight kids had gone from not knowing who they were to wearing Burberry shirts, saying 'madferit' and growing their barnets out. It was as though the press had held a mirror up to us and we fell in line with the uniform.

> The media that exists outside of Manchester gets thrown back at us, and it becomes amplified again. So just the very simple tropes, the simple myths, get amplified over and over again. So that sometimes the people involved in Manchester, instead of putting a stop to it and saying, 'It's not like that', just go along with it.
>
> – Jay Taylor[12]

> I mean it's a bit of a weird analogy, but there's a similar thing with elegant Parisian women. Okay, they're always told there's this notion, you can buy books, *How to Think and Dress like a Parisian Woman*, because they are held up as being some kind of model for womanhood. And in my mind's eye I can kind of see the look, you know. And so the Parisian women, there's a lot of them who are quite happy to buy into that image because it's all around them and it's being talked about and it's real in some ways, and there's plenty of others who spend their whole lives fighting against that. I spent a few months hanging out with a bunch of Parisian lesbians, you know? And this is in 2016, I lived in Paris for a bit, and they were always shaking their heads about the image of French womanhood

> as seen and represented by this myth around the elegant 'Parisian Woman'. It's almost like an off-the-peg identity. You know, so instead of having a made-to-fit suit that actually works for you, and the contours of your body, you walk in somewhere and you just pick a suit off the rack and that will do. Whole identities are created like that, human beings maybe don't want to explore other options for their identity so the most obvious is the one they'll pick, and it probably makes life a hell of a lot simpler.
>
> – Dave Haslam[13]

> When I won the Mercury Prize, I went up and made the dumbest speech of all time, talking about good things that happen to good people, referring to myself. Stuff I regret saying to this day, and throwing the cheque away and all that nonsense. I suppose that I had this, I think a lot of us suffered at the time in the nineties in the Manchester thing, I was doing my best to survive in the media world. So I kind of thought I had to be this version of a mild-mannered Liam Gallagher. I don't mind admitting it. I've never really talked about this, but nobody gave you lessons in how to behave, you know, and I think they do nowadays.
>
> – Badly Drawn Boy[14]

It's understandable why Damon would feel the need to try and fulfil an expectation of how a Mancunian singer is supposed to act. His mannerisms were a slip through nerves on a stage he didn't expect to find himself on. He was far from alone; many of us were aping the Manc in the mirror being held up to us and living vicariously through the Gallagher brothers. I always found it a bit strange when blokes of a certain age try to look and act like people younger than them. It's normal for teenagers to mimic their idols, but it is a bit weird when you're over thirty and asking a five-bob barber to give you a feather cut. It wasn't just Mancs trying on this new image, people from across the UK were doing the same thing, famously lampooned by comedian Harry Enfield.

> Yeah, again it's that Northern thing – they do it to Scousers as well. We all have a laugh and stuff like the Harry Enfield thing. I think that was more piss-take of Southerners who were trying to be Mancunians because of the success of Oasis. There's a lot of people, who I knew, who went to public school in Cheshire, or they were from Birmingham or wherever, and everybody was trying to be from Manchester. That was a quite a pivotal time around '96, because Oasis were *the* band, the cooler, edgier band – everybody wanted to be more like them than Damon Albarn, because [Blur] were known as the posh band – which is just ridiculous now, when you think about it. It was the press doing that thing where they're pitting people against each other. I'm sure it was somebody like Richard and Judy who lived in Manchester, whose kids were really well spoken but then went to school and started talking with pretend Manc accents, because that was seen as cool. I think that's what that Harry Enfield take was. They went to Manchester for the weekend and Kevin and Perry came back like Liam Gallagher because they thought that was dead cool.
>
> – Natalie-Eve Williams[15]

This 'trying on' a perceived Mancunian outfit wasn't a new phenomenon and typifies the strength of the media's portrayal of the city and its culture.

> I did an interview the other day with a kid who's doing a degree at, whatever it's called, the Fashion College in London. I think his thesis was on dance music in the early nineties. He had this idea that everybody in the Haçienda wore a bucket hat, a long-sleeved T-shirt and some flowers and a pair of Kickers, and that the club was full of that person, and it wasn't at all. You know, you had people in fetishwear, there were people with dreads. There were people in waistcoats and so many weird and wonderful outfits, but what happens is that one image does the rounds and becomes the representation of what everyone dressed like and then people buy into that image. You see it now with kids wearing bucket hats and stuff.
>
> – Elliot Eastwick[16]

This so-called 'Proper Manc', I think, is a caricature of Oasis – so I always say some people are Mancunian by pure accident of birth, I chose to become one, and I think Mancunian is more of an attitude, a go-do-it attitude. And to be honest, you've got to be really, really careful, if you start saying what's a 'Proper Manc'. It's about celebrating our mixture, that openness. It's celebrating radical thought, that's Mancunian. Manchester has always been a welcoming city, and Manchester started with nothing, and actually it was built on immigrants from the UK and overseas. Go into the old Town Hall, you see on the ceiling the flags of all the nations we used to trade with. Look at the roads, Poland Street, Dantzic Street. Look at the buildings, Asia House, Rhodesia House. Trade is impregnated into our city. It's a city that's always been welcoming.

– Tom Bloxham[17]

To me it was more a case of being Asian made me feel more Manc – because growing up I did not feel English, and I don't identify as being English or British, I always thought of myself as being Manc rather than English. And it was little things like I remember going to the cricket when I was pretty young with a mate and it was England versus Pakistan and I think we were sat in with the England fans – 'cause that's where we could get tickets – and like we'd not done anything to sort of show we were supporting Pakistan or anything. But loads of blokes, like grown-up men, started pointing at us and chanting, 'You've never had an Empire!' And like this is to us, as kids, and it's like, 'What the fuck?!' It wasn't even a case of they were hooligans and they were gonna beat us up or anything. They were kind of doing it for banter. But to us it was just so weird that they thought, oh, these two Asian lads over there. Let's start chanting to them, 'You never had an Empire!' But I never felt that in Manchester because everyone seemed from everywhere. Like my Dad had a shop in the precinct and it was such a community feeling like he'd have friends or regular customers that would just come in and sit down and have a chat for a few hours. He had Jewish mates, he had Irish mates, he had Italian mates that would come in … again it's that sort of feeling as if Manchester is a community of

> people who are all different but still belong to the same community, like you're all Mancs. And that's really nice.
>
> – Nooruddean Choudry[18]

When there is a robust presumed identity of how a population is supposed to look it can be dangerous and a source of fuel for racism.

> What's weird is that I'd say in the eighties I got a lot of shit. I got a lot of 'slitty-eyed' bullshit, literally on the street – then it just kind of disappeared. Then, when I would come into the city centre in the mid-nineties, it was virtually non-existent. With my colour, for the first time actually, when I moved into the city centre, I didn't feel I was different. I felt like I was just part of everyone else I was hanging out with. It just didn't really matter who I was. It wasn't until Brexit that I experienced racism again. The day after Brexit, it was literally carte blanche, like I'd not had any kind of any racial shit all throughout the nineties and 2000s, until 2016. The day after Brexit I was crossing the road and a van driver decided to just pull up next to me and stop and do a racist Chinese accent. What the fuck is that about? And that evening I was DJing at the Mint Lounge on Oldham Street and I come out for a quick cig break and a group of girls come up and I thought they were going to ask what time it was, or for a lighter, and one goes, 'Wax on, wax off'. And I was like what the fuck is that? It was such an eye-opening experience. I knew this was gonna happen but I didn't really expect it so soon. It felt like a lot of people were just holding it all in for twenty-odd years and then when Brexit happened it was like people went, 'Shit, we can be fucking racists again now!' I always thought we lived in a society where there are racists around but at least they will be surpassed by society as a whole. I was never living in a kind of a sugar-coated, rose-tinted world of 'no one's racist anymore'. There were always pockets of tensions in areas where you were instinctively aware of it, but I guess with Brexit it allowed them, empowered them. But amongst my friends, amongst the people I know, especially the whole Northern Quarter area, during that time it just didn't exist.
>
> – Stan Chow[19]

> I think growing up we were used to seeing our parents be dead meek and deferential because they'd come here from somewhere else. They were used to it. They accepted racism, like they came over here and were just told 'people don't like us' and they just accepted that and that became a normal thing to them, but it also meant that they had to be a bit meek if they did face it, to just ignore it or sort of just let it happen. But our generation was different. We were more like, 'Why the fuck should we take it? We were born here and we speak like everyone else. Why should we be ashamed of who we are?' So we wouldn't cower away from it.
>
> – Nooruddean Choudry[20]

Different ethnicities have gone unrepresented in Manchester, as have the different classes. Sociologists at the University of Manchester found that Mancunians are 'more working class' than the rest of Britain.[21] This is a source of pride for the city, and, given our successes, it typifies the underdog spirit with which we often like to associate ourselves – yet coming from a working-class background and how we speak has been a hurdle.

> I think it's a working-class thing, a lot of where that comes from. I think we always feel like we have to prove ourselves a little bit more. Everything now has changed, thank God, there's a load more stuff happening up north, but even when I was like a teenager, there was still very much that mentality of 'thick northerners' and 'It's grim up north', if you went on telly or on radio (with a couple of exceptions) with an accent like ours. I heard it when I first did Manchester music. I did an interview with, I think it was Rick from the Space Monkeys – he'd done his top five Manchester tunes and he'd put up a link on his Facebook, and somebody had put, 'Oh my God, where did you get them then? Where did you get them two from?' Because we weren't BBC. We weren't talking 'properly'. I remember somebody phoning Alan Beswick about our accents. And he told them, 'It's about Manchester music. They're not newsreaders … that's how they talk. They've got Manchester accents. They're from Manchester!' For a long time, it was like you were 'common', or you were made to feel

> ashamed, people speaking down to you because of your accent. Now, half the time it's easier to kind of play up to that, because that's what people expect.
>
> – Natalie-Eve Williams[22]

Mancunians' strong working-class identity has also come at the expense of how we under-represent and under-celebrate different classes. A person's wealth shouldn't separate their identity as being Mancunian in the same way you wouldn't do it because of colour or creed. Yet there seems to be a problem with celebrating that a lot of Manchester's success stories have come from affluent and middle-class people such as Emmeline Pankhurst, L.S. Lowry, Tony Wilson, and Elizabeth Gaskell.

> I've always had an irrational chip on my shoulder about middle-class people. I think part of it is maybe for me because I went to the grammar school and I didn't feel part of it at all. Like I will slag off middle-class people, but then I think some of my favourite politicians are middle class. Like Tony Benn was sort of upper middle class, and Jeremy Corbyn, he's not a working-class hero, he's from an affluent sort of family and he's proper middle class, so it's funny that there's this ingrained attitude about not liking anyone from a class that isn't yours. Like every middle-class person I've met has been properly sound and lovely, so it's mismatched but it is always there.
>
> – Nooruddean Choudry[23]

Toxic masculinity

> Toxic masculinity is what can come of teaching boys that they can't express emotion openly; that they have to be 'tough all the time'; that anything other than that makes them 'feminine' or weak'.[24]

The part of the presumed 'Proper Manc' stereotype I struggled with most was how you were supposed to behave as a young man.

> I do like to think about the idea of toxic masculinity in notions of the North. Going back 150 years or more, it's often this symbol of the working man, the man in the factory, the miner, that's the symbol – obviously a lot of the mill workers were women, but I think that kind of 'Strong Manchester' identity is because the industrial past of the city is caught up with the idea of the male factory worker and then you ally that to football. And you basically get definitions of Manchester going back decades where women have been marginalised. So strong masculinities always been an important part of the image, and that goes right across the North. The post-industrialisation of Britain that began to happen at the end of the sixties and was accelerated by Thatcher has meant that a lot of people haven't had those symbols. You know, the manufacturing industries get taken away, and not only are you taking away opportunity, but you're also taking away the identity of the worker going to work. And that actually is the crisis of Northern masculinity. So it's almost like, what is it we do and why? Why are we here? What's our *raison d'être*?
>
> – Dave Haslam[25]

How do you become a man? What is a man? Why am I here? What am I supposed to do? How am I meant to behave? I never sought answers to these questions at home; I didn't find answers in school. To become a man in Manchester was to learn on the job; through trial and error, drink and drugs, fights and fun; by following in the footsteps of those that had gone before me.

The Farmers Arms was a testosterone-fuelled, foul-mouthed community centre where people didn't speak to one another but would shout over each other to win a debate. Everything competed. How much you could handle your drink, how you dressed, the team you supported, how good you were at pool or cards, the music you put on the jukebox, your taste in women; every aspect of your personality was up for ridicule. If you were the target for the abuse, you either had to retort quickly or accept that a salmon-coloured shirt on a Tuesday night was a little excessive. Aside from the bravado, it was more than just a place to get pissed with your mates. It was what urban sociologist Ray Oldenburg calls the 'third place'. Somewhere outside of work and home where we exchange ideas, socially interact, build relationships, and find our sense of place in the world. I was a regular before I was eighteen. The Farmers gave me a sense of place in a city that didn't care who I was nor what I wanted to do; I have never felt more at home in Manchester than with those people, in that pub, at any other point in my life. As the oldest sibling, I never had anyone to look up to.

The regulars in The Farmers were my dysfunctional extended family. I was a young wannabe writer with the funniest, toughest older brothers that would take the piss out of me at any given moment but would jump in to protect me whenever I was in danger. Was it hyper-masculine? Yes. Laddish? Of course, it was an environment filled with men. Did I ever consider it toxic? Not once. Where were the less poisonous surroundings? The behaviour in the local pub was a product of its time and the larger environment. The Farmers Arms wasn't an exception; it was the same culture you would find in all the pubs across the city.

> I think that we're a bit more acerbic, a bit more cutting, but the intention of the jokes is never to hurt each other's feelings. That way of interacting is just how people in the pub are – the fact that they're taking the piss is a sign of affection. They wouldn't bother if they didn't like each other. And they very rarely punch down – if you look at Eddie and Joan in *Early Doors*, they're treated quite gentle in the show, because otherwise it would be like savaging a dead sheep. But it's a bit like each person taking the piss is trying to place the ace down and outwit the other.
>
> – Phil Mealey[26]

It's more than black humour. I think it's happened to me on more than one occasion if my [southern] friends ever come up and they're settling in with us and they'll hear me and my mates from round here talking to each other and they'll go:

- *Do you not like him?*
- *Yeah.*
- *Why do you talk to each other like that?*
- *What do you mean?*
- *You're just horrible to each other.*

Me and my mates are just fucking awful, no respect for any boundaries. I remember when all this 'Yo Mama' stuff come out, but that has been us our whole lives. Taking the piss out of mums and dads and just going to the darkest places as quickly as possible. One of my favourites is where you and you mates will be having some banter and you'll be calling him all the names under the sun and mentioning the fact that he's got a withered arm and things like that and then somebody jumps in with the wrong comment and you're like, 'You what?!'

– Justin Moorhouse[27]

Being sharp and then hurting other people's feelings in the process because they don't know the culture. That's been a bit of a learning curve for me as more people move to Manchester because not everyone gets it, and I'm like, 'Oh god, no! If I'm horrible it means I care about you.' It's difficult to explain to them at times as they've not been immersed in it. I mean, it is a bit fucked up but that's how it is. I could give you the proper answer: so, a lot of the work I've done over the past few years deals with trauma and the impact of trauma, and I think that culturally speaking when you look at a lot of people's backgrounds in Manchester, there's a big Irish element. If you're not Irish, you're something else and there's these masses of immigration which is a trauma in and of itself. To be uprooted from your host culture and thrown into another culture is traumatic. I just started doing my family tree and I couldn't believe it, there wasn't anyone that did not do a dangerous job or live in a terraced house with fifteen other people, so that sort of hardness.

> Even if you look at the native white population, if you want to put it like that, most of them will have immigration in their backgrounds at some point, and even if they don't, what brought a lot of people to Manchester was the Industrial Revolution, and those guys were living in really tough conditions and I just think that to cope and get through you would have needed humour and you would have just had to put your feelings in a box and crack on with it. So I genuinely think that then becomes a culture: if your life is hard and that's how you interact with your family and your children, then that's how they're going to interact with their children, and then it moves down the generations.
>
> If I had to posit a theory, I do think that being uprooted from whatever nice bit of the countryside they were from, or if you want to add the paradigm of immigration, whichever country they were from, they were probably living in nicer conditions than Manchester during that time – and this is still the case for the kids I teach now, a lot of them are coming from middle-class West African countries to live in Beswick. That trauma doesn't give you the scope to indulge your feelings, and I think what has become particularly Mancunian is that you deal with that through a humour that is based on a wryness and a dryness. It's that acknowledgement that life is painful and shit, and the best thing you can do to deal with that reality is to laugh. And the best way you can bond with other people is to laugh with them. But the humour isn't negative despite how the outside world perceives it, it is showing that you know the other person so well but by poking fun at their weaknesses. There's an egalitarianism to it isn't there, like a 'You're no better than me, I'm no better than you.' I do think that you only tend to use it – to use educational terminology – with unconditional positive regard, so you only take the piss out of people because you love them. The obvious downside to this is then how emotions are expressed because it's usually only done in extremely unsentimental ways.
>
> – Steph Lonsdale[28]

If there is one thing I enjoy more than anything about being Mancunian, it is our innate ability to take the piss and have the piss taken out of us in equal measure; it is what I consider a pub sport. It wasn't toxic; and when I look back now, I still see the time, place, and people with the same fondness I did in my late teens. It was a belonging, and a culture, where none other existed. No one said, 'Hey, why don't you try this out instead of drinking yourself into oblivion this weekend?' I was one more domino standing in the pub, waiting to fall with the rest. At its worst, it could get violent: I've seen pubs erupt into chaos, where pint glasses were smashed into someone's face over a wrong word; where racism was used; where misogyny was rife, and women were seen as something to conquer rather than converse with. But, I hasten to add, these were the exceptions in my experience. At its best, it was a home from home. Where we learned about politics, music, and football; where we found employment (and equally lost it); where we bonded over beer and forged friendships for life. It was here where we lived, laughed, loved, and left stumbling into the night, only to return as quickly as possible to do it all over again. It was the only place we could be.

Where it would become problematic – toxic, to use the buzzword – was when it came to speaking about feelings. Through no fault of my parents, I didn't speak about emotions at home, so why would I do it anywhere else? Why would you reveal things about yourself you feared would be ridiculed? The irony is, of course, that every other man is holding their cards tight to their chest. It's all a pretence, isn't it? A form of protection. A way to fit in with the poise of the environment. A front. Men will wear the masks they think they're supposed to, which they're conditioned to, but they do talk. There are brief moments of honest communication between blokes often missed because of their brevity. Around the third pint, men's masks will slip, and whatever has been eating them up will usually be spewed out. Through a lapse in concentration or alcohol-fuelled confidence, they do seek counsel. The problem is that the friend you are confiding in is also three pints deep, with his shit going on that he can't deal with, so the solution is to talk over another drink, the fourth drink, the pint of no return. Few people go home after three, no one leaves after four.

Much later in my life, I was diagnosed with PTSD for things that happened during this period. I couldn't articulate the pain. My coping mechanism was to get off my face, confide in my mates, drink more, fight with people, get arrested, break shit, and find no solution but add more problems and compound the original. It became a self-perpetuating cycle of having a problem, drinking through it, and giving your situation some problematic company to join you when you inevitably return to the pub to drown your problems. It is incredible how quickly it can spiral out of control. It took me to the darkest corners that I managed to crawl out of by the grace of God, but it took leaving Manchester to do so. It chews me up now that I resented my parents – my Dad in particular, as he bore the brunt of my outbursts – for their inability to show me how to deal with my feelings. My Mum is an absolute rock, but I needed my Dad to show me, I thought, as he's a man. But how was he supposed to equip me with tools he didn't have? His solutions were no different from mine, and he'd learned from my well-oiled Grandad, who had from his father. I was carrying the hand-me-down woes passed on by previous generations of drinkers. We all were. I find the phrase 'man up' to be incredibly problematic, or the necessity for commentators to make out there's a weakness in discussing your mental health. I've lost many friends, who fit the archetypal image of a man, to drink, drugs, and suicide. These were 'Proper Men'; physically strong, hard-working grafters that spent their days digging the roads, working fifty-plus hours in the worst weather, and because of an insecurity about looking weak if they asked for help, it cost them their lives. I've had many friends go to prison through drunken behaviour that stemmed from their inability to process their mental state. I lost friends to addiction because what was an escape soon became a crutch, and then the crutch inevitably became a lifestyle. The aggression of the young men of the time – which I still see today – undeniably stems from their emotional state and the lack of knowledge of how to deal with it. Then you add in their environment, the unemployment, the drink, the drugs, and crime. It isn't a limitless vat we contain our feelings in; they will come out. Unfortunately, it can be in violent and tragic ways.

A history lost at sea

As has hopefully been apparent throughout the vignettes I have shared in this book, I spent my teenage years looking for an identity. A scenario we all go through. Growing up, I was white, just not the right white; I was not quite white, I was dirty white, as a friend's mother once quipped. My skin colour is like a weak cup of tea; you suspect there's more than milk in my cup; my Dad's skin is more akin to a builder's brew; it's glaringly apparent there has been some genetic alchemy in his mug. Then there is our hair. Jet black, straight as a short back and sides, but if it grows beyond an inch, it turns into this unruly hedge that only half a tub of the local chemist's wet gel will keep down. My Dad's hair becomes tight, thick black curls splashing back against his skull; mine emerges as loose ringlets that drop where they please. Yet I was told I was white, and my Dad was the darkest white man I knew. But that wasn't what other people saw. Mates called me a Jew, a Mexican, Peruvian, Bosnian, and a list of derogatory names meant as friendly fire; my sister was often called Pocahontas; my brother received the same sort of comments as me, and on far too many occasions I've heard my Dad called racist names to which he never replied, or rose to, because 'they were having a laugh'. Then when I was nineteen, the past came out. I got a phone call from my Mum asking me when I'd be back as they needed to talk. When I got home, it transpired that a drunken great auntie had told my sister at a BBQ that our Grandad wasn't our real Grandad – he is, and always will be: my love for that man is tighter than a DNA strand – but now I had more questions than answers.

My Nana Scott passed away when I began writing this book, but I was fortunate to speak to her about what had happened. In 1961, my Dad was born in Longsight, Manchester. A few months later, his biological father would leave the new mother and baby to join the Merchant Navy. The story as she told it was that he couldn't live in Manchester any more for the trouble he got into because of how he looked. His dark skin and black hair were targets for physical and verbal abuse. I can still hear the words she used to describe him from the bed she passed away in: 'He was so beautiful, David.' But the bullying got too much, 'everyone was jealous of his looks', and off he went. What sort of decisions go through a man's head where that becomes the option you take – to leave your new son and his mother? During his time in the Merchant Navy, he didn't fare any better, with the discrimination following him to sea. With no way to escape onboard a ship, he hit the bottle and began hitting back at those attacking him. He was dishonourably discharged and forced to leave the Navy because he stuck up for himself. Following this, he pursued work in the private boating industry to become a yachtsman on Peter Sellers' 'Amelfis'. He spent the sixties sailing around the Mediterranean with Sellers and his many famous guests, such as Britt Ekland and Ringo Starr. By the time he returned to British shores, my Nana had found my Grandad and our knowledge of him remained a mystery until many decades later.

My biological Grandad wasn't white. Within a generation on either side of my parents, my entire heritage is from elsewhere, from different countries, cultures, and continents. My bloodline is an amalgamation of migrant stories. How fitting, then, that I should live in this city? Is that not to be a Proper Mancunian?

I appreciate this now. The news at the time sent an already fragile head west. I had already been rattling around like an empty bottle on a night bus, trying to find out who I was. Perhaps it explains my interest in other cultures, my subconscious more in tune than the young head carrying it around. What was I, an unidentifiable other? The closest thing I've had to any distinct culture was through my Irish grandparents on my mother's side; still, my Gaelic credentials were dismissed. A friend's mother from Mayo said, 'You don't look Irish, David. You could be one of the Black Irish.' The term 'Black Irish' refers to Irish descendants with dark features, such as black hair, dark complexion, and dark eyes, and often associated with survivors of the Spanish Armada who sought refuge in Ireland. As marvellous as it would have been to have some loose lineage to the Spanish Armada, that theory falls way short of the mark; my mother's family couldn't be further from looking Spanish.

By the time I reached twenty-one, I had had enough. I didn't feel I belonged anywhere, let alone in Manchester. In this sea of life, where waves crash against us and the tide takes us to places we don't want to be, identity is the line with which we hoist ourselves for refuge. It reassures us of who we are; it is our dry land. I'd spent my formative years exhausting myself trying to find where the rope was: I couldn't find it in school, on the streets, in the pub, down the park, on the pitch, in work, nor through art. A future in this city felt as boarded up as the derelict shop fronts on Oldham Street. I was a shipwreck in an empty port. Manchester and I had nothing for each other. So that summer, I set off to Greece and didn't come back. For a bit.

9

(There is no) Conclusion

I've rewritten this conclusion countless times. The original idea was to paint the picture of what Manchester was like then and contrast it with how it is today. No matter how I try to crowbar that initial premise into a final chapter, it does not sit right with me (the publishers will have to accept it, sorry). This book is not about comparison, it is about documentation; it is a testament to the lives of those who have shared their experience of living in the city during the period we discussed. *Mancunians* is not a book about what has changed; it is about what was missed. It is a collection of voices demonstrating their existence when the city underwent a significant change. It is the writing back against the impression of how Manchester and its people were perceived. It is the population telling their own history.

As I put in the preface, 'It is never within the moment that we know what it means, but only after it has occurred.' With that in mind, I'm not comfortable with summarising what Manchester is like today in one last chapter. That is a book in itself, for another writer to write at a later date. To do otherwise would be to 'tell the story in broad strokes'.

An earlier draft of this chapter was set out in similar fashion to the previous ones, my thoughts interspersed with quotes to leave you, the reader, with a picture of events. There were great insights to behold. The CEO of a Youth Zone that said the provisions for young people have been improved but there is a long way to go; there was the revelation that today's gang members are the grandchildren of those from the nineties; people quipped about the fear of Haçienda nostalgia becoming a noose around the city's neck we needed to take off before we suffer the same inability to progress like Liverpool has with the Beatles. Football supporters either bemoaned or cheered how their club is run by owners whose takeovers started at the turn of the millennium. Music fans celebrated that Manchester is now a shattered glass of a scene, there is no one sound, or brand, and people of different sex, skin, and sexuality have more chance of making it. There were citizens disgusted at how many homeless people litter the city centre's streets as the apartment blocks whose shadows they sleep in cost thousands to rent. Manchester's bars and clubs were seen as a vast improvement but an expensive night out. Some people felt that Manchester had become a city for visitors; others were upset at local pubs dying out and being replaced by hipster bars. Many felt the Mancunian identity was changing due the latest waves of migration, or those people moving here to make money. Those that once saw the Gay Village as a haven felt that it wasn't the necessity it once was with the general public being more accepting of people's sexuality; others felt that Canal Street has now become a tourist attraction for hen parties and has lost some of its initial allure.

As extensive as I spread the net in the past, there are undoubtedly tales not told, voices unheard; to tell you, the reader, what Manchester is like today in a quote or two on different aspects is to dilute the representation. We should unpack the opinions with the same thoroughness as the previous chapters. How I, and the contributors, negotiate the city today is not the same as we did two decades ago. How a forty-year-old views the nightlife isn't the same as someone half their age. There are new voices that need to tell that narrative. I asked every contributor how today compared with the past, and it was the only question they had to really consider, the responses being 'well, it's different', and 'you need to ask someone younger', as they didn't feel qualified. If New York is the city that never sleeps, then Manchester is the city that won't sit still. It is different. *We* are different, not in how time has changed us, but Mancunians as a population. Our difference is our only constant; how it has been represented is a casualty of history.

If there is a success within these pages, it is that I have had the opportunity to share stories seldom told. The contributors' input was as much a discovery for me as I hope it has been for you. Collected, I believe that it has unintentionally challenged Manchester's greatest myth.

Manchester is *not* a melting pot. Mancunians are not a homogenised people. The people and place do not blend into one thing. Manchester is not soup. We don't talk with one tongue, we don't sing the same songs; our colours and creeds change like door numbers on a street. The actions of one person don't tell all our tales. We are panhandlers stopping cars for change under the Mancunian Way, developers truffling out a cheap property, parents mourning the loss of their child to mindless violence, imams ringing out the morning prayers at mosque, families heading to Shabbat in Cheetham Hill, greengrocers stacking yams on Hyde Road, newly arrived migrants seeking refuge. We are addicts selling stolen gear from the supermarket at the local pub, old timers propping up the bars, clubbers queuing in lines for lines, and troubled teens facing difficult decisions. We are parades that celebrate our sexuality, we are protesters fighting for acceptance. We are media types living in multimillion-pound apartments, elderly people being moved out of their homes in the name of progression. We are dynamic corporation leaders in glass skyscrapers where homeless people see their reflection in the streets outside. We are hipster restaurateurs culturally appropriating ethnic food, and emerging artists trying to carve a career whilst a civic nostalgia shackles them to the past. There are as many obstacles as there are opportunities, a contrast between conflict and community. The whole may be greater than the parts, but it is exactly because the parts are distinctly different that makes the place what it is: many worlds co-existing within a 44.6 square mile radius, we are the walking stories that make up a complex and compelling canvas. It is only when we look at the warts as well as its wonder can we solve the underlying problems overlooked as we celebrate our success. We are a multitude, people put together with the consideration of a four-year-old with a paintbrush. We are colourful, dull, irregular, sharp, dangerous, and ill-fitting pieces that on the face of it shouldn't be placed alongside each other but somehow manage to accompany one another as part of a larger pattern. To focus on a few is to skew the view, to miss the mechanics, to not take in the patchwork of the tapestry. We don't do things differently here. We each live differently here.

Manchester is a mosaic.

Acknowledgements

If I was to make this an extensive list of the people I owe gratitude to, this acknowledgements section would go on for as long as the book. I am fortunate to have found my life graced by so many great people that to try and name them all will undoubtedly mean a person will get left off, so I will keep this minimal.

To the contributors, those who appear and those whose interviews had to be cut for various reasons. This book would not exist without you. The majority of the people I spoke with I didn't know beforehand and, in spite of this, each person was incredibly open with their experiences of living in Manchester, with honesty and humour, often opening up different lines of thinking and linking me up with other people who could speak on other issues. I was adamant from the start that this would be OUR story and not just my interpretation of the time and events. I am so grateful for your time and allowing me to share parts of your life within these pages. Thank you.

To my closest friends. We do not see each other half as much as we should, as life has thrown us to the wind, but I am proud of you to a person for what you have become, especially knowing the hurdles that each of you faced along your journeys. Joseph Conrad said that 'you can judge a man's worth by his friends'. I have but a small circle, yet within it are the most supportive and sarcastic humans with questionable dress sense to walk the earth. I wouldn't change a thing about any of you (outside the ones that support Liverpool). I don't tell you dickheads enough, I love you.

To my parents. Where do I start, YOU are where I begin. I admire you both so much. All I ever wanted was to live a life to make you proud of me. To demonstrate that the hard work you both went through to raise me, Cameron, and Kelly was worth it. I wasn't the easiest of sons, a lad with his head in the clouds and an eye for adventure. I know I've put you through worry and heartache over the course of the past few decades, but through it all I know there has always been an invisible umbilical cord that I could pull on for safety. As Dad always says, Family Comes First; you have both shown that throughout my life. I would never take for granted what you have done for me. Thank you for everything.

To my sister and brother. You pair do my head right in. I am the eldest, yet it is you two that have your shit together. I'm glad you didn't follow my lead. Cameron, you have become the man I wanted to be. I can still see you in your Moses basket as a baby and me being gutted to have to share a room just at the age I might be bringing girls around. I see you jumping on my bed as a seven-year-old singing Oasis songs when I was hungover, and I see you now as one of the wisest, funniest, most carefree people that I look up to. You have become a great man, Meathead. Kelly, you were a massive pain in my arse. There was no age between us growing up and so what I experienced you did likewise, from running through Towyn Caravan Parks, to doing all-nighters in forests in Mossley. We drank, smoked, laughed, and fought together through our teen years. I never told you when we were kids, as siblings often won't, but you were, and are, the best of friends. You are an incredible mother. Smell, you have a heart of gold.

Niala. From my heart, thank you for having me as partner with you for half a lifetime and sharing the most memorable experiences, which I will always look back on in awe and love. Perhaps it is Just a Ride, but over the course of the rollercoaster we both know the highs outweighed the lows by at least seventeen to one. I am eternally indebted to you, for more than you think, and most of all for bringing me the three most beautiful gifts a man could ever want. There will never be anything but love.

To my daughters. My Angels with Mucky Faces, Snotty Noses and Untied Laces, my girls … You three are my purpose for walking this planet, you are the meaning of my life, you give me a reason to exist. You allow me into your world to see things through your eyes and I love getting lost in your imagination alongside you. Please remember to never allow life to put a ceiling above what you want to do in it, don't colour in between the lines that others draw for you. Your hearts and spirits will take you to places way beyond the clouds. You are a trio of smart, caring, inquisitive, beautiful tour de forces and I pinch myself all the time to say I had any part in bringing you here. Being your Daddy is an honour and I promise to stop at nothing to make sure that I can be one that you deserve and need. It is beyond love what I have for you, Maya, Roma, and Esme.

To Chris Hart and the staff at Manchester University Press. Thank you so much for the opportunity to write this book. *As far back as I can remember, I always wanted to be an author.* You are responsible for allowing me to realise a lifetime ambition and my gratitude for that is boundless.

To Natalie Rees and Clint Boon. Had it not been for you asking me on the podcast then none of this would have materialised, as Chris (above) wouldn't have heard our interview. I figure

I owe you at least a night out to say thank you (or half a pint to share, depending on sales).

Lastly, to the young lad that I hadn't seen or thought about for decades. To meet you again on this journey has opened my eyes to things I'd tried my best to forget. Writing this book has brought a lot to the front of my mind, to the extent that reliving certain events resulted in a relapse in PTSD. I found an old photograph of Us towards finishing this book and it was like I was right back there with you; the pain, fear and isolation we experienced in our youth began to haunt me again, the way it did for too long when we were just a kid. It seems we hadn't exorcised our demons, but hidden them in a time capsule. When we opened it this past couple of years the ghosts ran amok. You went through a lot of trauma that you didn't need to, mate. It is only Us that know the depths to which your heart and head have sunk to, how lonely life was, why you wanted to escape, and what it was you were running from. There are some secrets we will never share but I know that us holding onto the nightmare gives it its power. Maybe I had to reopen the wound for us to really heal, maybe, but enough damage has been done now, David, what's gone has gone. As these pages make their way into the world, my only hope is that we find a peace to live in the present, and not continue to drown ourselves in something which we had no control over in our past.

You did alright, man! You did alright.

Scotty

Notes

Preface: A view from the Low

1. Author interview with Bill Rice, 21 February 2022.
2. Author interview with Linda Walker, 21 February 2022.
3. Twitter reply from @thefibreman, 21 February 2022.
4. Twitter reply from @mrseed2022, 21 February 2022.
5. Author interview with Andy Bell, 22 February 2022.
6. Author interview with Jim Salveson, 1 March 2022.
7. Author interview with Claire Moruzzi, 8 March 2022.

'Manchester was miserable' / 15 June 1996

1. Author interview with Justin Moorhouse, 8 June 2021.
2. Elisa Bullen, *Manchester Migration: A profile of Manchester's migration patterns* (Manchester City Council, 2015).
3. Author interview with John Moss, 1 June 2021.
4. Author interview with Rachel Kelly, 2 May 2021.
5. Author interview with John Moss, 1 June 2021.
6. Author interview with John Moss, 1 June 2021.
7. Author interview with Anne Worthington, 7 June 2021.
8. Author interview with John Moss, 1 June 2021.
9. Author interview with Rachel Kelly, 2 May 2021.
10. Author interview with John Moss, 1 June 2021.
11. BBC On this Day, 'Huge explosion rocks central Manchester', 15 June 1996, http://news.bbc.co.uk/onthisday/hi/dates/stories/june/15/newsid_2527000/2527009.stm.

12 Todd Fitzgerald, 'Security guard who worked in Manchester following IRA bombing dies of asbestos-related cancer', *Manchester Evening News*, 6 January 2016, www.manchestereveningnews.co.uk/news/greater-manchester-news/manchester-ira-bomb-mesothelioma-cancer-10694237.
13 'Mr Major's statement following Manchester bomb – 15 June 1996', John Major Archive, https://johnmajorarchive.org.uk/1996/06/15/mr-majors-statement-following-manchester-bomb-15-june-1996/.
14 Author interview with Rachel Kelly, 2 May 2021.
15 Author interview with Anne Worthington, 7 June 2021.
16 Dr Joanne Massey, Manchester Metropolitan University, 'The bomb that made Manchester?', www.mmu.ac.uk/hlss/about-us/news/story/index.php?id=4438.
17 Author interview with Len Grant, 10 December 2021.
18 Author interview with Tom Bloxham, 27 November 2021.
19 Andrew Woodcock, 'Tory MP said Manchester lost Olympic bid because "no one wants to spend three weeks there"', *Independent*, 18 July 2019, www.independent.co.uk/news/uk/politics/damian-green-manchester-olympic-games-2000-tory-mp-minister-a9009746.html.
20 Author interview with Len Grant, 10 December 2021.
21 Author interview with Tom Bloxham, 27 November 2021.
22 Andrew Bounds, 'Manchester: The 1980s generation was not so mad after all – it is running the place now', *Financial Times*, 25 May 2010, www.ft.com/content/6d273ac6-66c8-11df-aeb1-00144feab49a.
23 Paul Taylor, 'Manchester paid the price for Thatcher's modernising', 8 April 2013, www.manchestereveningnews.co.uk/news/greater-manchester-news/manchester-paid-price-margaret-thatchers-2547173.
24 BBC News, 'Michael Gove criticised over racist and homophobic language in student speeches', 14 September 2021, www.bbc.co.uk/news/uk-politics-58562820.
25 John Harris, 'The great reinvention of Manchester: "It's far more pleasant than London"', *Guardian*, 3 November 2015, www.theguardian.com/cities/2015/nov/03/the-great-reinvention-of-manchester-its-far-more-pleasant-than-london.
26 Author interview with Len Grant, 10 December 2021.
27 Author interview with Len Grant, 10 December 2021.

'The city that lets down its pupils' / Youth

1 Judith Judd, 'The city that lets down its pupils', *Independent*, 18 June 1998, www.independent.co.uk/news/the-city-that-lets-down-its-pupils-1165701.html.
2 Author interview with Nathan Miles, 21 January 2022.
3 Office for Standards in Education, 'Inspection of Manchester Local Education Authority, June 1998', 1998, https://files.ofsted.gov.uk/v1/file/2763186.
4 Author interview with Mary McGuigan, 1 March 2022.
5 Author interview with Nathan Miles, 21 January 2022.
6 Author interview with Jay Motty, 20 July 2021.
7 Author interview with Nooruddean Choudry, 3 December 2021.
8 Author interview with Marsha Bell, 23 January 2022.
9 Author interview with Steph Lonsdale, 21 February 2022.
10 *Institute of Alcohol Studies*, Issue 3, 1998, www.ias.org.uk/alcohol_alert/issue-3-1998/.
11 Author interview with Nathan Miles, 21 January 2022.
12 Author interview with Jay Motty, 20 July 2021.
13 Author interview with Steph Lonsdale, 21 February 2022.
14 Author interview with Steph Lonsdale, 21 February 2022.
15 Author interview with Steph Lonsdale, 21 February 2022.
16 Author interview with Jay Motty, 20 June 2021.
17 Author interview with Marsha Bell, 23 January 2022.
18 Author interview with Nathan Miles, 21 January 2022.
19 Statewatch, 'UK: Ethnic injustice: More black and Asian people are being stopped and searched than ever before', August 2004, www.statewatch.org/media/documents/news/2004/aug/stop-and-search.pdf.
20 Author interview with Nathan Miles, 21 January 2022.
21 Author interview with Marsha Bell, 23 January 2022.
22 Author interview with Marsha Bell, 23 January 2022.
23 Author interview with Jay Motty, 20 July 2021.
24 Author interview with Nathan Miles, 21 January 2021.
25 www.theguardian.com/education/2000/mar/07/educationincrisis.uk

'It's the world of the drama series *The Wire*' / Crime

1. Author interview with Jay Motty, 20 July 2021.
2. Paul Reuter and Alex Stevens, 'An analysis of UK drug policy', UK Drug Policy Commission, 2007, www.ukdpc.org.uk/wp-content/uploads/Policy%20report%20-%20An%20analysis%20of%20UK%20drug%20policy.pdf.
3. Author interview with Jay Motty, 21 July 2021.
4. Neal Keeling, 'Binge drink capital of Britain', *Manchester Evening News*, 16 October 2007, www.manchestereveningnews.co.uk/news/health/binge-drink-capital-of-britain-1007178.
5. Peter Reuter and Alex Stevens, 'An analysis of UK drug policy', UK Drug Policy Commission, 2007, www.ukdpc.org.uk/wp-content/uploads/Policy%20report%20-%20An%20analysis%20of%20UK%20drug%20policy.pdf.
6. Z. E. Reed et al., 'Using Mendelian randomization to explore the gateway hypothesis: possible causal effects of smoking initiation and alcohol consumption on substance use outcomes', *Addiction* 117/3 (2021): 741–50.
7. Author interview with Anon, 28 July 2021.
8. Chris Elkins, 'Cocaine and alcohol', *Drug Rehab*, www.drugrehab.com/addiction/drugs/cocaine/mixing-cocaine-and-alcohol/.
9. Tony Thompson, 'Crack "epidemic" fuels rise in violent crime', *Guardian*, 17 February 2002, www.theguardian.com/uk/2002/feb/17/drugsandalcohol.tonythompson.
10. Author interview with Anon, 12 August 2021.
11. Sophie Goodchild, 'Cokeheads to be talked out of their habits', *Independent*, 1 September 2002, www.independent.co.uk/news/uk/politics/cokeheads-to-be-talked-out-of-their-habits-175426.html.
12. Author interview with Anon, 28 July 2021.
13. www.truecrimelibrary.com/crimearticle/benji-stanley/.
14. www.manchestereveningnews.co.uk/news/greater-manchester-news/dont-come-near-new-year-8369593
15. Author interview with Anon, 15 September 2021.
16. Author interview with Anon, 28 July 2021.

17 Ian Burrell, 'Bystanders caught in crossfire as gun gangs shoot it out in South Manchester', *Independent*, 19 October 2002, www.independent.co.uk/news/uk/crime/bystanders-caught-in-crossfire-as-gun-gangs-shoot-it-out-in-south-manchester-140484.html.

18 Karen Bullock and Nick Tilley, 'Shootings, gangs and violent incidents in Manchester: Developing a crime reduction strategy', November 2017, www.researchgate.net/publication/330173342_Shootings_Gangs_and_Violent_Incidents_in_Manchester_Developing_A_Crime_Reduction_Strategy.

19 Author interview with Anon, 26 May 2021.

20 www.casemine.com/judgement/uk/5a8ff71360d03e7f57ea72f2.

21 Author interview with Anon, 28 July 2021.

22 Cindi John, 'Manchester's gang busters', BBC News, 18 June 2014, http://news.bbc.co.uk/1/hi/uk/3816677.stm.

23 Author interview with Anon, 19 November 2021.

24 Author interview with Anon, 15 September, 2021.

25 Judith Judd, 'The city that lets down its pupils', *Independent*, 18 June 1998, www.independent.co.uk/news/the-city-that-lets-down-its-pupils-1165701.html.

26 Author interview with Miss Greene, 9 June 2021.

27 Author interview with Anon, 28 July 2021.

28 Author interview with Anon, 21 September 2021.

29 Author interview with Anon, 15 September 2021.

30 Paul Bracchi and Nazia Parveen, 'The shooting of a 7-year-old and a great city gripped by gangsterism', *Daily Mail*, 17 October 2015, www.dailymail.co.uk/news/article-3276722/The-shooting-7-year-old-great-city-gripped-gangsterism-quiet-cul-sacs-Manchester-suburb-home-bitter-turf-war.html#ixzz3zDCqJfYS.

31 Author interview with Anon, 28 July 2021.

32 www.casemine.com/judgement/uk/5a8ff71360d03e7f57ea72f2.

33 Chris Osuh, 'Top Tory compares Moss Side to *The Wire*', *Manchester Evening News*, 25 August 2009, www.manchestereveningnews.co.uk/news/greater-manchester-news/top-tory-compares-moss-side-928149.

34 Michael White, 'Chris Grayling is daft to compare Britain to Baltimore', *Guardian*, 25 August 2009, www.theguardian.com/politics/blog/2009/aug/25/the-wire-chris-grayling.

35 Author interview with Anon, 28 July 2021.
36 Author interview with Anon, 28 July 2021.
37 www.researchgate.net/publication/330173342_Shootings_Gangs_and_Violent_Incidents_in_Manchester_Developing_A_Crime_Reduction_Strategy.
38 Tony Thompson, 'Gang warfare in Games city', *Guardian*, 28 July 2002, www.theguardian.com/uk/2002/jul/28/ukcrime.
39 Author interview with Ian Hynes, 1 October 2021.
40 Author interview with Ian Hynes, 1 October 2021.
41 Author interview with Ian Hynes, 1 October 2021.

'He's going to have sex with that girl on stage!' / Nightlife

1 Author interview with Nathan Miles, 21 January 2021.
2 Author interview with Anon, 16 February 2022.
3 Author interview with Stan Chow, 27 April 2021.
4 Author interview with Tom Bloxham, 27 November 2021.
5 Author interview with Jay Taylor, 19 May 2021.
6 Author interview with Tash Willcocks, 25 November 2021.
7 Author interview with Guy Garvey, 15 June 2021.
8 Author interview with Badly Drawn Boy, 16 June 2021.
9 Author interview with Andy Hargreaves, 28 April 2021.
10 Author interview with Tash Willcocks, 25 November 2021.
11 Author interview with Andy Hargreaves, 28 April 2021.
12 Author interview with Stan Chow, 27 April 2021.
13 Author interview with Tash Willcocks, 25 November 2021.
14 Author interview with Tash Willcocks, 25 November 2021.
15 Author interview with Guy Garvey, 15 June 2021.
16 Interview with Dan Hett, 2 August 2022.
17 'Manchester's Electric Chair returns with DJ Harvey', *Decoded Magazine*, 11 August 2021, www.decodedmagazine.com/manchesters-electric-chair-returns-with-dj-harvey.
18 'Unseen footage from Electric Chair … Manchester Dances On', *Ransom Note*, www.theransomnote.com/music/news/unseen-footage-from-electric-chair-manchester-dances-on.
19 Author interview with Sacha Lord, 10 March 2022.

20 Author interview with Sacha Lord, 10 March 2022.
21 Author interview with Sacha Lord, 10 March 2022.
22 Author interview with Emma Goswell, 20 January 2022.
23 Author interview with Emma Goswell, 20 January 2022.
24 Author interview with Marsha Bell, 23 January 2022.
25 Author interview with Nathan Miles, 10 January 2022.
26 Author interview with Marsha Bell, 23 January 2022.
27 Author interview with Nathan Miles, 10 January 2022.
28 Author interview with Steph Lonsdale, 21 February 2022.
29 Rachael Healy, '"We weren't allowed feminism – we had the Spice Girls": The two comics unpicking ladette culture', *Guardian*, 6 January 2022, www.theguardian.com/stage/2022/jan/06/we-werent-allowed-feminism-we-had-the-spice-girls-the-two-comics-unpicking-ladette-culture.
30 Author interview with Steph Lonsdale, 21 February 2022.
31 Author Interview with Mary McGuigan, 1 March 2022.
32 Author interview with Leon Mike, 1 March 2022.

'A different success for Manchester' / Music

1 Author interview with Natalie-Eve Williams, 6 April 2021.
2 https://blim.org.uk/report/.
3 https://midiaresearch.com/blog/be-the-change-women-making-music-2021.
4 Black Lives in Music, September 2021, *BLIM*, https://blim.org.uk.
5 Author interview with Andy Votel, 4 August 2021.
6 Author interview with Tunde Babalola, 26 January 2022.
7 Anon quote from music industry figure, 1 March 2021.
8 BBC News, 'Urban Cookie singer Diane Charlemagne dies at 51', 29 October 2015, www.bbc.co.uk/news/entertainment-arts-34666593.
9 Author interview with Tunde Babalola, 26 January 2022.
10 Author interview with Tunde Babalola, 26 January 2022.
11 Author interview with Tunde Babalola, 26 January 2022.
12 Author interview with Darren Lewis, 26 January 2022.
13 Author interview with Tunde Babalola, 26 January 2022.
14 Author interview with Darren Lewis, 26 January 2022.

15 Author interview with Tunde Babalola, 26 January 2022.
16 Author interview with Karen Gabay, 11 May 2021.
17 Author interview with Sylvia Tella, 12 December 2021.
18 Author interview with Sylvia Tella, 12 December 2021.
19 Author interview with Sylvia Tella, 12 December 2021.
20 Author interview with Sylvia Tella, 12 December 2021.
21 Author interview with Sylvia Tella, 12 December 2021.
22 Author interview with Aziz Ibrahim, 14 December 2021.
23 Author interview with Aziz Ibrahim, 14 December 2021.
24 Author interview with Aziz Ibrahim, 14 December 2021.
25 Author interview with Aziz Ibrahim, 14 December 2021.
26 'Finley Quaye Unplugged at Tallyrand', https://discover.events.com/gb/england/stockport/e/music/finley-quaye-unplugged-talleyrand-stockport-road-1030-377876597.
27 Author interview with Karen Gabay, 11 May 2021.
28 Author interview with Karen Gabay, 11 May 2021.
29 Author interview with Dave Haslam, 10 May 2021.
30 Author interview with Badly Drawn Boy, 28 April 2021.
31 Author interview with Andy Hargreaves, 28 April 2021.
32 Author interview with Guy Garvey, 15 June 2021.
33 Author interview with Andy Hargreaves, 28 April 2021.
34 Author interview with Guy Garvey, 15 June 2021.
35 Author interview with Andy Hargreaves, 28 April 2021.
36 Author interview with Guy Garvey, 15 June 2021.
37 Author interview with Richard Jupp, 12 May 2021.
38 Author interview with Guy Garvey, 15 June 2021.
39 Author interview with Richard Jupp, 12 May 2021.
40 Author interview with Guy Garvey, 15 June 2021.
41 Author interview with Richard Jupp, 12 May 2021.
42 Author interview with Andy Hargreaves, 28 April 2021.
43 Author interview with Jay Taylor, 19 May 2021.
44 Author interview with Badly Drawn Boy, 28 April 2021.
45 Author interview with Andy Votel, 4 August 2021.
46 Author interview with Badly Drawn Boy, 28 April 2021.
47 Author interview with Andy Votel, 4 August 2021.
48 Author interview with Badly Drawn Boy, 28 April 2021.

49 Author interview with Andy Votel, 4 August 2021.
50 Author interview with Andy Votel, 4 August 2021.
51 Author interview with Andy Votel, 4 August 2021.
52 Author interview with Badly Drawn Boy, 28 April 2021.
53 Author interview with Guy Garvey, 15 June 2021.
54 Author interview with Badly Drawn Boy, 28 April 2021.

'Did horse semen lead to their downfall?' / Football

1 David Ward and Libby Brooks, 'Bus driver gets life for boy's murder', *Guardian*, 24 April 1999, www.theguardian.com/uk/1999/apr/24/davidward.libbybrooks.
2 Author interview with Jay Motty, 20 July 2021.
3 Author interview with Emily Brobyn, 24 February 2022.
4 Author interview with JP Dolan, 5 March 2022.
5 Author interview with Jay Motty, 20 July 2021.
6 Author interview with Emily Brobyn, 24 February 2022.
7 Author interview with Jim White, 26 April 2021.
8 Author interview with Andy Mitten, 28 April 2021.
9 Author interview with Ste Howson, 20 May 2022.
10 Author interview with Jay Motty, 20 July 2021.
11 Author interview with Nooruddean Choudry, 28 April 2021.
12 Author interview with JP Dolan, 5 March 2022.
13 Author interview with Andy Mitten, 28 April 2021.
14 Author interview with Ged Tarpey, 5 January 2021.
15 'Ged Tarpey: From Maine Road to LA', Professional Footballers' Association, 2 October 2014, www.thepfa.com/news/2014/10/2/from-maine-road-to-la.
16 Author interview with Ged Tarpey, 30 April 2021.
17 Author interview with Steve Armstrong, 17 March 2022.
18 Author interview with Emily Brobyn, 24 February 2022.
19 Author interview with Jay Motty, 21 June 2021.
20 Author interview with Jim White, 26 April 2021.
21 Author interview with Jim White, 26 April 2021.
22 Author interview with Jim White, 26 April 2021.
23 Author interview with Jay Motty, 21 June 2021.

24 Author interview with JP Dolan, 5 March 2022.
25 Author interview with Emily Brobyn, 24 February 2022.

'And Tony Wilson didn't even say it!' / Media

1 Author interview with Justin Moorhouse, 8 June 2021.
2 BBC Comedy, 'The Royle Family', 25 September 2015, www.bbc.co.uk/comedy/theroylefamily/index.shtml.
3 Author interview with Phil Mealey, 15 February 2022.
4 Author interview with John Thomson, 30 June 2021.
5 Author interview with Phil Mealey, 15 February 2022.
6 Michael Imperioli, 'Pax Soprana', *Talking Sopranos* podcast, Episode 6, 4 May 2020, https://talkingsopranos.simplecast.com/episodes/episode-6-pax-soprana.
7 Author interview with Phil Mealey, 15 February 2022.
8 Author interview with John Thomson, 30 June 2021.
9 Author interview with Phil Mealey, 15 February 2022.
10 Author interview with Phil Mealey, 15 February 2022.
11 Author interview with John Thomson, 30 June 2021.
12 Author interview with Phil Mealey, 15 February 2022.
13 Author interview with John Thomson, 30 June 2021.
14 Quoted in 'The Making of East is East', https://eastiseast.co.uk/about/.
15 Author interview with Nooruddean Choudry, 3 December 2021.
16 Author interview with Justin Moorhouse, 8 June 2021.
17 Author interview with Justin Moorhouse, 8 June 2021.
18 Author interview with John Thomson, 30 June 2021.
19 Alan Morrison, '*24 Hour Party People* review', *Empire*, 1 January 2000 [review date from *Empire* website is 2000, although film release date was 2002], www.empireonline.com/movies/reviews/24-hour-party-people-review.
20 Author interview with Elliot Eastwick, 21 April 2021.
21 Author interview with Justin Moorhouse, 8 June 2021.
22 The opening lines to L.P. Hartley's *The Go-Between*: 'The past is a foreign country; they do things differently there.'

23 Louis Staples, 'Twenty years on, *Queer as Folk* remains a more radical and fearless tribute to gay life than many LGBT+ shows today', *Independent*, 23 February 2019, www.independent.co.uk/voices/queer-as-folk-stuart-vince-nathan-russell-t-davies-lgbtq-discrimination-tv-culture-20th-anniversary-a8793316.html.
24 Author interview with Emma Goswell, 20 January 2022.
25 Author interview with Emma Goswell, 20 January 2022.
26 Author interview with Emma Goswell, 20 January 2022.
27 James Sherwood and Chas Newkey-Burden, 'Debate: *Queer as Folk* has shocked TV audiences with its explicit portrayal of gay men', *Independent*, 28 February 1999, www.independent.co.uk/life-style/debate-queer-as-folk-has-shocked-tv-audiences-with-its-explicit-portrayal-of-gay-men-great-says-james-sherwood-finally-there-s-a-tv-show-telling-it-like-it-is-not-so-says-chas-newkeyburden-qaf-is-a-dangerous-parody-of-1073722.html.
28 Author interview with Kurtis-Lee Spittle, 28 January 2022.

'Proper Manc' / Identity

1 Author interview with Jay Taylor, 19 May 2021.
2 Author interview with Jay Taylor, 19 May 2021.
3 Quoted in Tom Jacobs, 'How stereotypes take shape', *Pacific Standard*, 24 July 2014, https://psmag.com/social-justice/knowledge-process-information-scotland-stereotypes-take-shape-86697.
4 Helena Vesty, 'Coronation Street at 60: The real story of the Salford neighbourhoods that inspired the famous cobbles', 6 December 2020, www.manchestereveningnews.co.uk/news/greater-manchester-news/coronation-street-anniversary-itv-history-19325571.
5 Author interview with Mary McGuigan, 1 March 2022.
6 Author interview with Stan Chow, 27 April 2021.
7 Author interview with Justin Moorhouse, 8 June 2021.
8 Author interview with Dr Rob Drummond, 12 May 2021.
9 Author interview with Stan Chow, 27 April 2021.
10 Author interview with Mary McGuigan, 1 March 2022.
11 Author interview with Mary McGuigan, 1 March 2022.
12 Author interview with Jay Taylor, 19 May 2021.

13 Author interview with Dave Haslam, 10 May 2021.
14 Author interview with Badly Drawn Boy, 28 April 2021.
15 Author interview with Natalie-Eve Williams, 6 April 2021.
16 Author interview with Elliot Eastwick, 21 May 2021.
17 Author interview with Tom Bloxham, 27 November 2021.
18 Author interview with Nooruddean Choudry, 3 December 2021.
19 Author interview with Stan Chow, 27 April 2021.
20 Author interview with Nooruddean Choudry, 3 December 2021.
21 Cited in Yakub Qureshi, 'Study finds Manchester is home of new "affluent" working class who love gym and rap music', *Manchester Evening News*, 22 April 2013, www.manchestereveningnews.co.uk/news/greater-manchester-news/study-finds-manchester-home-new-2993715.
22 Author interview with Natalie-Eve Williams, 6 April 2021.
23 Author interview with Nooruddean Choudry, 3 December 2021.
24 Maya Salam, 'What is toxic masculinity?' *New York Times*, 22 January 2019, www.nytimes.com/2019/01/22/us/toxic-masculinity.html.
25 Author interview with Dave Haslam, 10 May 2021.
26 Author interview with Phil Mealey, 15 February 2020.
27 Author interview with Justin Moorhouse, 8 June 2021.
28 Author interview with Steph Lonsdale, 21 February 2022.

Index

Index

Index

Index

Index

Index

Index

Index

Index